The Transformative Cinema of Alejandro Jodorowsky

The Transformative Cinema of Alejandro Jodorowsky

George Melnyk

BLOOMSBURY ACADEMIC
NEW YORK • LONDON • OXFORD • NEW DELHI • SYDNEY

BLOOMSBURY ACADEMIC
Bloomsbury Publishing Inc
1385 Broadway, New York, NY 10018, USA
50 Bedford Square, London, WC1B 3DP, UK
29 Earlsfort Terrace, Dublin 2, Ireland

BLOOMSBURY, BLOOMSBURY ACADEMIC and the Diana logo are trademarks of
Bloomsbury Publishing Plc

First published in the United States of America 2023
Paperback edition published 2024

Copyright © George Melnyk, 2023, 2024

For legal purposes the Acknowledgments on p. viii constitute an extension of this copyright page.

Cover design: Eleanor Rose
Cover image: Portrait of Alejandro Jodorowsky © Herve BRUHAT / Gamma-Rapho / Getty Images

All rights reserved. No part of this publication may be reproduced or transmitted in any form or by any means, electronic or mechanical, including photocopying, recording, or any information storage or retrieval system, without prior permission in writing from the publishers.

Bloomsbury Publishing Inc does not have any control over, or responsibility for, any third-party websites referred to or in this book. All internet addresses given in this book were correct at the time of going to press. The author and publisher regret any inconvenience caused if addresses have changed or sites have ceased to exist, but can accept no responsibility for any such changes.

Library of Congress Cataloging-in-Publication Data

Names: Melnyk, George, author.
Title: The transformative cinema of Alejandro Jodorowsky : from surrealism to psycho-magic / George Melnyk.
Description: New York : Bloomsbury Academic, 2023. | Includes bibliographical references and index. | Summary: "This book analyses the complete cinematic work (1968 to 2020) of Alejandro Jodorowsky"– Provided by publisher.
Identifiers: LCCN 2022028581 (print) | LCCN 2022028582 (ebook) | ISBN 9781501378805 (hardback) | ISBN 9781501378775 (paperback) | ISBN 9781501378799 (epub) | ISBN 9781501378782 (pdf) | ISBN 9781501378768 (ebook other)
Subjects: LCSH: Jodorowsky, Alejandro–Criticism and interpretation.
Classification: LCC PN1998.3.J63 M45 2023 (print) | LCC PN1998.3.J63 (ebook) | DDC 791.4302/33/092–dc23/eng/20220924
LC record available at https://lccn.loc.gov/2022028581
LC ebook record available at https://lccn.loc.gov/2022028582

ISBN: HB: 978-1-5013-7880-5
PB: 978-1-5013-7877-5
ePDF: 978-1-5013-7878-2
eBook: 978-1-5013-7879-9

Typeset by Deanta Global Publishing Services, Chennai, India

To find out more about our authors and books visit www.bloomsbury.com and sign up for our newsletters.

To my brother Lubomyr

Contents

Acknowledgments — viii

1. Reappraising Alejandro Jodorowsky's Cinema — 1
2. A Brief Summary of the Life and Times of Alejandro Jodorowsky — 11
3. In the Beginning: *La Cravate* (1957) and *Fando y Lis* (1968) — 25
4. The Birth of a Cult: *El Topo* (1970) — 43
5. The Ascent of and the Descent from *The Holy Mountain* (1973) — 63
6. The Interregnum: *Dune* (1974–6), *Tusk* (1980), *The Rainbow Thief* (1990) plus Jodorowsky's comics/graphic novels — 83
7. The Auteur Reborn: *Santa Sangre* (1989) — 97
8. A Magical Childhood: *La danza de realidad* (*The Dance of Reality*, 2013) — 117
9. An Absurd Youth: *Poesía sin fin* (*Endless Poetry*, 2016) — 137
10. The Therapist on Film: *Psychomagic, A Healing Art* (2019) — 157
11. Jodorowsky Redux: Evaluating the Art of a Fabulist — 169

The Auteur Filmography of Alejandro Jodorowsky — 181
Bibliography — 186
Index — 196

Acknowledgments

This book would not have happened without the keen support of Katie Gallof at Bloomsbury, who first recognized the importance of publishing the second book in English ever to study Jodorowsky's total cinema. She was a responsive editor, who answered all my queries and kept the process moving along smoothly. She made the whole writer–publisher process as painless as possible. An equally important contribution was made by Daniel Lindvall, editor of *Film International*, who published two of my articles on Jodorowsky in his journal. Their publication inspired me to propose the book.

There were a number of individuals who helped me realize the project. Don Wetherell and Irene Kmet sourced the book *Midnight Movies* for me in Vancouver and then scanned an important chapter on *El Topo* and *The Holy Mountain*. Adam Puskar was invaluable in accessing difficult-to-get Jodorowsky work. Especially crucial was Julia Berry Melnyk, my dear wife, who had to put up with my blurting out insights into Jodorowsky's films at any hour. Her tolerance for listening to what I had discovered is inspirational. I also want to express my gratitude to the resources of the University of Calgary Library which provided me with many of Jodorowsky's films plus online access to numerous articles and interviews. The library's database is extensive and served as an essential research tool that speeded up my writing. This book was written without a grant and solely out of an interest in Jodorowsky's filmmaking. I hope this book will encourage more people to discover or to rediscover his cinematic genius. His films do not grow tired or old. They simply grow, alive with nuance.

1

Reappraising Alejandro Jodorowsky's Cinema

Alejandro Jodorowsky was ninety-two years old when I began researching and writing this book in 2021. I had no idea whether he would be around to see this book's publication and what, if anything, it might mean to him should he ever see it. I suspect that at this late stage in his life he would have little interest in what others had to say. During his film career he had both an abundance of praise and a surfeit of ridicule. My imagined disinterest on his part enabled me to pursue my own, self-directed journey in reappraising the contribution of his cinema. In fact, I made a point of not interviewing him for the book because he had given so many interviews and had said so much (and yet so little). My audience for the book is not Jodorowsky, but all those who are drawn to his work. I spent the time writing this book because I wanted others to appreciate what he has done, while understanding some of the limitations of his achievement. The perils of writing an assessment of his cinema involves the usual quicksand created by academic dogmas that point to their own analytic genius, thereby sucking the lifeblood out of creativity. Added to this is the difficulty of ascertaining the true facts of his peripatetic and transnational existence, especially since he has been so adept at beguiling and mesmerizing. At times it seemed almost impossible to escape his phantasmagorical imagination with one's sanity intact. But I persevered, emerging from his Alice-in-Wonderland universe with an equal measure of awe and analysis.

Jodorowsky has invested himself at the deepest personal level in his cinema because he sees it as transformative and life-changing for those involved in its making as well as those who view it. The demand that his cinema be transformative turns him into a self-styled therapist, a healer of the psyche, and a transformer of personal identity. I experienced this power after viewing Jodorowsky's second autobiographical film *Poesía sin fin* (*Endless Poetry*) in 2016 at the Vancouver International Film Festival. His son Adán, who was at the screening as his father's representative and the lead actor, spoke of how his acting in the film had redirected his life. There is a scene in the film in which Adán, who plays his father as a young man, is required to shave off the hair of Jaime (Alejandro's father and his grandfather). Jaime is played by Adán's older brother Brontis. Jaime (Brontis) is pleading with Alejandro (Adán) not to go. Brontis is not wearing a wig. It is his real hair that is being shaved. The act is real. Adán is unable to complete the shaving of the head, so the real Alejandro completes the act. Jodorowsky often did only one take of a scene and with the shaving there was only one take possible. The symbolic meaning of these father/son/grandfather relations will be discussed later in the book. What is important here is the seamless unity of reality and fantasy that Jodorowsky believes leads to transformation. Adán was unable to shave his own brother's hair as the film required, but he took the act and its meaning to heart. He recounted to the audience how he had gone to the Atacama Desert in northern Chile after the shoot, where he shaved off his own hair as a symbol of his own transformation. The act in the film was envisioned by his father as a sign of transforming his bedeviled relationship with his father. Adán's failure to complete the act forced Alejandro to intervene and enact the scene. Alejandro unwittingly performed an act of psychomagic, a concept about changing oneself through performance that he had conceived and promoted for many years. Furthermore, his conception of the scene and his intervention, fits with another of his theories—metagenealogy, in which the traumas of past generations, which remain unresolved, carry forward into the future.

When Adán shaved off his own long locks he told the audience that this act was meant to signify the end of his earlier attempt to distance himself from his father through his own musical career under a distinct name. After Atacama he returned to using his birth names. In this way Alejandro's problematic relationship with his father is reconstituted in the problematic relationship Adán had with him, except that now there is a resolution. Adán went even further in expressing Jodorowsky's cinematic androgyny (the melding of reality and fantasy) when, at this 2016 film festival, he wore the same kind of hat as his father wore at Cannes in 1973 where he was launching *The Holy Mountain* (Cobb 2007, 12). The admixture of the actors' roles with their real-life identities and the "reality" of what happens in the film and its imitation afterward is radical and thought-provoking. It convinced me to see Jodorowsky's films as having a special power.

Alejandro Jodorowsky has dipped his fingers into many artistic pots, all of which provide inspiration for his creativity. Filmmaker, novelist, cartoonist, poet, playwright, graphic novelist, psychotherapist, shamanistic healer, actor, mime artist, Tarot master, and theater director are all professions he has practiced with a high degree of success. This heterogeneous production has made him an outlier in the cinematic universe because he has expressed himself successfully in so many diverse ways. At the same time this diversity of genres has meant that his cinema cannot be separated from his other work. This study of his films takes into account the relationship of his films to his other creative work because they are connected and intertwined. His career as a filmmaker has been fraught with controversy and his films have generally been a financial disaster for its producers. Because of a dispute with one of these producers his earlier films were unavailable in the United States for thirty-two years (1975–2007). This added to his marginalization in the cinema world plus the fact that he did not make an auteur film in the twenty-four years between 1989 and 2013.

Since his films were made over a period of over sixty years (1957–2019) means this study ranges over many different artistic subjects and has to take into account huge shifts in cultural taste, new film movements, and technological innovation that has occurred over that period of time. The result is a wide range of source material. The primary sources for this book are his films. Second are his writings and pronouncements on his films. Third are critical commentaries by others about his films and his other creative work. Fourth are interviews with him. Fifth are general studies of surrealism, and avant-garde and cult cinema that provide a context in which to situate his work. Sixth are his non-film writings—fiction, poetry, autobiography, graphic novels, and nonfiction books. Seventh are biographical elements that relate his life to his films. Taken together they provide the chain of dots that connect his early work with films that he made much later.

There is a small body of critical work about his cinema and only one major book in English published so far plus a short monograph on one of his films. Ben Cobb's inaugural study *Anarchy and Alchemy: The Films of Alejandro Jodorowsky* (2007) captured the intensity and magic of his vision. Unfortunately, it has been out of print for many years. Most of the academic and popular commentary is found in articles or book chapters in English, Spanish, Portuguese, and French. It ranges from the gush of celebrity journalism and enthusiastic fandom to rigorous and sometimes opaque scholarship. This wide range of reactions is not easy to reconcile when trying, as this book does, to provide a holistic view of his cinema and its author. Because Jodorowsky is an unusual filmmaker with a troubled, roller-coaster film career, the assessments made of his achievements and failures vary widely in tone and appreciation. This is not surprising due to the changing tastes, evolving academic discourse, and distinct historical contexts that occur when films cover a fifty-year span.

What Others Have Said

There have been a number of labels applied to Jodorowsky and his film work. He sees himself as an artist and an avant-garde auteur, who writes, directs, and acts in his work. Externally, the most common label applied to him is that of "cult director." The term "cult" has religious connotations. It is applied to small, idiosyncratic religious entities led by charismatic leaders. In cinema the term refers to directors who make unusual or peculiar films that appeal to a specific group of followers. What constitutes a cult film or a cult film director varies. Whatever or whoever the term is applied to separates that entity from the mainstream, relegating the film or the person to a particular subculture. In the case of Jodorowsky the term first appeared after his 1970 film *El Topo* generated what the media termed a "cult following" after its midnight screenings in New York in the early 1970s. The cult concept was used in both a cultural and a religious sense. In a retrospective article about the impact of the film in New York, film critic Eric Benson wrote:

> For six months, beginning on Dec. 18, 1970, it [*El Topo*] played once a day at the Elgin Cinema in Manhattan's Chelsea neighborhood, at midnight (1 a.m. on Friday and Saturday)—selling out virtually all its screenings and attracting a heady crowd of hippie-intellectual royalty. Dennis Hopper saw "El Topo," loved it and recruited Jodorowsky to recut his next film. John Lennon saw it, returned several times and persuaded his manager, Allen Klein, to buy the distribution rights. (Benson 2014)

These late-night screenings were associated with drug-taking and hallucinatory experiences, then valorized in counterculture circles as ways to enlightenment. Cultists find satisfaction in being counternormative in their taste, enjoying the sense of belonging to an exclusive group, and feeling superior to those who cannot appreciate the transgressive appeal of their hero or the art. Unfortunately, the continued application of this term to Jodorowsky locks him into a fringe category of cinema that separates him from such renowned twentieth-century auteurs as Kurosawa and Bergman. While the history of Jodorowsky's early reception as a filmmaker may support the use of the term, it does an injustice to the depth of his later cinematic creativity.

His films are anti-conventional, transgressive, profane and sacrilegious, sexualized, bizarrely violent, and definitely subversive. This book argues that these qualities turn his films into major works of art with a thematic and visual unity, as well as providing a profound sense of the absurdity, hypocrisy, and ambiguity of the human condition. His films are much more than some kind of freakish display. They go to great lengths to exploit the contradictions in official cultures and ideologies, including religious ones. There is also an ongoing sense of pain and tragedy in his work that lifts it to a masterful level, albeit one that is idiosyncratic. Jodorowsky may be classed a *cineaste provocateur*, a creator of visual provocations that stab at bourgeois complacency and subvert all that sees itself as sacrosanct. His work is much more than simply an assault on complacency; its goal is the resanctification of the human psyche. This quality alone lifts his films out of the B-movie category. There are other values in his films that contribute to lifting his stature to a nobler plateau. They are evident in labels other than "cult" that have been widely applied to him, beginning with the term "surrealist."

Surrealism is an honored European art movement that made a significant impact on Jodorowsky's visual content and style. It was an outgrowth of the earlier twentieth-century Dada art movement which made fun of the seriousness associated with art. Surrealism was Dada's child and it operated from the mid-1920s up to the Second World War. *Un Chien Andalou* (1929), a silent short by two prominent surrealists, Luis Buñuel and Salvador Dali, embodied the "shock and awe" aspects of the movement by portraying the slicing of a supposedly human eyeball with a razor. It was just the kind of provocation that would appeal to Jodorowsky. When he arrived in Paris from his country of birth, Chile, in 1953, surrealism was passé, but its historic engagement with dreams, the subconscious, the spontaneous, the irrational, the outrageous, the irreverent and the absurd became integral to his art. Surrealists elevated the convoluted workings of the human psyche and its symbolic associations into artistic assaults on conformity, morality, and conventional aesthetics. Maurice Nadeau, the grand historian of surrealism, wrote about the dream world that surrealists venerated and in which the artist and anyone else becomes "acquainted with strange creatures ... moves in landscapes never seen before ... performs enthralling actions" (Nadeau 1967, 48). Each of Jodorowsky's films contains dreamscapes as do his many other artistic creations from graphic novels to plays.

The term appears often in media pieces about him. A 2004 interview with Jodorowsky was titled "A Delirious Surrealist" (*POV* 2004). A 2014 *Taste of Cinema* article is titled "Filmmaker Retrospective: The Surreal Cinema of Alejandro Jodorowsky" (Evans 2014). A *New York Times* review of his 2019 documentary film on his therapies is subtitled "A Surrealist Therapy" (Kenny 2020). The use of the term is concentrated in popular media though academics have also used the term. "Caracteristicas surrealistas no filme *A montanha sagrada*, de Alejandro Jodorowsky" (Surrealist Characteristics in Alejandro Jodorowsky's Film *The Sacred Mountain*) is the title of a 2014 Brazilian article (Garcia 2014). My own "Surrealism in the Autobiographical Cinema of Alejandro Jodorowsky" is part of that approach (Melnyk 2016). Why the term appears more often in the popular media and journalistic discourse may be because of the diversity of views, approaches, and foci that academic discourse follows, while journalism is tied to general categories easily or seemingly easily grasped by its audience. In the popular lexicon, the term "surreal" can be used as a catchall term for anything unusual, out of the ordinary or bizarre, while in the academic universe its meaning is more precise. Since Jodorowsky was not part of the formal surrealist movement, the surrealist elements in his films would make him a post-surrealist filmmaker with a predilection for surrealist values.

The final labeling consists of a collection of designations that together produce a composite identity that he has accepted and even fostered as a sort of "bad boy" of cinema. In the contemporary media he or his work attracts such pop descriptions as "psychedelic zaniness" (Kohn 2020), "the last survivor-practitioner of underground freaky radicalism" (Bradshaw 2020), and "a puppeteer of grotesque fantasy and psychedelic excess" (Kan 2018). In academic circles descriptive terminology is more circumspect. An academic reviewer of a book on Jodorowsky's *El Topo* stated that "Jodorowsky is difficult to classify" (Martin 2009). He was referring to the multiple genres in which Jodorowsky has worked, with a resulting difficulty of classification. Other famous filmmakers have stuck to their métier and so made it easier for scholars to locate their work in genre theory. One academic termed Jodorowsky a filmmaker of "charismatic authority" (Guida 2015, 539). A charismatic personality is suspect in academic circles, where it is often associated with populist demagoguery or religious cults. For some, Jodorowsky has presented himself as a self-proclaimed spiritual guru, which raises a flag about his cinema. The idea of a difficult-to-label maverick can be engaging for some, but it is negative for others, especially for those who wish to situate him in some kind of canon.

He has been accused of initially creating "arty exploitation," a category related to productions of low-budget horror films with sexual content. Fellow auteurs David Lynch and David Cronenberg began in the same genre but then migrated to art-house status (Cerdán and Labayen 2009, 102). Jodorowsky was able to make the same transition later in life. One aspect of Jodorowsky's filmmaking that has appeared in academic analysis is his Jewish identity and how it is manifested in his filmmaking. The release of his two autobiographical films—*La danza de realidad* (*The Dance of Reality*) and *Poesía sin fin* (*Endless Poetry*) in the 2010s—was a stimulus for this discussion. An early example is "Arbol genealógico y álburm de familia: dos figuras de la memoria en relatos de immigrantes judios" (Genealogical tree and family album: two memory figures in Jewish immigrant narratives) (Massmann 2005) and a later example is Blanc-Hoang's "Meta-performance and Jewish Identity in Alejandro Jodorowsky's *The Dance of Reality*" (Blanc-Hoang 2019). Most often these academic studies discuss the influence of Jewish mysticism and the history of anti-Semitism in Latin America on Jodorowsky's autobiographical work, whether literary or cinematic. His Jewish roots add a further factor to his other ethno-national identities—Chilean, Mexican and French.

Another fact that is often noted by academics is his film's religious symbolism. Titiana Lee Marques's 2014 article "Climbing the Holy Mountain—Alejandro Jodorowsky's Mystical Cinema/Subindo a Montanha Sagrada—O cinema mistico de Alejandro Jodorowsky" adds some of Jodorowsky's films to the category of sacred cinema. Earlier Henri-Simon Blanc-Hoang produced a doctoral dissertation titled "Allegorias del Mesianismo en la obra de Alejandro Jodorowsky" (Messianic Allegories in the Work of Alejandro Jodorowsky) (2005), while Adam Breckenridge wrote a valuable essay titled "A Path Less Traveled: Rethinking Spirituality in the Films of Alejandro Jodorowsky" (2015). These articles affirm the spiritual dimension in his films, which is one of the attributes that lifts it from cult or art exploitation status.

While popular commentary uses labels that highlight the more sensationalist aspects of his films, of his career, and of his personality, academics work hard to fit his work into acceptable scholarly concepts and theoretical frameworks. This book is a combination of the populist and the academic. It seeks to blend both worlds into a readable and insightful text that offers a view of the man, his films, and his fiery imagination that can be understood by layperson and scholar alike.

What This Book Is About

This book is meant to build on Ben Cobb's pioneering study *Anarchy and Alchemy* (2007) by including a discussion of his three subsequent films, *La danza de realidad* (2013), followed by *Poesía sin fin* (2016) and *Psychomagic, A Healing Art* (2019). Cobb provided detailed synopses of Jodorowsky's films, the historical and textual background to their production, brief discussions of his other graphic and narrative works, and a lengthy interview with his subject. Cobb is a British journalist, who later migrated into the world of fashion magazines. David Church, a scholar of Jodorowsky's work claimed that Cobb's book was "limited by its semi-academic tone and narrow degree of analytical depth" (Church 2007, 69). The limitation he is referring to is its lack of theoretical grounding promoted by film scholars. For most readers the lack of analytical depth and a semi-academic tone would be welcome. A more important drawback is his book's monolingual sources. This volume incorporates insights from academic work in English, French, Spanish, and other languages.

This volume makes use of the insights of numerous scholars to create a wider and fuller picture of Jodorowsky than can be gleamed simply from journalism or from recent scholarship limited to a specific film. When academics perceive an issue they search out commentaries by their peers to help guide them in their interrogation of that issue. Often they apply a particular theory or theories to the issue. The result is both a critique and an evaluation. The main issue that this book addresses is Jodorowsky's status as a filmmaker. Does he deserve to be elevated to the upper echelons of filmmaking and if so, why has he not achieved that status? For example, this is only the second book in the English language published on the totality of his cinema, while major auteurs tend to have significantly more studies published on their work. The reasons for this marginalization vary. First, there is the barrier created by his diffuse identity as an artist working in various genres. Second, there is his promotion and practice of idiosyncratic and unorthodox psychotherapeutic theories, which are relegated to New Age self-help literature. Third, there is the quarter-century break in his film production after 1990, as well as the equation of his work with the term "cult." Another reason that may have contributed to his marginalization is his persona as an accomplished mythmaker and publicist of his own image. This book looks beyond these publicity antics to explore the reasons for his shifting status as a filmmaker. In the process it argues that his film work deserves a major reappraisal.

While reviewing the literature on Jodorowsky's work and reflecting on an extensive body of interviews that offer his own insights and interpretations, this book aims to provide an interpretative framework for his work and his life that allows a more profound Jodorowsky to rise from the ashes of a tarnished reputation. In particular it explores the way he integrates theatrical practices and ideas, transformative psycho-healing therapies, and his work in comics into his cinema. This integrative practice is unorthodox for filmmakers, but fundamental to understanding Jodorowsky's achievement as a filmmaker. It is his integrative practice that makes demands on film audiences. When a filmmaker insists that his films become psychologically transformative happenings, then scholars become nervous. This kind of demand is beyond their scope of scholarship, so they try to explain his films using tried-and-true categories that apply to film practice as a separate and distinct art. While his films use all the usual elements—mise-en-scène, cinematography, actors and costumes, scores, scripts and plots, editing, and special effects—they offer much more than routine film productions. By bringing noncinematic elements into his films, Jodorowsky challenges those who work within the parameters of orthodox film studies. They in turn are led to question the validity of this approach and whether it makes a genuine contribution to the art form. This book intends to answer the question of whether his films are masterpieces of transformative cinema or whether they are something less.

2

A Brief Summary of the Life and Times of Alejandro Jodorowsky

Most biographical information on Jodorowsky that is easily accessible is online and usually presented in a few paragraphs as a prelude to a discussion of his films. This cursory treatment does little to illuminate the ties between his life and his art and how location, ethnic and national identities, art movements, and national environments influenced his creativity. The main print source of biographical information are his own autobiographical writings, which have to be approached with caution. These works are *Donde major canta un pájaro* (1992) translated as *Where the Bird Sings Best* in 2015; *La danza de la realidad* (2001) translated as *The Dance of Reality: A Psychomagical Autobiography* in 2014 and repurposed in 2013 as a film with its original name; *El maestro y las magas, memorias* (2005) translated as *The Spiritual Journey of Alejandro Jodorowsky* in 2008; and the cinematic memoir *Poesía sin fin* (2016) translated as *Endless Poetry*. His other writings contain sporadic autobiographical/anecdotal testaments.

Because of Jodorowsky's tendency to see the real world through a mythopoetic lens, none of his autobiographical works are an objective source of biographical information, though some are more factual than others. For example, the quote that follows from *Where the Bird Sings Best*, a book that tells the story of the family's migration from Eastern Europe to Chile in a mind-boggling 386 pages of hyper-magic realism, describes his father Jaime:

> Jaime split in two. Everything he saw became a mirror. Then he was three and four. He realized he could multiply until infinity and be in innumerable places at the same time. Again he laughed. For so many years, an entire lifetime, he'd been one, a prisoner of an imagined body. (Jodorowsky 2015, 310)

While the hall of mirrors image is intriguing, the view it presents of Jaime is totally metaphoric. Jodorowsky provides the factual (his father named Jaime) a completely imagined makeover. In an example such as this one, differentiating between the real and the imagined is easy, but Jodorowsky does not care to be obvious in all cases. Until such time as a legitimately researched biography comes to be, this chapter's biographical sketch is dependent on secondary sources (what others attribute to him), which may not always be accurate, and on primary sources (his own accounts), which are also suspect. Readers beware. While this summary errs on the side of caution, it cannot be considered an accurate, fully documented statement. It rests on shaky ground, but at this point, there is no other ground on which to stand.

Jodorowsky was born on February 17, 1929, a few months before the world fell into the Great Depression and not long before fascism and militarism rose from the scattered ashes of a failed capitalist order. Alejandro Jodorowsky Prullansky (his full name) was born in Topocilla, Chile. His parents were Jewish immigrants to Chile, who came from Ukraine after the Russian Revolution, first fleeing east to China. Jaime Jodorowsky Groisman(n) was his father and Sara Felicidad Prullansky Arcavi was his mother. They operated a dry goods store in this coastal town that served as a port for copper exports. His father (1901–2001) lived to be 100 and died in Haifa, Israel. He is parodied in both of Jodorowsky's autobiographical films. While it was in Topocilla that the boy's journey into the phantasmagorical began, it was in Santiago, the national capital, that he launched his artistic career. The family moved there in the late 1930s. During the next fifteen years that he lived there, the future filmmaker experienced the volatile political atmosphere of the time and the distant atmosphere of the Second World War. Although it was a conservative Catholic country in many ways, there was a strong left-wing current as well. A prominent example was the future Nobel Laureate, Pablo Neruda, who was a member of the Communist Party and a senator, who had to flee into exile after the party was banned in 1948.

Jodorowsky attended university after the Second World War but did not stay long. About this time he supposedly became acquainted with the soon-to-be celebrated poet Nicanor Parra (1914–2018), whose best-known book *Poemas y anti-poemas* came out in 1954. Parra went to the United States in 1943 and returned after his studies abroad in 1953, the same year that Jodorowsky sailed to France. It is doubtful (though possible) that Jodorowsky would have met Parra before 1943. Perhaps Jodorowsky attended the school where Parra taught. It is also unlikely Jodorowsky would have met him at the university, where Parra began to teach when he returned, since he had left university life in 1949, started his own theater group, and then left for France the same year Parra returned to

Chile. Parra is a character in *Poesía sin fin*, where he is presented as a cultural figure, originally revered by Jodorowsky. In the film he rejects Alejandro's youthful rebellion for the security of teaching. Jodorowsky is the inspired rebel, while Parra is a timid figure. What influence Parra had on Jodorowsky is yet to be determined. What is clear is that in his twenties Jodorowsky saw himself as part of Chile's avant-garde cultural scene, its issues, and its personalities.

The poetry that had first attracted him soon gave way to the performing arts. He preferred to *embody* the expression of words and ideas rather than limiting them to the page. He did some clowning at a circus and then started to direct theater in his early twenties, forming his own group, the Teatro Mimico, which he led till 1953, the year he wrote his first play *El Minotaura* (The Minotaur) and went to France. His name for the theatrical troupe illuminates his early artistic vision, as does the title of his first play. Mime and the fantastic are the two polarities of his then artistic communication. His work in theater is worth exploring in some detail by a knowledgeable theater critic or scholar because it laid the foundations of his future art, including cinema. The following is only a cursory discussion.

Mimico is Spanish for mimic. It means to imitate or copy and is associated with mime, a form of expression used in clowning, which is a silent art. Mime and a clown's use of a painted face and gesticulation to convey meaning without words is the essence of performative communication. The term "mimic" is rooted in the Greek term *mīmikós* and refers to mimes and miming, which had been practiced since the fifth century BCE. Jodorowsky's early emphasis on silent performances suggests that the art he was interested in was highly physical and a blend of the comic and the tragic. Audiences had to work to understand what was being wordlessly performed and narrated. This level of engagement by the audience appealed to Jodorowsky.

The Minotaur is a classical Greek mythological creature that is half man, half bull. The conjoining of human and animal and the transference of attributes from one to the other in both directions projects Jodorowsky's attachment to the grotesque and the fantastic. In Greek myth the Minotaur is trapped in a labyrinth, which reflects the labyrinthine theme that appears in Jodorowsky's later work. The monster is named after Minos, King of Crete and a son of Zeus, the most powerful of Greek mythological gods. Minos feeds the creature human flesh. The monstrous is an ongoing aspect of Jodorowsky's vision because it links the grotesque to the fantastic. What is also significant is that the Minotaur belongs to European mythology rather than South American pre-Columbian cultures. Clearly Jodorowsky was drawn to Europe as the cultural center of his universe. At that time European culture was a destination for many artists. Why did he go? The lure of artistic adventure and challenge was part of it. Not feeling fully attached to Chilean society was another. Perhaps experiencing anti-Semitism was another reason, or simply wanting to expand his understanding of mime could also have been a driver. For many young people, distant places with reputations for sophistication are a lure. Whatever his reasons, the departure for France marked the end of his Chilean apprenticeship and the beginning of his blossoming as a distinct artist attuned to European trends.

He arrived in Paris the year Stalin died. Jodorowsky was an unknown theater director and playwright from South America searching for a place in a vibrant avant-garde theater scene. He brought with him his attachment to clowning and miming and his desire to shock and provoke theater audiences. He was quickly absorbed into the performing arts—first by studying with Étienne Decroux, who was a radical innovator and theorist of pantomime. Decroux went to the United States in 1957 and established a school there before returning to France in 1962. Jodorowsky did not go to the United States with him, but one of Decroux's students, the famous Marcel Marceau, created a mime troupe that Jodorowsky joined and for which he wrote several routines. It was during this immersion in European mime that Jodorowsky, only four years after arriving in Paris, produced his first film. The short *La Cravate* (*The Severed Heads*) is twenty minutes long, has a cast of twenty, and is based on a Thomas Mann story. The 1957 film is performed completely in mime.

A few years later he abandoned Paris to move to Mexico City. This soon-to-be megacity was a cosmopolitan cultural center for the Spanish-speaking Americas, and home to a nationalistic, anti-American government. Again Jodorowsky arrived as an outsider, but he adapted quickly to working in theater. He premiered his fellow artist Fernando Arrabal's play "Fando y Lis" in Mexico City in 1961, which he later turned into his first feature film (Kerik 2018, 120). For the rest of the 1960s he lived in both Mexico City and Paris, traveling back and forth between two radically different worlds. When he was in Paris in 1962 he co-founded the Panic Movement (named after the mythological god Pan) with his Parisian collaborators Fernando Arrabal and Roland Topor. The result was a theater of extreme provocation. Its "happenings" combined the outlandish, the surreal, the absurd, and the profane. The group's most infamous play, the four-hour-long *Mélodrame sacramental* (Sacramental Melodrama) from 1965, contained nudity, flagellation, a heart nailed to a cross, and the butchering of two live geese. The spectacle incorporated ideas from Antonin Artaud's Theater of Cruelty, which was not so much about cruelty as such, but, rather, the use of coded symbols (the cross or nudity) in such a wild and irreverent way as to break through stereotypical comprehension and thereby build a visceral bond between the illogic and madness happening on the stage and the bewildered audience, whose complacency had been destroyed.

He had married the French actress Bernadette Landru and their first son Brontis was born in 1962, while they were living in Mexico City. Brontis later appeared in Jodorowsky's film *El Topo* as a young boy and again in two of his later films *The Dance of Reality* and *Endless Poetry*. Alejandro began working in the comic book/cartoon genre while in Mexico. In 1966 he joined with the Mexican cartoonist Manuel Moro to produce *Aníbal 5*, a comic book series, which later took on a new life with a French edition illustrated by the well-known comic book artist Jean Giraud (Mobius). It was re-released in 1990 with art by Georges Bess. Jodorowsky had written a sci-fi script for the work, in which a sex-crazed superhero tries to protect earth from cosmic terrorists. At the same time he was creating his own weekly comic strip titled *Fábulas pánicas* (Panic Fables), which appeared in *El Heraldo de México* from 1967 to 1973. These panic stories (and his theatrical happenings) were meant to create "panic" in an audience. While doing his comic strip and directing theatrical productions in Mexico, he wrote and directed his first feature film, *Fando y Lis*, a 96-minute black-and-white film that caused a riot when it was screened at the Acapulco Film Festival in 1968. When it screened in Mexico City there were fights in the audience. The film was very loosely based on Fernando Arrabal's play of the same name, which Jodorowsky had directed earlier. By shocking audiences and fomenting outrage, he knew he had touched a nerve. The film's plot involves a couple, one of whom is paralyzed, journeying through a desert wasteland in search of enlightenment, but discovering only horror and madness. Because of its inflammatory content and audience reaction the film was banned in Mexico until 1972.

The publicity only encouraged him to begin another film, the "cult" classic *El Topo*, his most famous and, some might say, noteworthy film. What is interesting about *El Topo* for this biographical sketch is how it became the turning point in his film career. He was able to make a film in Mexico and find an audience in the United States. He had been fortunate to sell *Fando y Lis* to a US distributor. It screened in New York for those interested in nudity and mayhem, but *El Topo* had a much bigger impact. Why? *El Topo* rode on the coattails of the popular Italian "Spaghetti" Western genre inaugurated by Sergio Leone in the mid-

1960s using American actors in such moody, little dialogued, yet powerfully scored films as *A Fistful of Dollars* (1964), *For a Few Dollars More* (1965) and *The Good, the Bad, and the Ugly* (1966). They were popular in the United States because of its home grown tradition of film Westerns. *El Topo*'s lead, played by Jodorowsky, is a lone gunslinger whose laconic personality was easily relatable to an American audience steeped in the Western genre and its valorization of male individualism. That it was the United States that lifted his film career to new heights is worth reflecting on. Even though his films subverted the Western genre, certain American audiences found the weird plots and bizarre imagery worth the price of admission. Likewise, the American film industry was always in search of business opportunities, especially when controversy was at play.

In the sixties Jodorowsky was an avant-garde theater figure in Paris, a director of (he claims) 100 plays in Mexico City, a comic strip creator, and an auteur filmmaker. What is the connection between the three art forms? Each has a visual aspect and each has a literary aspect, that is, a text. The performed word or the written word is encapsulated in imagery, whether on an illustrated page, a theatrical stage, or in a film scene. Jodorowsky always wanted to give the verbal a visual presence. This approach grew out of his foundations in mime in which communication was nonverbal and embodied.

El Topo attracted the attention of Allen Klein, a powerhouse in the American music business. He fronted the money for Jodorowsky's next film *La montaña sagrada* (The Holy Mountain). The film was released in 1973. Jodorowsky played the lead as he had done in *El Topo*, as well as other key production roles from directorial to music. The film plot centered on a powerful alchemist who leads a group of businessmen in search of enlightenment on a holy mountain. Jodorowsky's business deal with Klein gave Klein world distribution rights to both *El Topo* and *The Holy Mountain*. It turned out to be a deal with the devil. When Jodorowsky refused to make a film that Klein wanted him to do, Klein kept both these seminal films from public viewing for over thirty years. This basically undercut Jodorowsky's film career and he was left to fend for himself in a cinematic wilderness. It was not until the two men reconciled in the 2000s that the films returned to circulation (Jodorowsky 2005, 237–40 and Rose 2009).

Jodorowsky explained early on that he had left France because of his being viewed as an outsider. "I lived in Paris for ten years. The French didn't accept me because I was a 'Chilean.' I moved to Mexico." The latter also did not accept him, nor did the Americans later on (Cerdán and Labayen 2009, 104). Yet, throughout this period he went back and forth between the two countries that supposedly did not accept him. A short sojourn in the United States associated with work on *The Holy Mountain* ended quickly, when he returned to France. His was a peripatetic, unsettled existence in the 1960s and early 1970s. In the end it was Paris that provided the kind of refuge for his creative freedom which he was seeking. He has made it his permanent home for the past fifty years.

While shuffling between countries and continents and languages, he embarked on various consciousness-expanding journeys in both Mexico and the United States including Zen Buddhism with Ejo Takata in Mexico City. *The Spiritual Journey of Alejandro Jodorowsky* (2008) provides a kaleidoscopic description of his various experiments with religious traditions, including the practices of Indigenous female shamans and folk healers in Mexico. In the prologue he states: "Though I have written these memoirs in novelistic style, all the people, places, events, books, and quotations by sages are real" (Jodorowsky 2008, ix). While the book is not written in the hyper-magic realism of *Where the Bird Sings Best*, its portrayals need to be considered fictionally enhanced. Jodorowsky's Zen master had been trained as a Buddhist monk in Japan before arriving in Mexico City in 1967, where he became a well-known local figure, creating a Zen study center named "Zendo Aguila Blanca" (White Eagle Zendo). Eagles and mountains provide a regular theme in Jodorowsky's work. He was drawn to Zen Buddhism's mystical/mysterious mind-benders known as koan, paradoxical riddles or stories so contradictory that they undermine logical reasoning in order to produce an insightful revelation. As for the four women he called "magical" in his book, he says their shamanistic practices became "life-changing" for him (Jodorowsky 2005, x). The concept of magic is a rich one associated with trickery, alchemy, entertainment, and allusion. Magical women became an integral part of his cinema imagery.

Jodorowsky was approached in 1974 by a French consortium to direct Frank Herbert's 1965 science-fiction novel *Dune*, a work that had garnered international attention after winning the first ever Nebula Award in 1966 for American published science fiction and fantasy and sharing the 1966 Hugo Award, the most prestigious award in that genre. Jodorowsky was not the first nor the last to attempt to make a film version of what has come to be considered to be a grand epic of twentieth-century science-fiction literature in English. Among the figures who got involved in the film's production were Jean "Moebius" Giraud, who storyboarded Jodorowsky's script, H. R. Giger, who became famous for his work on the film *Alien* a few years later, and the science-fiction creator Dan O'Bannon, who also went on to write the script for *Alien*. The pop musical group

Pink Floyd was hired to write the music. Unfortunately or fortunately, depending on your viewpoint, the script never made it to the screen. No film studio put up the required funding, after several million had been spent in preparatory work. The making and unmaking of Jodorowsky's *Dune* was chronicled in a 2013 documentary by Frank Pavich titled *Jodorowsky's Dune.*

A decade later David Lynch made his version of *Dune* but it was poorly received. In 2021 Denis Villeneuve, who had become well known for his 2017 sequel to another well-regarded science-fiction film *Blade Runner,* released his version. On the whole, the film received positive, though not enthusiastic, reviews and grossed about $400 million in worldwide theatrical release, barely enough to make back its $165 million budget after adding its advertising and promotion budget to the total (Boxofficemojo.com 2022 and Agar 2021). Perhaps Jodorowsky was fortunate not to have made it, since his genius lay in auteur films. But like any filmmaker he had to make a living and accepting well-paid non-auteur assignments was part of it. His own account of this *Dune* episode in his life concludes with his refusing to call the project a failure. "Failure does not exist. It is a concept of the mind. Instead, let us call this a *change of path*" (Jodorowsky 2005, 230). He went on to say, "because we [Giraud and Jodorowsky] could no longer express our visions in cinematic form, I proposed we work together on graphic novels" (Jodorowsky 2005, 230). And they did, to much acclaim.

Linking his cinematic work with comic books as a continuation of his cinematic vision is important because it shows that Jodorowsky did not delineate one art form from another. It was simply a new manifestation of who he was and what he imagined. Moebius was an established comic book artist to whom Jodorowsky brought a script in 1977 that eventually became a 54-page graphic novella titled *Les yeux du chat* (*The Eyes of the Cat*), published in 1978. The protagonist is a blind boy, a character reflective of the many figures in his films who have disabilities.

He was able to do some film work as well. A French film company named Les Film 21 along with another French company Yang Films hired him to direct a French language film shot in India titled *Tusk* in English. It never received American distribution and is generally considered a failure. His inability to create or fund an auteur film like his previous three films meant that his visionary creativity moved to another field—the graphic or comic novel, where he had creative control. It is in this arena that his propensity for the fantastic, for science-fiction imagery and settings, plus surrealist narratives found its fullest expression during the 1980s. Anyone who wants to get a better understanding of his cinematic production must examine more closely this specific imaginative outpouring.

As a practitioner of the performing arts he was used to working with others. As a filmmaker he also worked with others and as a graphic comic creator he collaborated. This suggests strongly that he was comfortable working in a team, as long as his narrative vision was in charge. His major comic breakthrough came with *L'Incal* (1981–7), (*The Incal* in English), a science-fiction series that he realized with Moebius. Published in *Métal hurlant*, first when it was a quarterly and then when it became a bi-monthly magazine issued by *Les Humanoïdes Associés* of which Moebius was a member, *The Incal* concerns a private detective named John Difool, who embarks on a space odyssey adventure that leads to cosmic enlightenment. No doubt, both Jodorowsky's and Moebius's work on *Dune* found its way into this legendary graphic work. The value and importance of the comic is evidenced when *one page* of the original artwork was sold for 37,500 euros by Christie's in 2019 (Christies 2019). It was published in the United States by the *National Lampoon* magazine under the title *Heavy Metal*. It has come to be considered one of the seminal works of the adult comic book genre. Unfortunately, his successful work in the comic book genre contributed to his marginalization as a filmmaker. In the eyes of some critics and academics, his comic book fame associated him with a "lower" and highly pop culture segment. But one could argue that his association with the graphic comic was not in vain or a radical departure. It served as a narrative bridge from his 1970s work on *Dune* to his return to the cinema in 1989 with *Santa Sangre* (Holy Blood), a Mexican–Italian co-production filmed in Mexico. The protagonist, like all his protagonists, is a male. He escapes from an asylum and in a bizarre turn of events becomes his mother's arms, which are used to kill any woman he loves.

The last installment of the original French language *L' Incal* (there would be future iterations) appeared in 1987, with a new series starting in 1988. *Tusk* was released two years later. Clearly, a project like this could easily be two or more years in the making. So the move from the graphic novel genre to auteur cinema happened quickly and, in a way, seamlessly like the move from *Dune* to *Les yeux du chat*, suggesting that his scripts in the graphic novel genre were a form of narrative expression related to his cinematic imagination. *Santa Sangre* was the final installment in the grand trilogy of his auteur films that began with *El Topo* and it concluded the tetralogy that began with his first feature film, *Fando y Lis*. Four films in about twenty years does not make a substantial body of work, nor does the fact that very soon thereafter, his filmmaking ended. In 1990 he was a director for hire on *The Rainbow Thief*, a film that starred Omar Sharif and Peter O'Toole of *Lawrence of Arabia* (1963) fame. He subsequently disowned the film and stepped away from filmmaking for almost a quarter century.

Jodorowsky had divorced in 1982 and was living in a large apartment in Paris with his son Adán (Jodorowsky 2005, 235). While working on comics in the 1980s, he also integrated the experience and teachings of the Indigenous or folk healers he had frequented in Mexico into his own self-conceived psychotherapeutic practice termed "psychomagic." He published a book on his practice in 1995 titled *Le théâtre de la guérison, une thérapie panique* (*The Theater of Healing: A Panic Therapy*), a title that the publisher insisted on because the term "psychomagic" was unknown, but in France the Panic Movement was known. The project had originated in the late 1980s with Gilles Farcet, who did a series of interviews with Jodorowsky on psychomagic that eventually became the book. The book appeared in English translation in 2010. After the public success of the book, he practiced this therapeutic art on "two advice seekers per day, from Monday through Friday, in one-and-a-half hour sessions," the way any licensed psychotherapist might (Jodorowsky 2010, iii). He described his technique this way:

> After establishing their genealogical trees—siblings, parents, aunts and uncles, grandparents, great-grandparents—I advised them on psychomagic acts, which would produce notable results. This was how I developed a certain number of guidelines, which permitted me to teach this art to a large number of students, many of them already established therapists. I granted private sessions for two years, at the end of which I began to write *La danza de la realidad* (The Dance of Reality) [the first installment of his autobiography that came out in 2001]. (Jodorowsky 2010, iii)

Another aspect of his time in Paris was his engagement with the Tarot, a medieval system of fortune-telling cards that he related to his psychomagic therapy. In 2004 he published a major work on the subject, *La vía del tarot* (*Way of the Tarot* in 2009) with Marianne Costa. But all these diversions into books did not add significantly to his income. In a 2009 interview a British journalist concluded that "writing comic books is still his principal way of making a living" (Rose 2009). Beginning in the 1990s, nongraphic writing, including plays, poetry, fiction, and nonfiction became his passion. From the 1990s into the 2010s he published dozens of books, sometimes two per year, including works of hundreds of pages. To go from the brief texts in graphic works, including *Avant l'incal* (1988–95), *Le Lama blanc* (1988–93), *La Caste des Méta-Barons* (1992–2002), *Juan Solo* (1995–9) and numerous others, to inaugurating a writing career involving tens of thousands of pages of text is not a natural transition. It could very well have come about because of his numerous nonliterary activities that he sought to document and proselytize, or it could have come about because of an experiential maturity (he was in his sixties and seventies when this flood of writing occurred), or it could have been that his engagement with graphic comics was not sufficiently engaging to satisfy him, while he was still unable to return to the expensive art of cinema for financial reasons. By the end of the first decade of the 2000s, he was a semi-forgotten figure in the cinema world since he had stopped making films, but he was able to keep himself intellectually and artistically present to an audience through his writings as well as new iterations of his popular comics using the art of new artists.

The artistic and creative relationship between the graphic comic genre and his cinema is captured in the concept of "pictorial enunciation," which considers the image in graphic works and cinema as equally important as the text in telling the story. Jacques Samson in his article "Modern Strategies for Pictorial Enunciation in Comics" raises issues of signification, rhetorical strategies, and metadiscourse in the "modern comic" which contribute to it being "resistant to banal representationalism" (Samson 2014, 152). Both Jodorowsky's comics and his films resist banal representation because they direct the viewer/reader into a sophisticated zone of consciousness and psychological turmoil. Neither his comics nor his films are simple fantasies. They are complex scenarios with twisted Manichean characters, mythic plots, and deeply symbolic costuming set in ethereal and problematic environments.

His fictional and nonfictional writings can be surreal literary escapades or versions of real events and people that have been raised to a "comic book" level. They are characters and situations that are presented in an otherworldly way. What follows is an example of his literary writing from *Where the Bird Sings Best* which expresses that exaggerated cinematic/comic book tone. The narrator is describing a Tarot reading:

> Up ahead, on card number eleven, Strength, a woman with a huge head joins a luminous yellow lion. With her mouth closed, she listens, and he, with his jaws open, speaks, transmitting the message that pours into her the Infinite Profundity. (Jodorowsky 2015, 48)

In a more stylistically prosaic work, *The Spiritual Journey of Alejandro Jodorowsky*, he writes in a similar tone of cosmic mystery:

> These words fell like rain on the lips of a thirsty wanderer... I realized I was alive for a duration of time that was infinitesimal with the eternity of the cosmos, and what a privilege, a gift, and a miracle this life was. This instant of my existence was the same instant in which the stars are dancing, in which the finite and the infinite were united. (Jodorowsky 2005, 156)

The style of his ebullient prose in his books contrasts with the "sound byte" prose style required in comics and often in films. In the former he waxed eloquent, while in the latter he embraced brevity. The following example of dialogue in the film *The Dance of Reality* reflects a style that is similar to the text space in a single frame of comics:

> *Alejandro as a child*: The darkness is swallowing everything. It's going to devour us.
> *Sara*: Alejandrito, do I love you?
> *Alejandro as a child*: Yes, Mama.
> *Sara*: How much?
> *Alejandro as a child*: From the sky to the earth.
> *Sara*: This is not my love, it comes from God. I am merely the sender. As God creates all, so we all radiate His love. My son, the darkness loves you as much as I do, for it is God's shadow. (*The Dance of Reality* 2013, IMDb)

Both his graphic novel texts and his films originate in his life as a theater director and playwright. He wrote his first play while still in Chile, and then occasional plays until 1971, during which he was expressing the ideas of the Panic Movement. Then followed a long break of twenty-seven years in playwriting after which he wrote some new plays until 2009, about the time he turned to working on his first film in many years. The upsurge of playwriting in the first decade of the 2000s corresponded with the upsurge in his prose writing mentioned earlier. Jodorowsky's writing, whether prose or script, should be considered a single stream that split up when it encountered a barrier such as the cost of filmmaking. Yet, it remained the same creative water flowing in different channels.

The conclusion that can be drawn from this cross-genre connectivity is that Jodorowsky's films are not examples of occasional, sporadic spikes on a creative graph dominated by other art forms, but a continuation of a common artistic explorative journey with related themes and methods. The vision was singular, but its expression was multiple. That multiplicity had two main avenues—the dialogue of the comic book frame, a film, or a play plus the prose of a novel or nonfiction. Jodorowsky's vision was the bridge.

After an overly long hiatus another cinematic spike appeared on his creativity graph. It involved two films—the first was a second documentary about himself—*Jodorowsky's Dune* (2013), that was made by Frank Pavich and included interviews with Jodorowsky, the artist and designer H. R. Giger, the film's producer Michel Seydoux, and the writer Dan O'Bannon's widow. The author of the novel, Frank Herbert, had died in 1986. The documentary premiered at Cannes. The second was his autobiographical film *La danza de la realidad* (*The Dance of Reality*) that was also released in 2013, and also premiered at Cannes, where both the documentary and the feature film won awards.

The Dance of Reality was finalized in 2010/11 with on-location shooting in 2012. With a purported budget of three million dollars, the film was a French–Chilean co-production involving Michel Seydoux, formerly the producer of his 1989 film *Santa Sangre*. The three million-dollar budget realized only a half-million-dollar theatrical-release gross (Boxofficemojo.com "The Dance of Reality" 2014). The financial failure became a barrier to getting funding for the second installment in his memoir—*Poesía sin fin*, which he overcame through crowdfunding on the internet. Those who contributed on Kickstarter were offered poetic money bills with his face on them. You were supposed to spend the bills on nonmaterial goods such as "the poetry of the universe" (Kastrenakes 2015). The ploy paid off. According to Kickstarter, Jodorowsky raised over $400,000 from 3,500 backers, surpassing the campaign's goal of $350,000 (Kickstarter, "Poetry without End" 2015).

Endless Poetry premiered at Cannes, received fewer awards and nominations than the first film had, and grossed about the same amount—half a million. What the full cost of the film was to his company Satori Films is unknown. However, Jodorowsky and his company faced a $200,000 law suit over a loan from a backer of the film. Ordered to repay the loan, Satori Films (94 percent owned by Jodorowsky) declared bankruptcy in 2020 (Ramanchandran 2020). Before this happened, there was enough money remaining for Satori to fund a documentary film about Jodorowsky's practice of psychomagic that was released in the fall of 2019.

Psychomagie, un art pour guérir (*Psychomagic, A Healing Art*) was a feature-length documentary that incorporated his son Adán's music and cinematography by his wife Pascale Mondandon Jodorowsky, whom he married in 2007 and with whom he has worked on various art projects. The English-language reviewers were either perplexed by the film or confused by its intent. Ultimately they were dismissive because his art-inspired therapeutic technique seemed bizarre. Considering what happened financially to the three films he made in the 2010s, it seems unlikely that there would be funding for new cinema projects, but with Jodorowsky one never knows.

3

In the Beginning

La Cravate (1957) and *Fando y Lis* (1968)

La Cravate (The Severed Heads 1957)

Jodorowsky released his first film when he was twenty-eight. *La Cravate* (a.k.a. *Les tétes interverties/The Transposed/Severed Heads*) can be translated as *The Tie*. It is based on the Nobel Laureate Thomas Mann's 1940 novella, *The Transposed Heads: A Legend of India*, which tells the story of a love triangle involving two men, who switch heads for the love of a woman while under the influence of the beheading goddess Kali. The original Indian folktale was transposed into Jodorowsky's film via Mann's European imagination. The film is performed in mime.

In the film Jodorowsky plays a young man who desires a woman. She rejects him, so he resorts to trading in his head for others until he finds the right one that will appeal to her. He acquires the various heads in a shop run by a woman, whom he eventually falls for. After its premiere (supposedly in Rome in 1957) the film was lost until 2006, when the print was rediscovered by the son of two principals in the film (Ruth Michelly and Saul Gilbert) in his mother's attic in Munich (https://letterboxd.com/film/the-severed-heads/). Other sources claim the city was Berlin. The fact that there was probably only one copy or very few indicates its novice status. The film was added to the box set of his films released on DVD in 2007.

The film itself has a cast of fifteen, a significant number for a short film. Most of the cast appear only as human heads, whose bodies are hidden by the set design of full-height cardboard shelving. Likely they are members of the Marcel Marceau mime troupe of which Jodorowsky was a part. The production credits include Saul Gilbert, Ruth Michelly, and Jodorowsky, which is indicative of a collaborative effort.

The film begins with the young suitor Jodorowsky fidgeting with his long, wide purple tie (the kind artistes might wear in the nineteenth century) while entering a shop to buy flowers to use in wooing the object of his desire. He is pushed aside by a bully who wants first choice. The film's emotional driver is music by Edgar Bischoff which resembles that of a circus organ grinder's repetitive melody. Jodorowsky picks a flower that is dark blue. He takes it to the woman he desires to impress her as she reclines on a chaise lounge. She has a buxom figure and is wearing a purple dress. The color of her dress matches Jodorowsky's tie. Purple is a signifier that Jodorowsky will use in the future.

The woman rejects him, so he returns to the shop in the hope of becoming someone that she might like. Once he switches heads, his own head is put in a box on a shelf and marked with an asterisk. Various suitors, all supposedly Jodorowsky with a new head, are in turn rejected. The final suitor with the head of the original bully who had traded in his head earlier is also turned away. When all fails Jodorowsky removes the purple tie and turns it into a hangman's noose because he can no longer take the rejections. Then he stops and decides to get back his original head. When he finds the box that is supposed to have his head it is empty. The symbolism is clear. He has lost his head psychologically speaking and is without an identity. He has a nightmare in which various mimes go by him wearing different hats, symbolizing different identities. Meanwhile, Jodorowsky's head reappears in the bedroom of the female shopkeeper, who has taken a fancy to him and has taken his head home. We see her playing chess with apples and pears as pieces, symbolizing the battles of the sexes. Jodorowsky appears and she offers him a flute to play, which he does as a god Pan figure, and then being sleepy she goes to bed. As she lies there looking up at him, a tear rolls down his cheek as he realizes where his true love lies. Jodorowsky tries to exchange his original head for the bully's that he currently has on, but fails. The shopkeeper wakes up and makes the exchange. Now Jodorowsky is whole again.

The film ends with Jodorowsky throwing away the purple tie and embracing the severed heads shopkeeper who is wearing a blue dress similar to the color of the blue flower he had brought to his first object of desire. The word "fin" appears at the end of the film composed of torn pieces of the purple tie. The purple phase is over and the blue phase has begun. The color purple here represents a false obsession, while the color blue represents authentic love. The colors are near each other on the palette, which suggests that the distance between good and evil, true and false love is not great. Purple has various meanings: villainy being one of them, and hierarchical power represented by royal or episcopal purple is another. It is this latter meaning that he uses in future films. Blue is a more attractive color suggesting stability and contentment. It is also the color most often used in paintings of the goddess Kali, who is the patron divinity of the original story. The symbolic role of color to represent various states of emotional awareness is suggested at the beginning when the film's credits run over a background of a purple swatch, a blue flower, and a wave of red across the purple tie symbolizing love. The color red eventually becomes Jodorowsky's cinematic symbol of life.

A number of signature aspects of Jodorowsky's future films make their first appearance in this short. He plays the lead as he does in most of his auteur feature films. Acting the central role displays his attachment to performance and his love of the stage. His continuation of this custom in future films suggests that the internal transformations an actor must undertake to be convincing in his or her role are also dear to him as a form of expression, but also as a way of assessing his ability to engage an audience with a captivating persona. It also points in the direction of Jodorowsky's implanting his person (and later his family) in his cinema as a way of grounding the films in his personal universe. Second, the mixing of the grotesque (head swapping) and the comic (the head swapping business is a shop like any other) is an approach that will be revived in the later films. Third, the use of mime, that is, wordless communication through body language, belongs to a specific historic moment in his artistic endeavors, which he continued to varying degrees in his later films. Fourth, the emphasis on symbolic colors is crucial to the other auteur films, except for *Fando y Lis*, which is black and white.

The Peruvian academic José Carlos Cabrejo observes: "Many of the director's characters . . . once they go through times of confusion of what is real with what is dreamed or imagined, they rediscover themselves. The Jodorowsky mime embodied on screen is the first of them" (Cabrejo 2019a, 20). Here is the first sign of his commitment to transformation as the single most important aspect of his films and life. Of course, all films have a dramatic arc that involves change. While this film is typical of the kind of transformation/insight one might see in many other romantic comedies, the centrality of self-knowledge and self-transformation for Jodorowsky has its start here. Acceptance of one's true self allows change to happen when assumed identities fall away.

What *La Cravate* explains about Jodorowsky at this early stage in his film career is his deep attachment to the idea of masks and masques, the former rooted in ancient Greek plays, in which players wore masks expressing their identity, and the latter rooted in a European form of courtly entertainment, where masked figures in elaborate costumes performed, danced, and recited. The human heads in the film are presented as masks that offer a new identity. Mimes do not use masks. Instead their faces start out as blanks that take on various forms of emotional expression. A white face, used by both clowns and mimes like Marcel Marceau, is part of that initial blankness. A white face offers either a sad or a happy persona against which other emotions can be displayed. Several years after making this film, Jodorowsky created a seven-minute mime for Marcel Marceau titled *The Mask Maker*.

La Cravate is an adaptation like his next film *Fando y Lis* and like that film it is a very light adaptation, meaning that the connection to the original inspiration, whether it be a novella or fable or play, is transformed by Jodorowsky into a narrative imprinted with his own style and content. It may be claimed that *La Cravate* is a broader metaphor of his own transposition from one country (Chile) to another (France) and his needing to take on a new culture, a new language, and therefore a new identity. Since Jodorowsky was an immigrant in France, who had to learn a new language after arrival, his working in mime, including this film, removed this drawback.

As a film it is unremarkable and innocent in tone. The complete absence of the kind of provocative material that dominated later was most likely the result of the film's collaborative structure, as well as the general norm for mime performances. It lacks the quality of a successful calling card for future cinematic work. The film is much more mime-influenced than surreal in its execution. It has a two-dimensional quality with little depth of field in the filming and the sets are similarly flat. It is inexpensively thrown together and reflects more of a stage play than a movie set. Jean Cocteau, a prominent French playwright and the filmmaker behind a 1932 surrealist-style film titled *Le Sang d'un poète* (*The Blood of the Poet*) is said to have introduced Jodorowsky's film (at the premiere perhaps?), but that introduction is not part of the film itself, so it is uncertain what his role was, if any. That the film was hidden away for half a century indicates that its makers paid little attention to its promotion. It is more of an exercise than a serious attempt at filmmaking. Nevertheless, it was a portent of things to come.

In contrast to this little film is the emergence in France at this time of the La Nouvelle Vague or New Wave cinema, deeply engaged with political and social issues and stylistically different from French film up to that point. Two major films of that movement, François Truffaut's *400 Blows* (1958) and Jean-Luc Godard's *Breathless* (1960) stand in contrast to this first film by Jodorowsky. He was not part of this movement or of the cinema scene in general. He was attuned to theatrical performance and did not see himself as a filmmaker at this stage, which he was not. His interest was human relations expressed in a symbolic way. It would be ten years later and in another country that he would be ready to do another loose adaptation and begin his real journey as a filmmaker.

Fando y Lis (1968)

Jodorowsky first went to Mexico with the mime master Marcel Marceau and then he moved there. Mexico is Spanish-speaking but vastly different from Chile. It has a revolutionary history and an established secular, liberal tradition. He could work in his native Spanish tongue and so move away from mime, and he could bring what he had learned in Europe to Latin America. But most importantly, he could now be in charge of his own productions like he had been in Chile. He began his working life in Mexico by staging avant-garde plays by European playwrights such as Ionesco and Beckett, as well as stage adaptations of works by Kafka and Nietzsche (Cerdán and Labayen 2009, 104). He also returned to Paris to co-create the Panic Movement and launch its outrageous happenings. He had previously run into problems in Mexico with his plays to such a degree that he had to do them as one-offs in order to avoid their cancellation. These one-time-only events were Jodorowsky's way of continuing to build an audience that appreciated his subversive staging. Single events also allowed him to avoid trouble with the authorities. He termed these events *efímeros*, which refers to a short-lived or ephemeral occurrence. His European Panic events are in harmony with the spirit of his Mexican *efímeros*. In turn these happenings created an artistic guide for his filmmaking.

Fando y Lis is based on a play written by his colleague in the Panic Movement, Fernando Arrabal, who had come from Spain to France in 1955 at the age of twenty-three, just a few years after Jodorowksy arrived from Chile at the age of twenty-four. They were both of the same generation and from Spanish-speaking cultures. Jodorowsky acted in the play, which tells the story of a man and a woman on a quixotic journey to the magical city of Tar. The play was meant to confuse the audience, undermine rationality, and convince it to accept and even join in the staged mayhem. Jodorowsky described the play as having "a childish purity in a sadomasochistic world" (Cobb 2007, 46). When he returned to Mexico he could see the play working as a film. Jodorowsky established his own film company named Produciones Pánicas and enlisted the help of individual investors, who raised $300,000 (about $2.6 million in 2022 dollars) (Cerdán and Labayen 2009, 105). This was a sizable budget for its time and place, especially for a Mexican film shot in black and white.

Another inspiration for Jodorowsky to turn to cinema may have been the work of the Spanish surrealist Luis Buñuel, who had renounced his Spanish citizenship in 1949 and become a Mexican. His film *El ángel exterminador* (*The Exterminating Angel* 1962) won the critics' prize at Cannes. A bit later Buñuel did another film in Mexico that also won a prize at the Venice Film Festival. All this would have been known to Jodorowsky, who may have seen an opportunity for himself to get into the field in a serious way. When he did make his first feature he used Carlos Savage as its editor. Savage had been the editor in all of Buñuel's Mexican films (Cobb 2007, 47). Curiously, Jodorowsky had already returned to cinema in a modest way while in France, when he made *Teatro sin fin*, an eighteen-minute documentary composed of assembled footage from the May 1965 Panic Movement performance of *Sacramental Melodrama* staged at the Paris Festival of Free Expression. The title of the film is repurposed in his 2016 film *Poesía sin fin* (*Endless Poetry*) because the idea of the abolition of boundaries, of being without end, is central to his philosophy of film. *Teatro sin fin* begins with a well-edited sequence of shots of ballet-like dancing figures accompanied by symphonic music. The imagery and the music lulls the audience into a sense of gentleness, but soon the mood changes with staccato drumming accompanying naked female dancers giving off clucking sounds and twisting to the drumbeat. Then figures in sadomasochistic leather outfits appear. They make animal-like screams and guttural noises to continue the mayhem. The film's movement from the benign to the obscene and from the gentle to the violent was a pattern repeated in *Fando y Lis*.

In the mid-1960s, Jodorowsky was fully into the god Pan-inspired anti-theater event when a Mexican publisher brought out his book *Teatro Pánico* (*The Theatre of Panic*), expressing his ideas on ephemeral happenings. The book may be considered a kind of closure for the theatrical part of his creative life. Nevertheless, his artistic vision remained grounded in the Panicism that he had helped found. Filming the *Sacramental Melodrama* happening and using clips from it in a short film could have been his way of expressing a desire to overcome the ephemerality of such events by allowing parts of it to be shown over and over again. Since he was totally new to feature films, his determination to make *Fando y Lis* must have been very strong.

The film was shot on weekends between July and December 1967 and then premiered the following year at the Acapulco Film Festival (Cerdán and Labayen 2009, 105). The film proved to be so unsettling that Jodorowsky was attacked by the audience and had to flee. The film was eventually banned by the Mexican authorities. The controversy caught the attention of an American distributor, who hoped it would appeal to the soft-core porn market because of its nudity, sexual content and violence. Jodorowsky is quoted as saying "the scandal it . . . opened . . . doors for me" (Cerdán and Labayen 2009, 106). The scandal confirmed the importance of notoriety for success in the film business.

The move from theatrical happenings to cinema involved transferring his philosophy of the *efímeros* from the stage to cinema. That philosophy is explained in *Teatro Pánico*:

> *Todo es teatral y nada lo es.* Los límites entre le "efímero" y la realidad se harán tan ambiguos como los límites entre pintura y escultura. (Burgos 1984, 212)

> [*Everything is theater and nothing is.* The boundaries between the ephemeral happening (efímero) and reality become as ambiguous as the boundaries between painting and sculpture (tr. the author).]

Jodorowsky's espousal of the blurring of boundaries in art forms arose from the ambiguous boundary between theater and cinema, which are both performative events with directors, actors, sets, and so forth. The blurring can also be applied to representation and the "real" world, that is, the blending of the producing experience of the presenters with the attending experience of the audience. His aim was to establish a single emotional field shared by both actors and audiences. The illusion, whether cinematic or theatrical, must be turned into a real experience similar to the one Jodorowsky observed with the conjuring of Mexican shamanistic healers. They were able to convince the audience and the patient that what was happening was "real." This was the magic that Jodorowsky wanted to reproduce in his films.

The mixing of the real and the fantastic was at the core of the Panicism he loved so dearly. The flyer for the Acapulco screening suggested that the physical violence in the film was "real" (Cabrejo 2019a, 24). This is precisely the kind of provocation that Jodorowsky wanted to foster. However, creating a single reality without boundaries between an audience and performers in a live theater is easier than doing the same thing in a cinema screening. The former (theatrical) involves a single space shared by live actors and audiences, though there is a physical divide between stage and seating, which can be overcome psychologically. Having a live-action event on stage, whether a musical concert or a play, can be more engaging for an audience, especially if it can stand up, be close to the action on the stage, and be free to move with the action. The sense of participation can be high. The suspension of disbelief required by "watching" a film on a screen can be harder to achieve since most film audiences experience films in a sedentary state that encourages disengagement. This is why oral sound and music play such an important part in feature film narratives. They augment normal visual engagement.

How successful was Jodorowsky in translating Panicism from the stage to the screen? His short film *Teatro sin fin* does convey some of the intensity and mayhem of the four-hour happening, but one is aware of simply watching something that had once been. One does not feel involved the way an audience member would at the event itself. The screen mediates events. It is a representation to its audience, while the stage shares a common space and time with its audience. Working to overcome this cinematic distancing was Jodorowsky's biggest challenge in making *Fando y Lis*.

The brochure that accompanied the premiere of the film in Acapulco stated that the film should be viewed as a combination of Dante's Hell in the *Divine Comedy* and Homer's *The Odyssey* (Cabrejo 2019a, 23). This combination of trials to be overcome and a final descent into the abyss is played out under the guiding light of surrealist ideology and practice. Besides the classical literary allusions, Jodorowsky mentions the folktale of Hansel and Gretel, who outwit the witch who wants to eat them for dinner, as an inspiration. In Jodorowsky's vision Fando and Lis do not escape evil in the end. They are devoured. As is appropriate for a fairy tale, the film begins with a voice-over announcing "Once upon a time …" The voice-over, identified in Cobb's published script as the character of Fando's Father, describes the city of Tar as a rejuvenating mecca, suggestive of the Spaniard Ponce de Léon's legendary search in the sixteenth century for the fountain of youth in Florida. But the voice-over for all its seductive tones is accompanied by still images done as late medieval woodcuts displaying brutality. The father creates a fairy tale for his son that ends in tragedy.

Synopsis of the Film and Its Meaning

The film has four parts, just like the play. Jodorowsky calls these sections "cantos," a narrative form associated with epic poems such as Dante's *Divina Commedia*

(*Divine Comedy*), referenced by Jodorowsky earlier and translated as "song" or "chant." Certainly the words of the voice-over, whispered in a storyteller's inviting tone, have poetic qualities. Cobb took up this connection to poetry when he described the film as a "surreal cine-poem" (2007, 46). The elaborate symbolic richness of the film, its metaphoric allusions, and its multiple dimensions certainly give it a poetic quality.

The film has a prologue that begins with a reclining Lis, dressed in white, eating flowers. The scene suggests a state of innocence belonging to humanity's first parents in the biblical Garden of Eden, but that state of grace is subverted by her eating the flowers rather than just smelling them, a hint of a troubled future. Her idyll is disrupted by a voice-over narration (Jodorowsky's) backgrounded by a series of medieval-like woodcuts with disturbing and threatening images. We are now in the first canto. The voice-over is enticing, claiming that "you'll find ecstasy" by going to the magical city of Tar. This is the message that Fando and Lis fall for. The young have idealistic fantasies about the purity of love and the state of the world. Soon after, a younger version of Fando and his father engage in a Buddhist koan dialogue about dismemberment and death. In this way Jodorowsky links Eros (love/life) with Thanatos (death).

An older Fando embarks on an epic journey to the ideal world of Tar, taking the beautiful paraplegic Lis with him. She is taken out of her Garden of Innocence, symbolized by her white dress, and placed atop an ugly utilitarian cart that a laborer might use to haul sacks of potatoes. Like the wagon in Brecht's play *Mother Courage*, this cart is rich in meanings linked to burden, toil, and the sorrow of the human condition. The young couple's journey through a post-apocalyptical landscape is epic only in the sense that it throws up a seemingly endless cast of fantastic characters who attack, lure, and distract them from going anywhere. While the film has a start and an end to the journey, it is not a typical road movie. It is more of a hallucinatory "head-trip" than a travelogue.

At the start, Fando and Lis witness a Fellini-like scene with jazz musicians providing cool music, a piano burning as it is played, and women in white moving languorously to the music. There are more such surreal scenes in the film. The action is disrupted by a cut to a female figure in black leather, a dominatrix with a whip, striding down into the scene. This technique of disrupting a peaceful scene occurs over and over again in the film. Jodorowsky wants this series of contrapuntal movements to show the tension between Eros and Thanatos and how the characters in the film respond to the good and the bad that confront them. Over time, the accumulation of all these threats and disruptions begins to affect Fando's mind and his attitude toward Lis. Initially he is seen by her as a savior, but then he turns into a torturer, rapist and, ultimately, her murderer.

The journey is disrupted by flashback scenes. The first is Lis as a little girl meeting a puppeteer played by Jodorowsky himself, who invites her to see the world behind the façade of puppetry that she finds so pleasing. She is lifted over the set and put on the other side, where she is forced to sign a contract with the promise of money if she will let herself be turned into a puppet he can control. It's a form of selling your soul to the devil. The scene is pure Jodorowsky, both as a former puppeteer himself and as commentary on the relationship between finance and art. The sequence ends with a strange, wreck-hopping dance in an auto junkyard in which Fando ends up being teased and lured by three bourgeois women, who blindfold him and then trick him into kissing a man. He is paid off in money, which he throws away in disgust. The theme of the contradiction between art and money is something that Jodorowsky felt right from the start. He used money to make his art rather than using his art to make money. The bourgeois figures in this film reappear as establishment characters in his other films with the same vile attitudes of smugness, hypocrisy, and exploitation.

Another theme that is perennial in his films is death, which has a strong inauguration in *Fando y Lis*. The burning piano seen earlier collapses upon itself as if it were a sacred pyre, on which one art form (music) dies in the hope of rising phoenix-like as another. The scene leads into Fando and Lis cavorting in a cemetery, which would have been particularly offensive to Mexican audiences at that time. The action is done in mime as an imitation of the silence of the grave. Fando and Lis uncover a doll which they take on the wagon/cart along with an antique gramophone and a drum, two symbols of reborn music. These three objects are reminiscent of props that might be used by a circus clown in a pantomime.

The second canto begins at the twenty-minute mark. It has the same mix of silent scenes and brief spurts of cryptic dialogue found in the first canto. Jodorowsky has adopted the use of intertitles at the beginning and/or end of a canto similar to the ones used in silent films. This reinforces the silent film character of much of the film and explains the kind of facial language that it uses to communicate, a combination of silent film expression and mime. His use of intertitles also adds to the fairy tale element in the film because it "pictures" or visualizes the language of the narrative and makes the audience aware of its being a story.

The story/journey appears as a series of disjointed episodes with very little purposeful relationship to one another. It is as if the underlying journey concept is inconsequential in the face of the experiences felt or actions undertaken by the two protagonists in each scene. What is the point of this? The disconnectedness is the essence of the film's structure and its defining reality. What happens in each scene is what holds the audience's attention, no matter how bizarre, unbelievable or even offensive it may seem. The journey *qua* journey or narrative flow is secondary. A turning point in what narrative arc there is comes when a wizard-priest appears as Fando is carrying Lis horizontally either on his back or in front of him. Together their bodies create a human cross. The cross motif is part religious (Lis is eventually viewed as a saint because of what she suffers) and part a statement of psychological burden. The wizard-priest is wearing a vestment which itself has a pattern of crosses so that the three of them are linked. He calls out to them and Fando asks him: "Is this the way to Tar?" And he responds: "It is if you think it is!" It's all in your mind as the saying goes.

Suddenly obese topless women appear. They have the body shape of ancient fertility symbols and they lead the couple into a mud hole filled with semi-naked bodies rolling and twisting like worms or snakes. At one moment Lis is shown standing in the mud hole as if she has been cured of her affliction. It is after this episode with the fertility symbols and the mud people that Fando begins to speak cruelly to Lis. His mind is now muddied or impure. The wizard-priest, like the Father who enticed him to take up the journey, has cast a spell on Fando and revealed his dark side.

Fando pulls Lis from the wagon and drags her on the ground and then abandons her when he meets three older women playing cards and feeding a boy that they kiss. Fando flees from them only to be confronted by more women, this time with bowling balls and a whip which they use on him. They put him into a shallow grave as he cries "Father, Father." His father is not there to save him. Ultimately, Fando is alone with his own personality and its light and dark sides. He has to navigate the contradictions himself. The scene switches to an abattoir piled high with cattle skulls with Lis lying on them and it ends with a man viciously excavating a doll's innards and then filling the cavity with snakes. Returning to Lis, Fando kisses her bloodied legs. Her body represents his return to reality and the task at hand, while his endless hallucinations represent the turmoil of his inner soul. He bounces from one to the other.

The third canto begins with an intertitle that reads "A man alone is always accompanied," which leads into a scene with transvestites prancing and dancing in the desiccated landscape through which he has been transporting Lis. They dress him as a woman. This cross-dressing scene echoes the earlier scene where he is fooled into kissing a man. One idea seems to be that Fando is easily transformed; the other is that sexual identity has a gender duality. Considering Jodorowsky's interest in making cinema transformative this scene of gender-transformation and gender-blending is more than just a psychoanalytical understanding of gender. It is tied to the importance of costume as an expression of gender, of the transformative power of costume in expressing personality as it would be in acting, and the central role played by costume in interpreting who and what we understand the person to be. Fando wears a black leather jacket that contrasts sharply with Lis's white dress. When he is dressed in other costumes, he becomes someone else.

The next scene involves a white-walled room in which Fando paints his name all over Lis's naked body and she reciprocates. Then they both throw black paint all over the white walls turning the room into a black-dominated mosaic. The whiteness (innocence) has been destroyed by blackness (evil). As in the earlier mud scene, Lis is standing, which only confirms that the reality of the cart she sits on stands in opposition to the fantasy of their dreams. As they walk out together (echoed in the finale), they become one with the room rather than being figures within it. Then they are on the road again where they are approached by a man with a syringe who extracts blood from Lis's vein, drinking it after telling her his blind companion needs it. This diversion into vampirism is part of the continuing abuse of poor Lis by men, just as Fando is continually being abused by women. These gender-based attacks blend their identities, so that in the end they are one and the same being.

While recuperating from this out-of-the-blue incident the audience is taken to a scene with a woman enthroned in a feather-resplendent chair. She offers to die for everyone. She is introduced to Fando as his mother, whom he eventually strangles with her personal blessing. The rationale for this act of matricide comes from his mother's responsibility for having his father executed. This tangled Greek tragedy ends the third canto. As the film moves into the fourth canto, the sense of death intensifies. The grand finale with the death of both Lis and Fando is at hand.

When Fando tries to have sex with Lis, she resists; so Fando chains her to the wagon/cart and calls out to men to see her naked. At first he watches voyeuristically and then describes her to them the way one might a piece of merchandise or a slave. The men fondle her and go away and the journey resumes. Fando's animosity toward and abuse of Lis is disturbing because it signals her new status as a commodity. At one point Lis complains to Fando, "We haven't gone anywhere." They haven't progressed to Tar at all because the journey is primarily internal rather than geographic. While Lis hasn't changed from her white-costumed innocence, Fando has become increasingly perverted in his attitude and actions.

He drags her from the cart and cruelly forces her to crawl on the ground. In return she throws away the drum and it is damaged. He is infuriated like a petulant child whose toy has been broken, and he attacks her, eventually killing her. He has become an incarnation of the duality of Eros and Thanatos, love and death. The fourth canto was introduced with the image of a two-headed human being and that is what he/she represents—love and hate, care and cruelty, attraction and revulsion. Lis, once the object of desire, is now the object of homicidal anger. An inanimate object (the drum) becomes more precious than a living person (Lis) and his embracing of that value leads not only to her murder but to his death as well.

The duality/singularity of the two-headed being is represented when Fando, after he has killed Lis, carries her body on his back and they become one body with their two heads touching. While it is clear that Lis and Fando are ultimately a single being with two sides (Janus-faced), this representation needs to be viewed in the context of a larger entity—a trinity of characters. Initially the film shows the father and son binary followed by the Fando and Lis binary, but it also suggests a trinity of Father, Fando and Lis, followed by the trinity of Fando, Lis, and the cart symbolizing journey, and then the objectification of the trinity concept in the gramophone, drum, and doll. The Janus-faced duality of every human's potential for both good acts and evil ones is placed within the familial trinity of Father, Mother, and Child. This family structure reappears in his next film, *El Topo*, where all binaries (man and woman) resolve into ternaries (man, woman, and child)—and they are repeated in every other film of which he is the auteur.

After retrieving Lis's body from a crowd of locals who cut off parts of her body as a kind of communion, Fando carries her on his back to a final resting place. Earlier her body is carried by a horse led by a one-legged man, mirroring her disability, but also prefiguring the use of characters in later films who have some other infirmity, disability or deformity. In the last canto the Father's voice-over tells Fando and the audience that "In Tar you'll wear a golden crown upon your head," which suggests that Fando's own death is about to happen. All the shallow graves in which Fando found himself earlier in the film are replicated in his final resting place, where he is covered in leaves which darken his body, while beside him is Lis's grave. This Romeo and Juliet finale is initially filled with lamentation associated with her death and atonement associated with his, but the film ends with a hallucinatory transfiguration/resurrection as a naked Fando and Lis, holding hands, run off into an Edenic forest. They are now free spirits. One can speculate that Tar is equated with death itself. In death, that is in Tar, Fando is freed from all his tormenting fantasies and the whole corpus of his dreaming. In death there is peace.

There can be a variety of interpretations of this fable and its events. Cobb offers a detailed and rational series of explanations, such as the mother's responsibility for Fando's father's death as the reason Fando strangles her or that his mistreatment by his mother in his childhood produced trauma that led to his killing of Lis. But there is a more symbolic interpretation that leads one to conclude that the murder of Lis and the suicide of Fando are one and the same since they are the two sides of one being. Everyone central to the story must die. Why? It can be argued that the journey to Tar is a metaphor for the life journey to death. All the traumas of childhood are relived in adulthood and the only relief from life's endless pain and suffering is the peace of the grave.

Does the film have a streak of misogyny because of Fando's violence toward his mother and girlfriend? On the rational level it would seem so, especially since so much of the violence done to his own person is by women figures and his seeking retribution could be justified by what he has undergone as a male. It would be a simple cause and effect. But on an irrational level the logic of cause and effect evaporates. If Lis is Fando and Fando is Lis and if the mother as stated welcomes her death and his father dies as a revolutionary hero, then the application of misogyny is too simple. Of course, the way the film is shot and edited makes it very difficult for a first-time viewer to grasp clearly the logical interpretations presented by Cobb. Things happen too fast and are often too contradictory and disjointed to facilitate a logical understanding. Cobb was trying to rationalize Jodorowsky's irrationality.

In the documentary film *La Constellation Jodorowsky* in which Jodorowsky is interviewed twenty-five years after he made *Fando y Lis*, he recounts that he had recently viewed it again and found it to be a "pure piece of art" that he made "instinctively" (Mouchet 1994, 19 min.) without any consideration for the audience. He claims that when making a film he is like "a mystic in a trance" (1994, 26 min.). This image ignores his preparation of a shooting script, his work as a director dealing with actors in every scene, his work raising funds to make the film and his experience with Mexican film unions, and all the editing and postproduction activities. But it does fit with his projection of the persona he likes to be cloaked in—the filmmaker whose only concern is art.

Jodorowsky's interpretation of himself as an artist is present in the film. First, there is Jodorowsky as the Father Narrator speaking over the intertitles, which imitates the role of the screenwriter. Second, there is Jodorowsky acting as the puppeteer and enticing the child Lis to become a puppet, which resembles the role of a director. Third, there is the persona of the wizard/priest who leads Fando and Lis down the road to perdition and salvation. Jodorowsky is the magician who makes the film appear out of thin air on the screen. In each of these roles, he is a male god-like figure holding all the power and all the authority.

Critical Response

Not only did the film experience public and official opprobrium in Mexico, it also received negative critical reaction in the United States even with the more salacious material removed. The *New York Times*, in a review titled "*Fando and Lis*, a Film Calculated to Shock," described the film as derivative of Fellini's work and the film's attempt to escalate the level of shock as ho-hum and ultimately uninteresting (*New York Times* 1970). The review considered that the imagery was intentionally constructed by the filmmaker simply to up the level of provocation without having any redeeming merit. What the American reviewer did not know was the film's roots in Jodorowsky's *efímeros* in which disturbing and contrary images were the norm. Nor did the reviewer know about Jodorowsky's intense work in the anti-theater of Panic. Instead, the reviewer used common points of reference such as the cinema of Fellini to explain the film. That only a couple of scenes (in Canto 1, the languid dancers in a field of rubble and in Canto 3 the dance of the transvestites) are clearly Fellini esque ought to have alerted the reviewer that the film had much more going on than this simple reference, but an American reviewer without any other point of reference could be excused from failing to grasp the film's importance. The mis-en-scène changes rapidly in the film, making it episodic and disjointed, and difficult to understand. This can be confusing and off-putting to a viewer unfamiliar with Jodorowsky's technique and its purpose, which is to disrupt linear chronological flow more or less completely.

One way to read Jodorowsky's abrupt and disorienting narrative junctures is to view them as cards symbolizing various states such as Death (the scene in the cemetery) or Desire (the scene of group fondling of Lis) or Love and Death (the scene of the kissed and then eviscerated doll packed with wormy snakes). Another is to view them as static tableaux that tell a whole story in a single image, which is the role of the woodcut images depicting various threatening and dire situations at the beginning of the film. Finally, the scenes can be viewed as dream sequences that are no more than jigsaw pieces without a logical fit or purpose. In most scenes he articulates enticement or allure.

The film is more than dysfunctional confusion. It contains within it the major themes of his future films, such as death (graves, coffins, and crypts), the importance of the symbolic (crosses, birds), the central role of dreams in understanding the psyche and its neuroses, and the essential fabulist nature of storytelling. Extravagant and symbolic costuming, nudity, dance, sex, and the role of muses, guides, mothers, and healers are all presented for the first time. At the core of his storytelling is the foundational image of the family. All these themes and elements evolve into cornerstones of his filmmaking.

The initial response of outrage and condemnation in the Mexican media and the blasé treatment as imitation of Fellini in the United States led to the film's hibernation. Even after *El Topo* made the filmmaker a celebrity of sorts, shortly thereafter *Fando y Lis* was simply too bizarre to resurrect. Academic attention came only after the DVD was released in 1999 (Fontana), which Cobb used for his 2007 book, and then it was re-released in 2007 (ABKCO), which made it accessible. But it was not until later in his career, after he reappeared as a filmmaker with his autobiographical films of the 2010s, that attention to it became more pronounced because it was added to box sets of his works.

A reasonable place to begin with academic critique is the claim of Spanish academics Cerdán and Labayen that Jodorowsky "may have been the first filmmaker to have successfully crossed over from exploitation to the mainstream, making films that simultaneously embrace both cult and exploitation categories" (2009, 102). Putting aside the debatable claim of his primacy, the matter of the "exploitation" nature of *Fando y Lis* needs to be addressed. They define exploitation films as those made "*to exploit* the audience" (2009, 102). Exploitation films are designed to have a "primal attraction" that uses "sensuality and shock, the chaos of their narratives, their ragged, fevered construction" to turn the audience's psyche from simply one of viewing to some form of participation (Schafer 2019, xii). One can attribute exploitive characteristics to *Fando y Lis*, but what

Jodorowsky does when using exploitive images is to simultaneously subvert them. For example, his presentation of nudity can be figurative, by which I mean the body takes on the characteristics of a figurine, static and unresponsive, and lacking in the erotic element that a typical exploitation film would exploit. In one scene in which semi-nude male and female bodies writhe in a pool of mud, their slithery motions are snake-like and anti-prurient. *Fando y Lis* may appear to fit the terms of exploitative cinema superficially, but under that surface is a cauldron full of intense imagery that conveys the idea that we live in illusion. The outlandish and bizarre costuming, the sometimes grotesque personalities, and the disturbing actions or performances are all ways of enforcing the idea that humanity lives in a dream-like state in which the imagination rules.

What about the "cult" characteristics? The film's public reception in Mexico was associated in the media as the work of a pornographer (Cerdán and Labayen 2009, 105). Its being slighted in the United States by reviewers and audiences certainly never gave it a chance to achieve the status of a cult film. The basic ingredients of strange and amazing characters, anti-normative behavior and illogical dialogue, and mind-expanding parodies of the human condition are all there. They simply don't blend into a single whole the way they did in his next film *El Topo*, which came out only two years afterward. *Fando y Lis* lacked cinematic refinement (its inherent visual and narrative choppiness and disorientation) because it was too heavily enmeshed in Panicism and because it was his first feature film, when he had no real experience as a film director. While each scene is complete in itself, its connection to other scenes and the overall narrative arc are uncertain. There is a contradiction in the film between narrative flow and dramatic scenes. Sometimes one feels that one is watching a three-ring circus simultaneously or seeing one short and complete sketch after another. The impressionistic flow of the film is confusing to viewers trying to understand what was happening and why.

There is some recent Spanish-language academic criticism dealing with *Fando y Lis*. The Peruvian academic José Carlos Cabrejo's 2019 study of the filmmaker, *Jodorowsky: El cine como viaje* (*Jodorowsky: Cinema as Journey*), devotes twenty-five pages to *Fando y Lis*. His treatment differs from this study because he relates a number of scenes to works by various other directors such as George Romero's *Night of the Living Dead* that came out the same year. David Church, who has studied Jodorowsky's films in several articles, concluded in 2007 that "the final product remains a disturbingly sadomasochistic piece of art" (Church 2007). Jodorowsky himself used the term "sadomasochistic" in his 1994 documentary interview with Mouchet (Cobb 2007, 46). But what Church does not mention is Jodorowsky's statement about the appeal of Arrabal's original play. It said that it is a story about "childish purity in a sadomasochistic world" (Cobb 2007, 46). The context is sadistic reality, but those who enter it are innocents. The presence of childhood scenes, in particular the molestation of Lis as a young girl, capture that duality perfectly. If *Fando y Lis* were simply a sadomasochistic film, contemporary viewers would label it a failure in that genre. While there are elements of sadomasochism as Jodorowsky gladly admits, he neither valorizes them nor exploits their luridness for its own sake.

The sadomasochistic label is a far cry from Cobb's evaluation of the film made in the same year as Church's. Cobb called it a cine-poem. The film is a hybrid of *efímero* theater and cinema, using the fable format as a generic template. It is focused on individual scenes of which some are "disturbing," as Church says, while others are "poetic," as Cobb says. But neither term captures the film's essence. Jodorowsky recently described his method of making a film as accidental. "I did not want to make compositions," he is quoted as saying, "as much as I wanted to create accidents and respond to them in their moment" (Nardonne 2020). The film is a series of scenes that Jodorowsky treats as accidents that he witnesses, and responds to as they occur. In such a context giving the film an overall label is problematic, and probably counterproductive.

Is *Fando y Lis* a transformative film? Not for the audience. Whatever impact it might have would quickly fade away and one's life would go on as before. However, for Jodorowsky himself the film was transformative because he went on to make a series of important films. If *Fando y Lis* had been the only film he had ever made, it and he would have become a footnote in the history of surrealist film. Instead, creating an outrage in Mexico became a portent of his potential cinematic power—one that he did not waste.

4

The Birth of a Cult

El Topo (1970)

Jodorowsky's fame as a filmmaker rests on *El Topo* (*The Mole*). This is a strange title for a film aimed at an American audience, yet its three-syllable name works well. The same was true of the Spanish title of the English-language film *El Cid*, a popular historical epic from 1961 starring Charlton Heston and Sophia Loren. Both titles are easy to pronounce, while adding an air of mystery. *El Topo* garnered notoriety when it was released in New York. Whether it is a Jodorowsky masterwork requires a patient parsing of this film's content and critical response.

Jodorowsky was forty when *El Topo* went into production. He was entering middle-age, a stage in life filled with energy laced with maturity. When his first feature film *Fando y Lis* got a US distributor he received a sense of an international potential for his Spanish-language, Mexican-made films. The Cannon Group that bought the distribution rights was a newly minted firm that had got its start producing dubbed versions of soft-core Swedish porn films. The appeal of *Fando y Lis* to Cannon was along the same vein. They saw it as catering to a New York audience that was looking for nudity, sexual content, and eroticism with a streak of violence. While *El Topo* also had these characteristics, it was radically different from *Fando y Lis* because of its broader vision, its narrative content, and its level of cinematic sophistication.

It was made on a $400,000 budget ($3 million in 2022 dollars), which is a 25 percent increase over the budget of *Fando y Lis* (Cerdán and Labayen 2009, 106). While *Fando y Lis* was rough around the edges because it was a learning experience for the untried Jodorowsky, *El Topo* became an expression of Jodorowsky's full-blown imagination. It was drenched in vivid color, replete with the sensibilities he had acquired from his discipleship with a Zen Master in Mexico, the shamanistic practices he had witnessed in Mexico, and his Panic-inspired sense of theatrical performance and exhibition. The film contains both American (the gunslinger) and Mexican (rural peasantry) iconography. In *El Topo* Jodorowsky is saying goodbye to the European influences that are part of *Fando y Lis* and fully embracing the visual metaphors of the continent that he had inhabited off and on for a decade. *El Topo* is a film that is both strange and familiar, foreign and domestic at the same time.

Jodorowsky presents a Mexico that fits the mindset of an American audience of its day, which saw that country as a place of backward sleepiness, oppressed peasantry, attractive women with low morals, the suffering-oriented religiosity of Spanish Catholicism, and an evil military. All of these stereotypes are present in his film. The reaction of Mexican critics, to whom Jodorowsky was already well-known for the scandal around *Fando y Lis*, was simply more outrage. To them Jodorowsky was exploiting an American caricature of Mexico and Mexicans, as well as adding to his reputation as a "pornographer." In *The Spiritual Journey of Alejandro Jodorowsky* the filmmaker relates how a media screening of the film in Mexico City resulted in a string of insults aimed at him. He was called "foreign vermin; raving egomaniac; donkey murderer; and so forth" (Jodorowsky 2008, 159). This surfeit of national self-consciousness on the Mexican side stood in contrast to a lack of understanding of the film displayed by American critics, who, on the whole, viewed the film and Jodorowsky as a fringe filmmaker. In labeling him marginal they were distancing themselves from the American zeitgeist of the late sixties and early seventies, that is, the youthful, drug-driven counterculture and the film's appeal to this spaced-out "midnight movie" crowd.

Vincent Canby, writing in the *New York Times*, termed it a "surreal fantasy" and he derisively quotes American critics from the counterculture media who called it "a weapon of spiritual revolution" (Canby 1971). *The Village Voice*, a paper associated with the counterculture, titled its review "Midnight Mass at the Elgin" in order to capture the ritual value of the film and its cult status. Canby concluded that "because the movie is without fundamental order it never succeeds in becoming anything more than a high class sideshow" (1971). Clearly, the snobbery of the reviewer irritated some, because the newspaper published a rejoinder review a few weeks later. Stating that the film is both "a very strange masterpiece" and "a monumental work of filmic art," the review concludes passionately and insightfully:

> But too facile a comparison between him and . . . Fellini—or, for that matter, Bergman, Sam Peckinpah or Sergio Leone—easily misses the point of his

originality, which consists precisely in bringing all kinds of disparate modes and motifs into a sort of orchestral harmony that both requires and transcends them . . . the architect is Jodorowsky alone.

If Jodorowsky must be compared to someone, let it be to that other South American fabulist, Jorge Luis Borges—not because their styles are similar (and they are surely poles apart politically), but because both combine an obsessive fascination with their continent's brutal past and an ardor for the wildest reaches of the imagination. (Schjeldahl 1971, D11)

The author of the review, Peter Schjeldahl, later became the art critic for the *The Village Voice* and then art critic for *The New Yorker*. He was twenty-nine when he wrote the review, a reflection of the age of the audience drawn to the film. John Lennon, the celebrity ex-Beatle, gave the film a major boost when he told audiences at a screening of his own short films at the Elgin to stay for the midnight screening of *El Topo*. The Elgin Theatre ran the film for months. Lennon's imprimatur not only made the film popular in New York, but he also got the Beatles manager, Allen Klein, to distribute *El Topo* and fund Jodorowsky's next film (Cobb 2007, 113).

Detailed information on how *El Topo* came about and how it was funded is sketchy. One account claims that "*El Topo* took four years to complete" (Mathijs and Sexton 2011, 14). Jodorowsky himself says it was made in a much more compressed time span. In *El Topo: The Book of the Film* that was published in 1971 he gives a lengthy interview (conducted in New York in December 1970) in which he claims it took nine months from conception to completion (Cobb 2007, 75). The two years between the release of the first film and the second is enough time to get financing and principal shooting underway. Both films were made in Mexico. Roberto Viskin produced *Fando y Lis* and then became the production manager for *El Topo*, while Moishe Rosenberg, who backed *Fando y Lis* financially, also backed *El Topo* (Cobb 2007, 75). Jodorowsky was working with the same principals and in the same milieu. Production could move along quickly, especially since he shot most scenes with just one or two takes. It could be that all the controversy generated by *Fando y Lis* and its American release appealed to his backers.

The film premiered in New York in the Elgin Theatre on December 18, 1970, after an invitation-only screening at the Museum of Modern Art attended by the owner of the Elgin (Cobb 2007, 111). He persuaded the film's distributor, Douglas Films, to allow midnight screenings. Word of mouth made it a chic happening until the middle of the following year, when John Lennon had his agent, Allen Klein, take over distribution through his company ABKCO. Alan Douglas continued his association with the film by publishing *El Topo: A Film of the Book* in 1971. The book has two parts—the first is ninety-four pages of film script and black-and-white stills from the film, while the second part consists of seventy-eight pages of an interview conducted by six people in New York in December of 1970. The book was also published in a British edition in 1974 and it remains the prime source of information about Jodorowsky's thinking at the time. Yet, one has to be careful about accepting his published words at face value, since the interview was done in the context of a euphoric reception for an unknown director using a translator. He was trying to explain the film and himself in Spanish to an Anglo audience that was fascinated by, yet ill-prepared to understand, his visual antics. Something he was quoted as saying in the interview section came back to haunt him much later. In fact, he may have seriously overstepped the boundaries of morality and may have gone so far as to engage in a criminal act of sexual violence in order to achieve what Cobb terms "a high level of authenticity" (74). Later in this chapter this matter is discussed more fully.

In terms of audience engagement the film proved highly successful. "People went to be mentally altered by the film, spiritually enriched or, at the very least, have an experience," writes Cobb (112). Jodorowsky at one point stated that he would "demand them to be [high]" in order to have the full experience (Dargis 2006). In the book about *El Topo* he explained the purpose of the film more fully: "I believe that the only end of all human activity . . . is to find enlightenment. I ask of film what most North Americans ask of psychedelic drugs. When one creates a psychedelic film . . . [the filmmaker] needs to manufacture the pill" (Jodorowsky 1971, 97). He clearly believed that viewing his film would give the viewer an altered state of consciousness, a high similar to that of an illicit drug. His use of the term "psychedelic" reflects the counterculture music and graphic art of the period, when altered visual reality and aurally-enhanced musical experiences were popular and viewed as a sign of enlightened, anti-normative behavior. The concept of a psychedelic movie is a leap beyond the surrealism of *Fando y Lis*. It suggests a mind-altering experience rather than simply a mind-bending one. The term "psychedelic" was resurrected in a 2009 interview he gave to *The Guardian* titled "Lennon, Manson and Me: The Psychedelic Cinema of Alejandro Jodorowsky." It placed the filmmaker within a time capsule as "the high priest of head-trip cinema" (Rose 2009). Eventually, *El Topo* joined the pantheon of what some have termed the "Acid Western."

For American moviegoers the film was a visual parade of bizarre imagery and subversive characters engaged in transgressive acts, while remaining comprehensible in terms of the cultural iconography and mythologies of the Western. Jodorowsky was seeking to appeal to the audience's subconscious, but whether that would result in a life-changing experience for a viewer is difficult to determine. He was pushing the envelope of visual shock in order to shake people out of their conventional lifestyle and consciousness. If the film is really a mind-altering pill, as Jodorowsky would have it, its power to transform a viewer would vary from person to person. There was also the impact on the film's participants, as well as Jodorowsky himself.

Jodorowsky states that he has sought "enlightenment" through filmmaking. By enlightenment he means finding "a way," so that a film's production (as well as its viewing) becomes a step or several steps on a personal journey to understanding and awareness (Jodorowsky 1971, 106). In the *El Topo* book interview he states emphatically: "I want to travel into the deepest areas of my being in order to reach enlightenment" (Jodorowsky 1971, 97). When one realizes that he not only wrote, directed, and starred in the film, but also conceived the music, chose the costumes, and designed the scenes, his level of creative involvement is significant and highly personal. The film became a singular expression of Jodorowsky's artistic vision.

The film carries in its genome many years of staging avant-garde plays, a decade of engaging audiences in one-off happenings, and the appeal of his recent Mexican brush with scandal. Jodorowsky's ambivalent relationship with Mexico after *Fando y Lis* is evident in his publishing a book about *El Topo* immediately after finishing its production. Editorial Novaro of Mexico City, publisher of his three previous books in Spanish on topics of Panicism, brought out *El topo, fábula pánica con imágenes* (*El Topo: A Panic Tale with Images*) in 1970. The 79-page book contained the original screenplay (with "uncut and uncensored" displayed prominently on the cover) and black-and-white photographs from the production. Why Jodorowsky would jump so quickly into bringing out the book only two years after the *Fando y Lis* debacle suggests that he intended to shock the Mexican audience once more by using his name-recognition for publicity purposes.

Jodorowsky's approach to personal transformation involves blurring the boundary between reality and fiction. That blurring is present from the start of the film in a scene in which he has his seven-year-old son Brontis (the naked boy in the movie) bury a picture of his real mother Bernadette Landru along with a teddy bear that he had been given by his father early on and which his mother had sent with him when she agreed to return Brontis to his father's care. This symbolic burial signifies a new beginning for Brontis under his father's control in both the film as well as real life (Jodorowsky 1971, 98). Jodorowsky's "way" or technique of transformation involves people carrying out symbolic acts, such as this one, to further personal enlightenment. He had no qualms about doing this with a child. In the film Brontis plays the role of the son of El Topo (Jodorowsky) and is referred to in the script by his birth name—again a blurring of reality and cinematic fiction. Likewise, the fictional cinematic father and son characters are a real father and son. Jodorowsky repeats his initial abandonment of the little boy in real life by having El Topo abandon his son in the film (Jodorowsky 1971, 101). In a 2013 interview, the now fifty-year-old Brontis talked about his childhood experience on the set that confirms that making the film was transformative because it brought him closer to the father with whom he had not lived for a while:

> I remember very simple things, how to do a hangman's noose, the big meals with everyone, the feeling of the sun on my skin because I was naked during the scenes all the time and the feeling of being very close to my father. That's the most important memory. I had a consciousness of a bond that was being created there. Not only of being father and son, but that we were doing something together. We were making a piece of art together. (Morgenstern 2013)

Unbeknownst to the seven-year-old, he was destined to act in later films by his father that also mixed fiction and reality in much the same way as happened in *El Topo*.

The Controversy

Jodorowsky may have seen his "way" of transformative cinema as a path to enlightenment, and the making of this film as a way of settling some personal psychological family debts (Jodorowsky 1971, 97). Unfortunately, this approach came to haunt him much later in life in regard to the sex scene between himself and his co-star Mara Lorenzio. In the 1971 book Jodorowsky is quoted as saying:

> When I wanted to do the rape scene, I explained to her [Mara Lorenzio] that I was going to hit her and rape her. . . . We went to the desert with two other people: the photographer and a technician. No one else. I said, "I'm not going

to rehearse. There will be only one take because it will be impossible to repeat. . . ." Then I told her, "Pain does not hurt me. Hit me." And she hit me. I said, "harder." And she started to hit me very hard, hard enough to break a rib . . . I ached for a week. After she had hit me long enough and hard enough . . . I said, "Now it's my turn. Roll the cameras." And I really . . . I really . . . I really raped her. (Jodorowsky 1971, 102)

This quote was used to cancel a 2019 retrospective exhibit of his films at El Museo del Barrio in New York. The matter had its contemporary origins in an article by Helen O'Hara in the UK newspaper *The Telegraph* that examined the veracity of the rape claim in which she asked: "Was this the most abusive shoot in film, or simply a director's misguided attempt at self-mythologizing?" (O'Hara 2017). Unlike 1971, when it passed unnoticed, the issue resonated in 2019 because of the American feminist #MeToo movement that sought to expose sexual predators, especially those in the film industry, with the case of the film producer Harvey Weinstein, who was convicted in New York of sexual assault in 2020, being the most notorious to date. Jodorowsky provides the context for his statement by saying that he "explained things to everyone. Mara, for example. When I wanted to do the rape scene, I explained to her that I was going to hit her and rape her" (Jodorowsky 1971, 102). Even if she consented to this act, it can hardly be considered genuinely consensual because of the power relationship of the director over this neophyte actor, who, according to him, had spent some time in a mental hospital after overdosing on LSD. He had hired her to live with and look after his two sons for six months (Jodorowsky 1971, 100). Was this an example of the sexually exploitative casting-couch syndrome that pervaded Hollywood studios for many decades? Was it a case of Latin American machismo? Was it Jodorowsky playing at being a sexual therapist as he suggests in the book (Jodorowsky 1971, 102)? Or was it just a fantasy?

In the film there is a suggestion of a sexual assault, but it is never shown. If it had been shown the film would never have been screened publically and it would never have been reviewed by the likes of Vincent Canby, Roger Ebert, or Pauline Kael. Obviously, they had not read his book prior to their film reviews. If a sexual assault did happen, it happened outside the frame of the released film. In the script about the scene El Topo says: "Moses found water in the desert. The people could not drink it because it was bitter. They named the water Mara" (Jodorowsky 1971, 24). He then gives her the name Mara because it means bitter water. The script dresses the whole scene in biblical allusions that equate El Topo with God, with Moses' miracle of bringing water from a rock, and even the Holy Ghost, where the script describes El Topo's violent sexual act (not shown in the film) like "a bullet—with the same power the Dove forced himself into Mary's ear at the Annunciation" (Jodorowsky 1971, 26). These biblical allusions make El Topo an angel, a man chosen by God, and a miracle worker. Cobb explains the scene as a religious allegory when he writes: "In an act that is less conventional rape and more violent religious awakening, El Topo forcibly shakes Mara's soul into life with a spiritual orgasm" (Cobb 2007, 85). Because of Jodorowsky's idea of transformative cinema, the boundary between fiction and reality is very thin, allowing performance or acting itself to be transformative. While the film presents a transformation as happening to Mara because she now has a different relationship to El Topo, this does not mean that the actor herself was somehow transformed. Jodorowsky implies in the book that the sex act (if there really was one) was consensual.

In response to the cancellation of the 2019 retrospective, Jodorowsky stated in a written statement:

> These words: "I've raped my actress," was said fifty years ago by El Topo, a bandit dressed in black leather that nobody knew. They were words, not facts, surrealist publicity in order to enter the world of cinema from a position of obscurity. I do not condone the act of rape, but exploited the shock value of the statement at the time, following years in the Panic Movement and other iterations of harnessing shock to motivate energetic release. I acknowledge that this statement is problematic in that it presents fictional violence against a woman as a tool for exposure, and now, fifty years later, I regret that this is being read as truth. (*Artforum* 2019)

While the "revelation" in the media may have produced opprobrium, the assessment in the scholarly media sought to contextualize the incident within a broader trend in a filmmaker's work. Feminist scholar Laura Jaramillo argues that violence against women in Jodorowsky's films is central to the "midnight movie" form of cult spectatorship, which has fostered a "postmodern spectatorship, characterized by distracted consumption and linked to cybernetic control" (Jaramillo 2020, 172). Considering the sexual violence of the male character in *Fando y Lis* in trying to force himself on the female character and the sexual violence portrayed in *El Topo*, the argument that there is a pattern is weighty. But the meaning and purpose of such violence remains debatable. As early as 1971 Jodorowsky defended his approach in an interview in which he stated:

> *El Topo* is not violent, it is a process I begin with violence but I finish it with love . . . our normal reality is war and violence and selfishness. You go to the normal reality, and construct your soul and your spiritual reality and all the human beauties. This is not violence, it is a process. (Gadre 2020)

Jodorowsky's film has been caught up in the wider issue of the portrayal of rape in cinema. Women commentators in the media have deplored the depiction of rape in cinema as part of a misogynistic, patriarchal worldview of male sexual privilege and an affront to women. No matter how valid such a critique of cinema history and certain films may be, judging *El Topo* solely through the lens of possbile sexual violence reduces its overall importance by discounting other aspects of the film. Until such time as the truth of what occurred and how it occurred in that one scene can be documented, the film deserves to be assessed in its totality.

The Film

The film begins with El Topo, all in black, with his naked seven-year-old son Brontis seated behind him on a black horse, riding down a sand dune. El Topo is holding up a black umbrella as they come to a pole sticking out of the sand. The script states that the pole works as a sundial whose shadow marks time and that marking time is the beginning of culture (Jodorowsky 1971, 8). The boy's nudity is indicative of childhood innocence. El Topo's namesake is the mole, so El Topo's black outfit, along with his black hair and full black beard, is the color of soil. His black outfit makes him a figure related to the underground world and to sin. In a desert landscape burned by the sun, the horse, the man, the boy, and the umbrella create a single figure that is the equivalent of the sundial pole casting the shadow of time. Both are solitary figures in a desert landscape. After dismounting, the first act of establishing time is El Topo giving a teddy bear and a photo of the boy's real mother to bury at the foot of the pole, which Brontis does. While the lone cowboy on a horse is an essential trope of the Western, the addition of the boy undermines that stereotype because it introduces fatherhood and nurturing, as well as an absent third figure, the mother. The horse plays the same symbolic role as the wagon carrying Lis and pushed by Fando. It is the "vehicle" of passage and the unification of father and son. But there is more to these vehicles of transport. The horse in this film and the wagon in the previous one represent an absent character. In the case of Fando and Lis, it is the authorial father who is present only in a voice-over and in the case of El Topo, it is the buried mother. As substitutes for these off-camera characters, the vehicles become a family threesome.

Throughout the film Jodorowsky works with binary relations, trinary relations, and quartets. The inaugural characters in *El Topo* face a typical Western genre's vast landscape, but end up being confined to a basic circular motion (the shadow moving around the pole as it follows the sun), much like Fando and Lis were confined in their imaginary journey to a barren ravine. While Fando and Lis were following the allure of fantasies created for them by their parents' generation, El Topo is the father of his own fantasy in a voice-over by Jodorowsky that says:

> The mole is an animal that digs tunnels underground searching for the sun. Sometimes his journey leads him to the surface. When he looks at the sun, he is blinded. (Jodorowsky 1971, 11)

Since he is like a mole El Topo is also blinded by the sun, with the sun referring to enlightenment. In a reversal of our normal perception of vision and enlightenment, it is light that causes El Topo's blindness. And after blindness comes the light/enlightenment of the underground journey. The film presents itself as a journey toward revelation and self-understanding.

The next scene has El Topo arriving at a massacre with numerous bloody bodies lying on the ground or hanging from the rafters in a church. They are Mexicans, one of whom asks to be shot because he is dying and in great pain. El Topo gives the child Brontis his pistol and has him shoot the man. In the first six minutes of the film we have four motifs, of which three are carried over from *Fando y Lis*. The first is allegory (the mole), the second is family (El Topo and Brontis), the third is journey (the horse), and the fourth is death (the massacre). There is also a new theme. Because *El Topo* mimics the Western genre (*Fando y Lis* was sui generic in its hodgepodge of genres from romance to horror), Jodorowsky has to play with the expectations the audience has for the genre. He references this by inserting "Livery Stable" in bold white letters on a building in the village, which is nonsensical in a Mexican town, but a fit with a frontier town in the American West. The "Livery Stable" is the prominent signage in a famous Western, *The Magnificent Seven* (1960), when three Mexicans ride into a frontier American town to buy guns. Jodorowsky is showing the film's pedigree.

The father and son are accosted by three banditos. This triad dressed in brown, black, and yellow are guffawing clowns (with appropriate circus music accompanying them). They are parodies of banditos from whom El Topo extracts information on the perpetrator of the massacre, a certain Colonel, some of whose henchmen are shown in the next scene machine-gunning children next to an ancient gramophone (echoes of Lis's gramophone), which then provides music for a bizarre homoerotic dance by this quartet of banditos with a quartet of Franciscan monks. The juxtaposition of celibates and murderers can be read in various ways depending on how much symbolism one wants to attribute to the scene, especially after the monks are stripped by their bandit captors, who then ride them, spanking their bloodied bottoms with spiny cacti in imitation of self-flagellation. Symbolism and silliness go hand in hand.

Then the first woman of the film appears, whom the script describes as dressed "out of Grimm's *Fairy Tales*" (Jodorowsky 1971, 16). Actually her brown dress is very similar to the Franciscan habits. For Jodorowsky color is an important expression of cultural grammars. She is dressed like a penitent at this point. This whole section of the film is highly religious in its overtones. First, she is presented as a servant of the Colonel in his church-like abode when getting him dressed in his military costume. When he goes outside, the Colonel is followed by a swarm of pigs, which are signs of his nature. He meets his bandito buddies, whom he tells to act as dogs and offers the woman to them sexually, but before they can assault her, El Topo bursts onto the scene with Brontis on his back. Various shoot-outs and knifings occur with lots of orange-colored blood everywhere, but nobody dies until El Topo castrates the evil Colonel, who then shoots himself because his machismo image has been destroyed. Since El Topo has vanquished the evildoers like any good knight in shining armor, the damsel in distress can play up to him in gratitude. He dumps his son Brontis and takes the woman behind him on his horse. His parting words to Brontis are "Destroy me. You no longer depend on anyone," which echoes the opening scene when he says little Brontis is now a man (Jodorowsky 1971, 21). The scene may allude to Jodorowsky seeing himself autobiographically as having gone off with another woman, leaving Brontis with his birth-mother. The scene ends with Brontis dressed as a Franciscan monk surrounded by the four monks, who miraculously are unscathed by their previous cinematic abuse. He is left in their care to reappear later in the film.

El Topo and the woman ride to an oasis in the desert where he gives her the Hebrew name "Mara" or bitter water. While he plays the flute like the Greco-Roman shepherd god Pan, Mara, who previously licked the reeds surrounding the pool of water, now finds the water sweet. The reference here is to Pan who mythology tells us created the pan flute after his beloved nymph was turned into reeds. This classical reference is recreated by Jodorowsky in this brief scene, but he then pushes it further in a subsequent scene with biblical references. Once El Topo and Mara leave the oasis (read Garden of Eden), they like Adam and Eve are driven into a hard desert world. She says: "How are we going to live here? We'll starve to death . . . we'll die of thirst" (Jodorowsky 1971, 25). Immediately El Topo responds by finding turtle eggs in the sand and brings water out of rock like Moses. She tries to imitate his miracles but fails.

He ends up on his knees while she circles him saying "Nada, nada . . . (nothing, nothing)" over and over again. He gets up, violently strips her, and as he is about to sexually assault her, the scene cuts to her floating face up in a lake, naked and screaming as if she was having an orgasm. Next she rides off to find turtle eggs and hits a phallic-shaped rock with a stone so that it spurts water as a sign of ejaculation. After "sacred" sex with El Topo, she too can work miracles. He now sits on the back of his horse as she is now in the saddle. They go off in search of four gunslinger masters, who are the four directions of the world and four aspects of El Topo himself. She tells him they must be destroyed.

Who is Mara in the film? Is she a sorceress? Is she a lover? Is she a muse? Is she a disciple? Or is she the master? The evolution of her role during the quest for the four Masters of the Revolver suggests that she may carry all these identities and more. When they reach the abode of the first master they are met by the double man—an armless man carrying a legless man carrying a gun. Figures with these disabilities become a mainstay in all his future auteur films. Perhaps they are inspired by the "Freak Shows" once common in traveling circuses, where humans with unusual attributes were displayed for a price. Or they may represent an antidote to the vanities of corporeal normalcy.

Prior to his killing the First Master, El Topo immerses himself naked in the pool of a desert oasis in a purification ceremony. Pools of water have been important from the start of the film and they continue to be a biblical referent. Moses being found in a bed of reeds and then bringing forth water from a rock in the Sinai are two examples. When the black-clothed El Topo on his black horse faces the naked master on his white horse, the musical score is an eastern chant signifying this is part of a religious ceremony. El Topo triumphs and is joined by another woman, also dressed in black, who offers to lead him to the second master. She is presented as a soul mate and guide. El Topo vanquishes the Second Master, who lives next to a gypsy wagon with a chained lion, which echoes a circus. Then it is time to go after the Third Master, but first the two women accompanying El Topo fight and eventually reconcile—the struggle of opposites who are, in fact, the same. In the script Jodorowsky comments on the importance of colors in regard to the scene of a black crow pecking at the bloodied ears of a dead white rabbit. "Black, white and red: alchemist colors," he puts in a footnote (Jodorowsky 1971, 43). The scene is followed by a pen full of dead white rabbits—the slaughter of the innocents in biblical terms. They belong to the third master who has watched them die as El Topo approaches. The Third Master is killed by El Topo. Now only one is left and we are only half-way through the film.

Like the others, the Fourth Master is bizarrely clothed/unclothed in the figure of a hermit. Equipped with a butterfly net he ricochets El Topo's bullets back to him until El Topo kills him. This concluding conquest throws El Topo into a frenzy as he revisits the dead masters, all posed in surreal graves. An image of a crucified goat carcass appears to make clear what is being alluded to. El Topo cries "My God, my God, why hast Thou forsaken me?" in imitation of Christ's words at the crucifixion. To continue the analogy to Christ, the script has the Woman in Black shooting him in his hands and his feet plus his side as a sign of "the fifth wound of Christ" (Jodorowsky 1971, 52). We need wait only for El Topo's resurrection, which occurs quickly when he wakes up in "an enormous grotto, sitting on a rock shaped like an altar" (Jodorowsky 1971, 53). Instead of having black hair and beard, he has a huge head of blond hair and his black clothes are now white, including a white loincloth. He is surrounded by humans with deformities, who are trapped underground because they are unsightly to those above ground. The Mole promises to free them.

At this point Christian imagery is replaced with shamanistic imagery when El Topo, who is now back underground where he belongs, consumes a large black scabbard beetle given to him by an old woman shaman. The scene is also accompanied by Buddhist chanting indicating a ritual moment in the same way it signaled one earlier. His consuming the bitter-tasting beetle, similar to the bitter-tasting water of the Moses metaphor, leads to his being reborn from under the shaman's Indigenously embroidered apron. His hair is cut off and he reappears with a shaved head and dressed in a Buddhist monk's brown robe. He is no longer a black-clothed gunslinger who vanquished the Four Masters of the Revolver. Aided by Small Woman, who represents the deformed people underground, he finds a Western-style American town, whose inhabitants worship the all-mighty dollar. Their adherence is symbolized by the all-seeing eye from the front of the American one-dollar bill, which they carry on banners.

The lowly *campesinos* of the town are treated like cattle and driven into pens. The well-dressed bourgeoisie of the town practice all the vices while maintaining their superior airs. An echo of an early scene in the film is an execution of five white-clad Mexican peasants. Into this den of iniquity rides El Topo (dressed as a Buddhist monk) on a donkey like Jesus riding into Jerusalem. The Small Woman and he entertain the townsfolk with a comic pantomime and collect money like buskers. As the two of them are about to leave the town, Brontis, now a tall young man, enters dressed in the brown cassock of a Franciscan monk. He goes on to perform a "miracle" for the townsfolk. We now have two miracle workers in the same place, one a symbol of Zen Buddhism and the other of Christianity. There is room for only one. The son replacing the father is the Freudian version. In *Fando y Lis* it is a matter of matricide and here it appears to be patricide. Murdering parents is becoming a theme. When father and son see each other they are shocked and like two magnets repel each other. Brontis, the monk, is then transformed into a version of El Topo, the gunslinger, warning his father that he will kill him once the tunnel that will free the underground people is finished. Brontis is made to regress into the same personification his father had when he abandoned him. In this way Brontis is cursed to repeat his father's mistakes and must begin a journey of enlightenment on his own.

The final battle between evil and good, between hypocrisy and truth, is about to reach its apocalyptic ending. As the underground people enter the town, they are met with armed citizens ready to kill them. El Topo tries to prevent the massacre, but fails. He then avenges the death of the innocents by killing the townspeople. Sapped by this act, he sits in a lotus position, pours oil over himself, igniting the fuel in a re-creation of the image of the Buddhist monk's self-immolation in Saigon in protest of the Vietnam War. He is now truly dead and the journey is carried on by Brontis, dressed in his father's gunslinger image. He takes the Small Woman with her child out of town on a sorrel horse. They now represent a new triune of the Holy Family. El Topo's grave is swarmed by bees who create "a river of honey" (Jodorowsky 1971, 93). The honeycomb motif appeared earlier and was associated with the death of the four masters. Its reappearance symbolizes that the mole has joined them in the afterlife. El Topo has entered the biblical land of "milk and honey," a reference to Israel. Bees in ancient religions were linked to the soul and its migration to paradise.

The film comes full circle by using a mythopoetic symmetry. The film begins with the father and son duo on a horse creating a triad similar to the one in *Fando y Lis*. The film ends with three figures on a horse. The absent mother of the beginning is now present at the end, and the absent father is replaced by the son. This "holy" family of father, mother, and child replaces the "unholy" triad of the father and the two women earlier in the film.

The family unit riven by conflict, trauma, and intergenerational transference first appears in *Fando y Lis* but it is refined in *El Topo*. The refinement consists in the clarity with which he presents the mythopoetic symmetry of the family triune and how he deals with the theme of the absent father and mother. The neurotic and broken family with children that need healing through his psychotherapeutic theories and practices of metagenealogy and psychomagic are more evident in this film. While his first film was tied to Eurocentric theories, this, his second film, transcends that surrealist-absurdist world with the articulation of his own worldview that he evolved through his decade-long Mexican experiences. *El Topo* is a homage to that world.

What the Critics Have Said

Jodorowsky himself has provided an extensive commentary on the film, beginning with the very long interview in his 1971 book, followed by numerous references to the film in some of his other books such as *The Spiritual Journey of Alejandro Jodorowsky* (2008), as well as in film documentaries. They offer explanatory comments on the symbolism in the film, its roots in various religious traditions, plus anecdotal stories about the production and its reception. He has spoken about the film in numerous interviews over the decades, all of which adds up to a voluminous and diverse commentary that defies easy summarization. In this study his own comments are reserved for the occasional quote to reveal his intention for an event or a scene. However, there is one assessment of his filmmaking that appears in his book on the making of *El Topo* that deserves to be quoted because of what it implies about how he saw himself at the time:

> Some people make films like novels: Truffaut. Some make films like political essays: Godard . . . Some make films like metaphysical stories: Bergman. But I want to make poems. (Jodorowsky 1971, 108)

Jodorowsky finds a place for himself in this pantheon of mid-twentieth-century film gods, as the poet of cinema. If we view *El Topo* as a version of an epic poem in the spirit of a grand odyssey filled with strange and wondrous creatures and miraculous events, we have a framework for appreciating all the exaggerated scenes and not-so-hidden symbols. This grand scale is an enhancement of the less glorious journey that he presented in *Fando y Lis*. However, Jodorowsky's own characterization of the film does not constitute a critical commentary.

Critical commentary can be broken up into two general categories—journalistic and academic. On the journalistic side there are the contemporary reviews in the United States, an important essay by the American critic James Hoberman from 1983, and Cobb's interpretation from 2007. On the academic side there are discussions in English, Spanish, Portuguese, and other languages covering a period of thirty years. Journalists first placed the film in the "cult" category, which academics came to address later on. Contemporary reviews in the United States included derision from Pauline Kael, who characterized Jodorowsky as "an exploitation filmmaker" who dressed up his product in sentimental religious imagery (Hoberman 1983, 97), and bemused praise from Roger Ebert, who denied the film was exploitative and considered it as having an "uncanny resonance" (Ebert 1970). James Hoberman's 1983 essay "*El Topo:* Through the Wasteland of the Counterculture" provided a 30-page plus discussion of both *El Topo* and his next film, *The Holy Mountain*, quoting both Jodorowsky and others in chronicling the film's reception as part of what was then called "the counterculture." This was a sociocultural movement that began in the 1960s among American youth opposed to the Vietnam War that focused on valorizing hallucinogenic drug usage, mood-altering cannabis, and rock music. After the war ended in 1975, the counterculture gradually disappeared. Hoberman views the film as a perfect match with counterculture sensibilities.

Cobb gives *El Topo* greater historical significance than Hoberman does, when he claims that the film "was a bridge to a new epoch of film culture [in the US]" by showing a new generation of young American filmmakers how to introduce "a European-style sensibility into American cinema" (Cobb 2007, 114). Both Hoberman and Cobb place the film into a time capsule. Does that mean that today it is no more than a fragment of historical nostalgia? Or does the film continue to have power and impact into the twenty-first century? Scholarship may help in answering this question.

Academics have had a long time in which to parse the film and relate it to his other work. Since religious symbolism is such an overt part of the film, it is best to start with that aspect. The four main religious traditions represented in the film are Judaism, Christianity, Zen Buddhism, and Indigenous shamanism. Jodorowsky was raised in a secular Jewish family. One academic considers *El Topo* to be a blend of the prophetic and revelatory narrative in the Jewish religious tradition as well as the Western genre (Lindstrom 2013, 127). Since the four sections of the film are titled Genesis, Psalms, Prophets, and Revelation, the biblical context is clear. One scholar prefers to view "Judeo-Christian" imagery as a unified presence in his work (Kahn 2013, 222). By this he means that the Chilean world of Jodorowsky's upbringing was genealogically Jewish, but culturally Judeo-Christian because Chile was a product of Spanish colonial Catholicism. By being exposed to both frameworks of thought it was easy for Jodorowsky to identify El Topo first with Moses and then with Christ.

The Zen Buddhism of the film centers on several key concepts—the master-disciple relationship, the solving of paradoxical koans or riddles, the lengthy path to enlightenment, and meditative purification. Jodorowsky discovered Zen Buddhism in Mexico City through his master Ejo Takata with whom he maintained a close relationship for three decades. Drawing on Jodorowsky's own writings, Ken Martin argues that the "death of the intellect" is Takata's enduring contribution to Jodorowsky's work (Martin 2018, 118). He goes on to explain that the rejection of reason as a framework for understanding reality ends up generating a "creative freedom to rewrite our personal narratives, that is, our identity and who we are" (Martin 2018, 124). This fits with the transformative mission that Jodorowsky gave his cinema and his own footsteps as an artist continually remaking himself through different art forms.

The shamanistic aspects of the religious traditions that Jodorowsky enunciates in the film are less studied, but it should be noted that in the rebirth-resurrection scene in the cave, El Topo is presented first as a babe in white (the baby Jesus) and then in the garb of a Buddhist monk. Jodorowsky emphasizes malleability of identity. He does so by presenting a seamless continuity in diverse religious traditions and their iconography that most likely represents his own relationship to religious beliefs and their mythological power.

Besides the religious aspects of the film, scholars have taken up other themes such as the role of landscape and disabilities in the film. A recent article describes Jodorowsky's films as narratives of displacement in which journeys and spiritual quests represent displacement, while the films themselves exist as "displaced entities existing on the extreme margins of global paracinema" (Melia 2019, 93–4). The first landscape that is displaced in *El Topo* is that of the Western by conflating both American Wests and Mexican Norths and by giving the genre itself a new mythology "of arcane religious iconography and Eastern spirituality while presenting a landscape that is at once familiar and utterly alien" (Melia 2019, 96). This may very well be the reason that New York counterculture audiences of 1970 felt that the film liberated them from the colonizing gaze and macho masculinity that are the tropes of the genre. At the same time, the various geographic, cultural, and linguistic displacements that Jodorowsky himself experienced in his artistic quest become a theme in his films. What is crucial about Jodorowsky's cinematic displacements/journeys/quests is that they are transcendent in the same way that the space journey in Kubrick's *2001: A Space Odyssey* (1968) is transcendent, culminating with a higher level of being for the survivor (Melia 2019, 103).

Landscape plays a symbolic role in *El Topo*. Its various elements have been chosen by the director to present landscape as an allegory—in this case, the meaning of wilderness or wastelands as spaces that test the human spirit. The Australian scholar David Melbye, whose country is filled with desiccated wilderness wastelands, discusses landscape allegory in cinema as "manifestations of a character's troubled psyches" and he conceives landscapes to be visual paradigms in "a cultural lexicon" (Melbye 2010, 1 and 3). While El Topo is certainly a troubled man-god, Jodorowsky's references to El Topo as a Moses and a Christ-figure emphasize the religious focus of the film. Miracles, hallucinations, and the quest for enlightenment associate the wasteland motif with visionary experience and power. As mentioned in the introductory chapter, Adán Jodorowsky, after starring in his father's 2016 film *Endless Poetry*, reported that he went to Chile's high-altitude Atacama Desert to cut off his hair and don a new identity. The wasteland as a site of visionary transformation is an established paradigm of change that Jodorowsky embraces. It first began in *Fando y Lis* with the barren, rocky ravine through which the protagonists travel. It serves as a metaphor for Fando's own desolate personality and his fruitless quest. The transformative part for Fando is his moving from lust to love as he dies.

A final academic observation that should be noted is the appearance of people with physical disabilities in the film. While this was hinted at in *Fando y Lis* in Lis's inability to walk and where people with crutches are part of Fando's death procession, the exhibition of amputees and people with deformities becomes central to the symbolism of *El Topo*. While their presence can be associated with Jodorowsky's general subversion of the Western and its classic emphasis on virility and physical prowess, the fact that these figures keep reappearing in later films that have nothing to do with that genre indicates that they are important for Jodorowsky as a universal statement. That El Topo has a child with "The Short Woman" after she has said he could not love her because of her short height is Jodorowsky's way of affirming inclusivity, as well as rejecting the norms of female beauty tied to Hollywood Westerns. David Church has tackled this issue head-on by discussing the theme of self-loathing or "bodily abjection" associated with physical disabilities and deformities (Church 2011, 4). He references *Freaks* (1932), a film about sideshow revenge as having an influence on Jodorowsky (Church 2011, 7) and other "exploitation" filmmakers. I'm not sure that this film was an inspiration for *El Topo,* but the film's extensive use of these characters (some might say they represent goodness seeking release from repression) does raise the issue of disability in film and its viewing by the able-bodied. Church considers the appeal of films like Jodorowsky's to be tied to the counterculture's view of itself as oppositional to social norms and values, so that it would embrace corporeal abnormality as a sign of its own rebellion (Church 2011, 9).

This may have been the case in 1970 but in the context of contemporary values, Jodorowsky's presentation of corporeal difference requires reexamination. Is it exploitative? Since Jodorowsky was well acquainted with circus culture from his days as a youth and considering the times and locations in which he experienced them, one could see him sympathizing with those who had been stigmatized, since he himself had felt anti-Semitism growing up. As inequalities generated by ableist biases become more fully addressed by society, Jodorowsky's frontal engagement with the issue in *El Topo* fifty years ago and in later films in which he portrays people with disabilities as powerful agents should be accepted as a genuine indictment of normalcy. Audiences today may be critical of his occasional lapse into comedy with these characters and they may view this film and others by Jodorowsky ambivalently because of changing sensibilities, but his intention to make unusual bodies part of the human community seems genuine.

A Half-Century Later Where Does *El Topo* Stand?

As cultures, popular tastes, and cinema history change, older-era films that can still resonate with audiences become fewer and fewer. While there is no doubt that in 1970, when the film was released, New York audiences of a certain kind thrilled to its novelty, absurdity, purported brilliance, and psychic energy. The film set them on a quest, at least while watching the film, to comprehend what they were viewing. Psychedelic drugs were an aid to some. But what can or should contemporary audiences make of *El Topo*?

So much has happened in cinema in the past fifty years that any breakthrough qualities the film may have had would no longer be viewed as such. Yet, the film has certain audacious attributes that continue to impress. If one asks if the film successfully subverts the Western genre that it parodies, the answer is a resounding yes. It's mix of Panicism, Absurdism, and Surrealism so exaggerates the tropes of the Western that they become hollowed-out and ineffective. That gives *El Topo* lasting value. But how should it be characterized? Is it primarily an "Acid Western"? An example of "Latsploitation" cinema? A film steeped in the "carnivalesque," or a religious allegory that combines Christian, Judaic, and Buddhist motifs? All these characterizations are present in the film and add to its complexity. I lean toward the religious allegory interpretation because his next two auteur films—*The Holy Mountain* and *Holy Blood*—in both title and theme reinforce the religious interpretation.

Is this film his masterwork? This question is relevant because *El Topo* is his best-known work. While Jodorowsky can style himself as the poet of cinema, others referencing this film might style him as the clown of cinema, but even that pejorative term carries connotations of seriousness. Jodorowsky's parodying the genre adds another hurdle to its being considered a masterwork. The film seems cartoonish in its conception and its dialogue seems suited to a comic book of laconic sound bites. Perhaps in a subliminal recognition of this attribute, Jodorowsky created a sequel to the film with a graphic novel *Les Fils d'El Topo* (*The Sons of El Topo*) whose first volume appeared in 2016 subtitled "Cain" and the second volume in 2019 subtitled "Abel." These subtitles suggest that El Topo himself must be the first man, Adam. Again we have religious connotations.

Religious symbolism is so omnipresent in the film and is often presented in such a heavy-handed way that one is not surprised that some audiences would find it excessive and counterproductive. Announcing over and over again that this is a religious journey leading to spiritual enlightenment can grow tiresome. Making sure the audience gets the references results in jarring transitions from scene to scene. The sexual content also seems campy, which suits the "Midnight Movie" style. The film's dramatic element is undermined by the comic book costuming of many of its characters. Yet, the film is highly successful in its subversion of the genre. For example, in the classic Western, the townspeople are usually victimized till the hero or heroes save them. In *El Topo* it is the townspeople who are the victimizers and the hero slays them. But the real value of the film is revealed by comparing it to his later films *The Holy Mountain* (1973) and *Holy Blood* (1989). The three films are his one and only trilogy. No one film in the trilogy need be considered a masterwork, but the trilogy as a whole certainly can.

5

The Ascent of and the Descent from *The Holy Mountain* (1973)

The instant notoriety of *El Topo* convinced Allen Klein to take a chance on a new feature film, *La montaña sagrada* (*The Holy Mountain*). It would be Jodorowsky's third film in five years. The rapidity with which this filmmaker became a *cause célèbre*, however minor, was a combination of his own provocative style of filmmaking and the nature of the American film industry. The ascent began when the pop music impresario Allen Klein (manager of the hugely successful pop band, The Beatles) took over the distribution of *El Topo*. American entertainment culture is all about taking advantage of celebrity status and Klein saw Jodorowsky as a potential star.

As early as his December 1970 interview for *El Topo: The Book of the Film*, Jodorowsky had announced that his next film would have a mountain-spiritual quest theme (Cobb 2007, 119). The way to express such a quest ranges from a cartoon of a guru sitting in the mouth of a cave atop a mountain while awaiting the queries of a struggling acolyte to the powerful narrative *Ascent of Mount Carmel* by the sixteenth-century Spanish mystic St. John of the Cross to which Jodorowsky made reference in the interview. *The Holy Mountain* contains both the comic and the profound. In *El Topo: The Book of the Film* he recounts his own mountain-related spiritual quest as beginning with Reyna D'Assia, a self-described daughter of the early twentieth-century spiritualist philosopher, G. I. Gurdjieff. She took Jodorowsky to Mexico's sacred Monte Alban in a spiritual quest that prefigured the film (Jodorowsky 1971, 179–80). Another Gurdjieff-related connection to this film is *Mount Analogue: A Novel of Symbolically Authentic Non-Euclidean Adventures in Mountain Climbing* by René Daumal (1908–44), which was published uncompleted in 1952. Daumal was a friend of one of Gurdjieff's pupils and the novel is meant to be an allegory of the thinker's method. Cobb makes a great deal of the similarity of the novel's plot with Jodorowsky's film. He writes:

> Jodorowsky took the book's premise, its storyline, endless textual details and even the way Daumal introduces his group members [. . .] The crossovers are so numerous. (Cobb 2007, 120)

But the precis of the fantasy novel's plot and characters who embark on a sea voyage to an unknown continent bears little outward resemblance to Jodorowsky's Mexican-infused film, his specific characters, and the alchemic structure that he gave it. While Jodorowsky may have used the novel as a stimulus, his own personal connection to the theme of mountaintop enlightenment is taken from a variety of religious traditions. For example, in describing his climbing the ancient Zapotec complex at Monte Alban, Jodorowsky tells us:

> We climbed extremely slowly, step by step. Chanting as if we were a magic mantra, she recited an exercise: 2; 4; 8; 16; 32 . . . 128; . . . 512; . . . 134, 217, 728 . . . 8,589,934,592 . . . and so on, arriving at an incredible series of figures recited with dizzying speed. (Jodorowsky 1971, 182)

Reaching the heights, while mouthing mind-stretching mathematical exercises, was just the kind of contrarian spiritualist mysticism that appealed to Jodorowsky. *The Holy Mountain* continued his previous creative trajectory by taking a concept from another creative work (a novella in the case of *La Cravate* and a play in the case of *Fando y Lis*) and then completely modifying its expression through his own artistic filters and interests. He did not adapt works to cinema. He transformed them. My conclusion that *The Holy Mountain* is not a film version of the novel *Mount Analogue* is supported by a close reading by independent scholar, David Pecotic, who concludes that "the two texts share few ideological or even structural elements [. . . and that the similarity be considered] a species of academic urban legend-making" (Pecotic 2014, 357). It is true that Jodorowsky was a fan of Daumal. In a 2020 interview he said:

> He, for me, is the best writer in France. Daumal discovered all of the things that Surrealism didn't want to see! He was the first to translate Sanskrit writings into French. Daumal also translated D. T. Suzuki's writings on Zen. He was a disciple of the spiritual teacher Gurdjieff [. . .] Daumal truly altered my mind. (Nardonne 2020)

Underpinning the significance of *The Holy Mountain* for his film career is the move from Mexican financing to American financing. While the film was made in Mexico, the money was Klein's. His company ABKCO Films put up US $750,000 ($5 million in 2022 dollars), which is modest by Hollywood standards.

It represented only half of the projected budget (Cobb 2007, 129). Jodorowsky complained during the shoot that he did not have enough money to film it properly (Greenfield 1972). The amount he did have reflected a nonstudio, independently-made film budget that required the low cost of Mexican production to be realized. Yet, it was a sizable increase over his earlier films, which suggested the possibility of even larger expenditures for future projects. In an article written during the production, Jodorowsky is quoted as saying that the next time he would "ask for more next time. Two, three million" (Greenfield 1972). Little did he know that this would actually turn out to be the case when it came to *Dune*.

Shooting began in Mexico in February of 1972 and was completed in August of that year. The shoot ended up with thirty-four hours of unedited footage that was then edited to about two hours (Galarza 2006, 46). In keeping with his philosophy of transformative filmmaking, Jodorowsky engaged in sleep-deprivation training and spent time training in the Arica method, a multidisciplinary way of transforming human personality created by the Bolivian Oscar Icahzo, who in 1968 established an institute in the northern Chilean town of Arica and then relocated to New York. Jodorowsky made a great effort to put himself into the mind-space of a guru or master since that is the part he plays in the film.

Jodorowsky's interlacing of his personal quests and his cinematic protagonists played by himself may have its roots in the way he saw himself as a person who adopts interchangeable personae. In a 1999 interview, he described himself as a blank slate awaiting fulfillment:

> My father was a Jew who tried to pass for a Russian. My mother was half-Russian, because a Cossack raped her mother, and she tried to pass for a Jew. So I was Chilean and not Chilean because I was the son of immigrants. So I was trying to pass for a Chilean, but never completely. I was never anything. Therefore, the only exile I know is the exile from myself. Because I was never myself. (Weiss 1999)

The idea of a spiritual quest may very well come from the need to find out who one is. He was searching for an identity primarily in the universal rather than in the particular. At this point, Jodorowsky was transitioning from being a theater director to being primarily a film director, but underneath these public identities he had aspirations of becoming a spiritual master. Films like *El Topo* in which he goes about slaying "masters," (perhaps a freeing of himself from his Zen Buddhist master in Mexico City), and *The Holy Mountain* become personal markers on his own journey to spiritual leadership. The films presented Jodorowsky in cinematic guise journeying to enlightenment, while in real life he would drop his sartorial disguises to engage in personal Jodorowsky-led teaching and healing. He did that when he had the actors participate in mind-altering exercises in preparation for their performances. Eventually, his embracing the identity of a spiritual master would lead to his own theories and practices of psychomagic and family psychotherapy.

According to Jodorowsky cinema is a place where "reality is transformed, as the story moves into a universe of mirages and reveries" (Houdassine 2014, 32). Because he saw his own personality and identity as open to re-creation, Jodorowsky conceived of identity as a mirage the way a film is. Because identity is a mirage it can be swept away by reverie or an awakening that allows personal transformation. Jodorowsky believed that the performative act creates an illusion or mirage that can liberate the actor from the illusions he lives by. Acting is a way to liberation.

While the auteur generates the film out of his own consciousness and existential experiences, the embodiment of those ideas requires engagement with the material world. Budgets, actors, technical crews, extras, casting, and so forth are demanding mental taskmasters. In an article about the shoot in Mexico City, Jodorowsky is quoted as saying:

> For *El Topo* I get $400,000 ... For this one, $750,000. Basileo, the dwarf, you have seen heem? He is fantastic, no? He can do anything. He has eight children. I pay him 400 pesos [$33] a day. He ask for 300. The old bums I use? I have to give them ten pesos. Ten pesos! (Greenfield 1972)

Robert Greenfield also describes Jodorowsky's *modus operandi* as a director on set, his then wife of eight years Valérie Trumblay, who has a part in the film and was with him during all of his feature films up to that point, and he even mentions and quotes Burt [Robert] Kleiner. Kleiner is the journalist who did an interview with Jodorowsky about this time that appeared in the June 1973 issue of *Penthouse* magazine and served as a source for Cobb's description of how Jodorowsky viewed the film (Cobb 2007, 127–8). The set was a complex ecology of humanity, both Mexican and American, from which the maestro Jodorowsky, waving his directorial baton, generated the film's energy.

Alchemy is an esoteric pseudoscience that claimed to be able to transform matter by knowing the secrets of its "spiritual" essence and deciphering its symbolic nature. The film itself is structured as an alchemic transmutation that turns ordinary characters into new, empowered ones, who are pure and enlightened. Jodorowsky had already begun the process by seeking to transform himself prior to making the film. Jodorowsky envisioned the film's imagery and narrative producing an alchemic change in the viewer—turning an ordinary consciousness into something new.

Jodorowsky has said, "Alchemy, like any process in human life, works to materialize spirit and at the same time spiritualize material. This is a concept that underlies all my artistic creations" (Cobb 2007, 125). While *El Topo* was guided by Jodorowsky's Mexican Zen Buddhist experiences, *The Holy Mountain* became a reflection of more esoteric thinking and practices. It was another step closer to his own interpretation of how the human mind operates and how it can be transformed. In this film he not only acted the part of an alchemist and structured the film as an alchemic process, but he also gave the film his own unique mysterious fusion. He combined the aesthetics of American psychedelic counterculture that he found in New York with Mexico's death-and suffering-obsessed Catholicism and the subversive, iconoclastic spirit of European surrealism. To this he also added a heavy dose of animal symbolism, the spirit of a masked carnival, and his now signature representation of people with disabilities. The result was an unusual cinematic experience for the makers and the viewers.

Jodorowsky avoided professional actors. He preferred using nonprofessionals to achieve the effect he wanted. He had already done this in *Fando y Lis*, whose leads were unknown actors and in *El Topo*, where his co-leads were also unknowns. By bringing "real" people into the film he was able to better represent the strange world he wanted to create. It was his way of uniting reality and fantasy. While depending on amateurs in the film, he was not adverse to some celebrity-name-dropping in regard to who wanted to be in his film or whom he had invited to be in it (Jodorowsky 2008, 221–2). The film was shot on the streets of Mexico City, in various other Mexican locations, and in Mexican studios. When he shot scenes in front of Mexico City's Basilica de Guadalupe, which honors the Virgin of Guadalupe, Mexico's most revered religious figure, outraged Catholics accused him of desecrating the shrine, which led to a scandal fanned by the media and recounted in his 1996 book *Antología pánica*. Jodorowsky was well versed in shocking people. He and Mexico seemed to be perpetually at odds. His minor celebrity status in the United States offered him solace.

Cerdán and Labayen point out that the first half of the film is "strongly influenced by Mexican iconography," which in Jodorowsky's hands becomes "exotic and baroque" (106). His exaggerated, spectacle-like treatment of Mexicans and Mexican identity using surreal and absurdist, blood-soaked images infuriated Mexicans. However, if one looks at the same images from the perspective of liberating Mexican viewers from their customary pieties and humdrum platitudes about what constitutes Mexican identity, then one can see that Jodorowsky had a serious agenda. What is not surprising is that Americans had no such qualms about the film, since it was not their identity being satirized. Here was Jodorowsky's secret tool: play to non-Mexican audiences who have only stereotypes to connect them to Mexico by exaggerating that country's culture so that it becomes an alien planet where all the madness of human life can be concentrated and universalized. This film turns Mexico into a Breughel-like world of strange and exotic rituals and misshapen creatures that nevertheless seem of this world.

Even though it was filmed in Mexican locations and with Mexican performers, it did not screen in that country till a couple of years after its premiere in Cannes in 1973, albeit in an edited and subtitled Spanish version. One critic of the film has written that Jodorowsky had created "a world that should see its consciousness/conscience altered, just like that of the spectator" (Garcia, E. 2012, 21). Jodorowsky confirmed this himself when he said: "I am a creator of consciousness. That is my product" (Biesenbach 2012, 252). It is as if he viewed his films as living organisms filled with mental processes that could mesmerize viewers into becoming wholly new creatures.

The Film

Jodorowsky's own comments on the film's production appear in various interviews. Almost thirty years after he made the film, he described *The Holy Mountain* as "a surreal film about a man (played by me) who makes a journey to a holy mountain to discover the lore of nine sages who have survived for 30,000 years" (Macnab 1999). While that is the single-sentence synopsis of the film that offers Jodorowsky's understanding of "mystical enlightenment," the complexity of the imagery that he put in the film required ingenuity (Macnab 1999). For example, Jodorowsky says in the same interview:

> We started to shoot without a script. I made a plan of exactly where we would go each day but not what we would do. We paid the keeper of the city's zoo and

at night he'd lend us animals, but when we wanted to shoot the procession of lambs on crucifixes I had to hire the lambs from a restaurant. When I finished the scene I gave the lambs back and they were eaten. (Macnab 1999)

However, in the 2007 DVD of the film which has extra features, there is an image of a page of a typed film script, so a script eventually appeared (Holy Mountain DVD 2007c). Jodorowsky also used storyboards for the film, which are rough sketches of each shot or scene (Biesenbach 2012, 115). They were displayed at the Museum of Modern Art in New York in 2012 as part of a retrospective. So he did use traditional filmmaking techniques to supplement his own spontaneity.

He brought a new aspect to this film, which was not in the earlier ones—the Tarot. In the Macnab interview, Jodorowsky explains that "in the Tarot the circle with nine points is a symbol which is supposed to explain the universe and every kind of character. The nine points correspond to the best-known planets." The concept of the nine planets or points can also be found in the Enneagram, popular at that time. It offers nine human personality types inscribed in a circle. Jodorowsky mentions the Enneagram in his discussion of the Tarot in an extra feature of *The Holy Mountain* DVD (2007). Of course, the nine planets are integral to astrological interpretations of identity and the future. The nine "sages" in his film therefore correspond to the nine points in the Tarot circle and the Enneagram, plus the nine planets used in astrological divination. The characters in the film are meant to symbolize these astrological signs and their qualities.

In his DVD bonus feature explanation of the Tarot, he says in English that the Tarot "will teach you how to create a soul." The Tarot's explanation of each card (the art of cartomancy) allowed its interpreter to influence the thinking of the one seeking to know either her or himself. Jodorowsky goes on to say that he did not understand how to approach the Tarot until he was able to view it as a total system, a mandala, which is an Asian religious art form, that represents the world on which one can meditate. The film itself becomes a kind of mandala of the world informed by the Tarot. While Tarot card readings are normally used to predict the future, Jodorowsky preferred to use his readings to determine the supplicant's essential.

A Tarot card that is relevant to Jodorowsky in this film is that of the magician, because of his role as the Alchemist. Jodorowsky seems to be at his best mixing all kinds of traditions and letting the symbols he incorporated carry numerous meanings. He could conflate the Tarot with Astrology and the Enneagram so that users or followers of each could see their preferred methodology in the film. Another example of conflation or syncretism is a scene that was cut from the film in which he has Whirling Dervishes (Islamic tradition) perform a dance on an Aztec ruin (Indigenous America), thereby having the circular twirling reflect the movement of the sun (*The Holy Mountain* DVD 2007, Scenes Cut).

Jodorowsky considered his training in mime to be a foundation he could use in making a film. He preferred facial and physical expression and bodily movement through space to convey meaning (Macnab 1999). In a later interview he said that he had put the dialogue into the mouths of the actors in postproduction, which is a kind of dubbing (Biesenbach 2012, 252). Postproduction was done in the United States to make it an English-language film, which is why it had to be subtitled in Spanish for Mexican audiences.

The plot of the film tells the story of a group of people on a spiritual quest. The goal of the group is the ascent of Mount Carmel, where immortals reside. The seekers give up all their possessions and embark on a journey of painful purification so that they may be worthy of enlightenment when they reach the pinnacle. The film's imagery itself utilizes well-known Judeo-Christian symbolism just as *El Topo* did. One of the main seekers is the Thief figure (a representation of the fool, beggar, or mendicant card in the Tarot). The Dwarf who wakes up the Thief at the beginning of the film plays a similar role in this film as the "the short woman" does in *El Topo*. The Dwarf and the Thief, like El Topo and the short woman, entertain tourists with their implausible relationship. Because of the Thief's resemblance to Christ, some people make a cast of his body and add the figure to crosses that they sell. A part of the statue of the Thief is sent upward as an offering using balloons in exchange for which a bag of gold is sent down. The Thief, keen on finding the source of the gold, climbs a tower (of Babel?) where he meets an alchemist who turns the Thief's excrement into gold. The Thief meets the group that will ascend the holy mountain. The individuals in the group embody the planets and they rendezvous at the house of the alchemist. A manufacturer of beauty products is Venus; a weapons manufacturer is Mars; an art dealer is Jupiter; a toymaker is Saturn; a worldly adviser is Uranus; a police chief is Neptune; and an architect is Pluto. Earth is represented by the Thief. The Alchemist represents Mercury, the most molten and malleable of the planets. The alchemist's assistant makes it a group of ten.

They travel to an island where nine immortals live atop a mountain. The number of the immortals and the seekers is the same, suggesting it is a one-to-one relationship. The seeker is the same as the imagined immortal. On the journey the group meets another group that has forsaken the search for enlightenment and engages in typical secular pleasures. The seekers leave them behind and renew their quest that offers each one a personal vision. The Thief (Earth) fails to reach the top and is sent down "to earth" ending up back in the city along with a woman and a chimpanzee, while the remaining members of the group meet the immortals only to discover they are mannequins and the mountain scenery is only a painted set. The film ends with this revelation about human fantasy and illusion.

Chapter by Chapter / Scene by Scene

The film begins with two Marilyn Monroe look-alikes kneeling in white dresses. Then the figure of the Alchemist (Jodorowsky) appears, dressed in black like El Topo was. He is kneeling, so the audience knows we are in a sacred space. He prepares a purification, using a white cloth bathed in pure water. The women are about to be wiped of their current identity and given a new one. The color contrast between the Alchemist and the Marilyn Monroe women and the significance of the colors began in *El Topo*, but it was already used in *La Cravate*. He uses the white cloth to wipe the makeup from the two women, removes their clothing, and shaves their heads. In this way the false idolatry of Hollywood iconography is gone. What emerges are two naked Buddhist-like nuns, or perhaps adults reborn as innocent babies. This act of head shaving (which involved cutting off the women's real hair) is a ritual found in various religious traditions. Head shaving imparts a new identity to the person and, when done in a religious context, identifies them as humans on a spiritual journey. This opening scene is infused with chant-like somber music, which adds to its religious character.

If an American audience could easily identify with the Western genre in *El Topo* because of the gunslinger image, then the Marilyn Monroe look-alikes have the same function. But who this black-cloaked and black-hatted figure is meant to be is not as easily identifiable. Alchemists are not part of Hollywood imagery. The esoteric setting of the opening scene (a room of Moroccan-style black-and-white tile) also makes the scene less accessible, but the religious denoting is obvious. The black-and-white design reflects the black-and-white contrast of the human figures. While the women are presented in a transparent way as symbols of light, the Alchemist is so draped in black that no light escapes. He is mysterious and unseen.

After a transition using a stream of psychedelic, mandala-like art indicating hallucination we see a white-clothed drunk (costumed as a Mexican peasant) lying on the ground, his face covered with flies. The camera follows a rivulet of his urine as it flows past a pile of discarded shoes on which are visible two Tarot cards—the Fool and the Crocodile. They are balanced by a shot of a real toad and a real panther, whose relationship to the cards is not clear. The cards and the animals add a level of mystery or mystification to the scene, and they indicate to the audience that everything in the film has a symbolic value and must be viewed as such. The drunk figure is the Thief (Horacio Salinas) who represents the state of humanity enchained, though the association with the good thief on the cross beside Christ is present as well. The good thief is mentioned in the Gospel of Luke as one of the two thieves, crucified along with Jesus, who asks that he be remembered when Jesus has ascended to his heavenly kingdom. This association indicates that the Thief in the film is one who seeks salvation, which is exactly what happens.

Suddenly, a handless and legless dwarf (Basilio González) appears to revive the Thief. He has a Tarot card on his back, continuing the symbolic nature of each major character in the film. Since most, if not all, of the viewing audience would be unfamiliar with the Tarot, the symbolism is opaque. The dwarf is approached by a swarm of naked boys with green-painted penises (the equivalent of the proverbial fig leaf used in Renaissance art to hide the genitals), who pluck a white rose from the Thief's outstretched palm which bears the mark of a nail wound (again a crucifixion allusion). The white rose is a sign of the Thief's inherent inner purity. The boys start throwing stones at the Thief who is now fully crucified (a New Testament reference to letting only the sinless ones throw the first stone in the stoning of an adulteress). The stoning wakes him up and he scatters the boys with a primal scream. Humanity has awoken, ready to be saved.

The presence of live animals in the film follows their use in *El Topo*, but here the animals are individualized (not a multitude of penned rabbits) which increases their symbolic impact. The symbolic meaning of the colors that clothe the characters is even more prominent than in *El Topo*. While El Topo's black garb suits a gunslinger as defined by the genre, the black garb of the Alchemist/Magician/Wizard is a vestment that is best associated with "the dark arts." The opening scene has the Alchemist using his large-brimmed, wizard-like black hat (think Harry Potter films) to cover and then reveal the changed faces of the women. Black is the color of night that turns visibility to invisibility. It is not a primary color as such. It is a mixture of red, green, and blue, which again suggests alchemy, transformation, and magic.

In the first few minutes the film establishes its basic visual method as a series of distinct and often contradictory images. Rather than accentuating the continuity of story, plot and character, Jodorowsky seeks to emphasize each discontinuous shot or scene in such a way as to turn the film into a series of tableaux or set pieces similar to a genre painting of the nineteenth century. We are asked to reflect on the meaning of each scene individually by analyzing what it symbolizes. The importance of each image/shot/scene on its own is amplified by the fact that the film up to this point is without dialogue. The visual clues are all the viewer has to decipher the meaning of what is going on.

The Thief and the Dwarf go into the city, where soldiers are executing students (a reference to the 1968 massacre in Mexico City) and parading with lamb carcasses that symbolize the innocent students they have killed. But then Jodorowsky uses a shot of the carcasses against the background of a cathedral, which some might interpret as a sacrilegious reference to Christ as "the Lamb of God." As tourists and the bourgeoisie of the city watch the killing, seven birds fly out of the chest of one of the executed students, symbolizing the rise of the soul to heaven. This chapter titled "The Initiation" ends with an American tourist giving the Thief an American dollar for filming the rape of his wife. Could this scene be a way of commenting on Jodorowsky's view of the relationship of filmmaking to transformation? It may be.

Chapter 2 begins with The Great Toad and Chameleon Circus which is performing the history of the conquest of Mexico. A scale model of Aztec temples is peopled by amphibian chameleons dressed in Aztec regalia. The chameleons are attacked by real toads dressed in conquistador armor emblazoned with red crosses while a German Nazi song serves as the soundtrack. The whole set is blown up with "blood" spattered everywhere. The next scene also begins with a sign "Christs for Sale" and ends with the making of a body cast of the Thief since he resembles church images of Jesus on the cross. The Thief finds himself in a room filled with a multitude of plaster casts of himself as Jesus, which drives him to destroy these "idols." The theme of idolatry, of craven images, and the attribution of divine representation to objects as a false religion is central to Jodorowsky's belief that spirituality is a psychological and inner state. Iconoclasm is central to Judaism, which prohibits images of the Divine.

Symbolic intensity, historical referents, and complex set design are made possible because the film is not bound by a genre and its conventions the way *El*

Topo is. These same features also limit its appeal to wide audiences. For example, the next scene shows the Thief carrying one of the plaster casts of himself followed by an entourage of prostitutes with a chimpanzee into a church, where the creature ends up eating up the face of the plaster cast in a bizarre ritual imitating the Last Supper. Then the effigy rises into the sky in a parody of the Ascension. One has to be deeply immersed in Christian symbolism and biblical narratives to make these associations. Not everyone is.

Now that the Thief is freed of his effigy he begins to climb a red tower that stretches into the sky. At the top of the tower he discovers the Alchemist (Jodorowsky) now dressed in white. A new initiation ritual begins in which the Thief is remade by having his old soul removed. Then he is offered "gold" by the Alchemist, which requires further cleansing in a pool with a hippopotamus. In order to create gold alchemically the Thief defecates into a glass pot, the contents of which are then used to distill the gold. The idea of "filthy lucre" and the Freudian discussion of the relationship between money and excrement are central to this ritual. The Alchemist tells the Thief that he can now turn his own excrement into gold. Of course, the great myth of alchemy was its ability to turn base metal into gold. This scene is Jodorowsky's re-creation of that myth. But there is another aspect to this gold scene that links it to the previous one of the conquest of Mexico. The Spaniards came for gold and the gold they took turned into the blood of countless Indigenous people.

The Thief and the Alchemist then appear in similar costumes (brown for the Thief and black for the Alchemist) in the roles of master and acolyte. They enter a room with Tarot cards painted on its walls. The sheer scale of the room's artifice of symbolic meaning is astonishing. How does an uninitiated viewer, who is a neophyte to Jodorowsky's ever-expanding and all-embracing system of religious references, find a portal into his world? Only in tiny glimpses. The volume of religious connotations can be grasped only sporadically. For example, when the Alchemist does his excrement-into-gold alchemy he wears a robe with Judaic symbols and a phylactery on his forehead, suggesting to me that the ritual is also meant to purge the Thief of his Christian messianic identity. Whether this is something Jodorowsky had in mind is uncertain, but in the end he would probably say that all interpretations only add to the majesty of his invention.

Eventually, the Thief himself is turned into a kind of Tarot card when the Alchemist adorns him with a wooden staff to indicate knowledge, a sword to indicate daring, a chalice to indicate desire, and finally a gold disc that indicates silence. The Thief now sees those who will be his traveling companions, whose effigies are now hanging on the wall where the cards used to be. They introduce themselves beginning with Fon, whose planet is Venus, the planet of love. He is a manufacturer of everything related to sensuality, has a large harem of wives, and has invented a line of masks that will allow a person to have any identity he/she wants till he/she dies (echoes of *La Cravate*). The factory scenes are accompanied by an American narrator's voice. The same technique is used for the others, who also do not speak other than through an alien female voice-over. Isla, the arms manufacturer, is next. She represents Mars and is making a drug to create "delusions of grandeur" and turn ordinary people into "wild beasts." In her segment, besides large doses of nudity, Jodorowsky introduces a flock of black swans, a new symbolic creature added to the mix. He also references American pop culture of the day with Isla's company producing "psychedelic" guitar guns and religiously themed guns for Buddhists, Jews, and Christians. This is religion as commodity.

Then there is Klen, who represents the planet Jupiter, which is the Roman name for Zeus, the supreme Greek god. Klen is in the art business, where he has created a machine for lovemaking. It is a bizarre contraption that creates an electronic beeping orgasm. Sel is a clown that represents Saturn. She rides an elephant. Her business is war toys and her company has created a comic book series that conditions youth to hate. Jodorowsky's attack on war and militarism is augmented when he introduces Berg, who represents Uranus. He is a political adviser who tells the president to gas millions of citizens. The reference to Nazi Germany is clear. The next companion is Axon, who represents Neptune. Axon is a chief of police, who engages in castration leading to death. One scene worthy of Cecil B. De Mille's film epics involves large numbers of lined-up soldiers, chanting and saluting, which resembles Third Reich parades. Like the others, Neptune is related to militarist imagery. He is followed by the last planet—Pluto, whose name is Lut. He is an architect who is promoting the City of Freedom project, where one pays to be free of family and a home—a critique of the illusions promoted by capitalism.

It has taken more than half the film to get to this point. Each scene describing the searchers contains extensive female and male frontal and rear nudity, along with weaponry, military figures, and caskets. Each scene is a circus of images that are excessive in every way. As the set designer Jodorowsky had free rein to create a setting that would accentuate his comic creations. Then these seven plus the Alchemist and the Thief begin the journey to find immortality. The switch to the actual search for the nine sages of the holy mountain begins with each searcher dressed in mendicant/penitent brown cassocks with a staff traversing a verdant green mountain landscape (the Alchemist wears the black version of the same cassock signifying his leadership role). There are ten people in total because the Alchemist has an assistant. The change to a natural landscape is a welcome relief for the viewer who has endured increasingly bizarre scenes and gross characters, plus a surfeit of nudity. Jodorowsky intended this scene to offer a feeling of escape from civilized madness. Their goal is to steal the secret of immortality, ergo "the Thief."

In this verdant landscape there are peasant healers and Indigenous plants with great powers that stand in striking contrast to the urban and industrialized decadence of the first part of the film. In preparation, the seekers submit to various ancient rituals. At one point in the ceremony Jodorowsky's Alchemist voice-over asks the seekers to give up everything, even their bodies and their past, because the ultimate reality is a form of nothingness. Their true bodies are the universe. This mesmerizing sermon by Jodorowsky liberates the seekers. They appear on top of a Mayan temple purified and ready to take their boat journey to the holy mountain. The journey by boat over water is a new departure for Jodorowsky's symbolism, which Cobb attributes to Daumal's novel, but it may go deeper (Cobb 2007, 163). The same motif reappears in his later autobiographical films and was present as a pool in *El Topo*. Jodorowsky was born by the sea in Chile and spent his childhood there, so water is an important symbol for him. The seekers in the small boat resemble the account in the Gospels of Jesus and his disciples crossing the Sea of Galilee. The association is confirmed before their departure when the Thief, standing on the pier, wants to work a miracle like Christ, and the Alchemist shows him how having all those loaves and fishes can turn to violence as boys fight over the spoils. As they depart there is a fascinating shot of the prostitute and the chimpanzee in a rowboat paddling after their boat with the chimpanzee doing a very credible job. Some critics associate her with Mary Magdalene.

Once they arrive on Lotus Island they are met by a strange Bavarian character in lederhosen, backgrounded by the Alps, who takes them to a cemetery, where they meet more strange characters, including one who promotes LSD. This scene is a reminder of the world that they have come from, the "base" of the holy mountain, which they are about to leave. Each seeker has a hallucinatory experience. One eats horse flesh raw on the hoof. Another is buried in a downpour of gold coins. Another drums out his violence, while two dogs tear at each other. The next one has sexual fantasies while a bull mates with a cow, while another prays to a witch in a tree that is covered in the carcasses of dead chickens she has slaughtered. She proceeds to castrate him. The higher they go, the more outlandish the enactments, culminating with one of the two women on the journey lying naked and covered with scorpions.

After this LSD-like hallucination the Alchemist announces that the group no longer needs him and that they are all masters now. He asks one of them to cut off his head. Miraculously, he survives the beheading and instead kneels over a beheaded lamb. He then takes the woman with the chimp (she is dressed in red) and tells the Thief that he should unite with her because one can only reach eternity through love. Once more Jodorowsky uses a trinity of characters to represent the family as the triangle of creation just as he did in *El Topo*. The trio depart as did the son of El Topo, the short woman, and the baby at the end of the previous film.

The remaining eight seekers reach a plateau with a round white table on which is drawn the Enneagram and at which sit their equivalent effigies. As they laugh they remove the mannequins and the Alchemist proceeds to proffer the moral of the story, which is that this is a film about illusion. It is time to end the film, to break its illusion and, with a command, the camera zooms back revealing the crew and cast of the film, the true reality of the creation of what the viewer has seen. This is Jodorowsky's version of "a happy ending" in which he tells the audience "the trip" is over and it is time to go "home" to the real world. When the film ends the magic ends. The credits roll and the 113-minute film is over.

Critical Response

The first public screening of the film occurred at the Cannes film festival in the spring of 1973. The actor Ingrid Bergman served as president of the jury for the feature film. All the other members of the jury were men, including the American film director Sydney Pollack, the British writer Lawrence Durrell, and the Mexican film producer Rodolfo Echeverria (Cannes 1973). Rodolfo was the brother of the President of Mexico (Luis Echeverria), so one can imagine what that meant politically for Jodorowsky's Mexican-made and Mexican-rejected reputation (Treviño 1979, 28). Jesús Salvador Treviño's valuable 1979 article on the new Mexican cinema of the 1970s, when Rodolfo reigned as the country's film czar, does not mention Jodorowsky at all, even though the article deals with numerous directors, both Mexican and foreign domiciled in that country. This erasure of Jodorowsky is a comment on his innovative and provocative imagery, whose use of the tropes of Mexican identity proved so offensive to its film critics.

The film did not even make it into the official competition for the best feature film at Cannes. It won no awards. Considering the detailed description of the various scenes provided previously, one can see immediately that the film did not fit any genre or normal expectation. It was a total outlier. It made its next public appearance in November in New York. The American media was not impressed. The *New York Times* review denounced the film for its abuse of animals, claiming they were killed for the sake of art (Klein 1974). Since the sheep were destined for the table and were sourced at a restaurant to which they were returned, this denunciation lacks validity. Church has claimed that the New York reviews were generally "lackluster" (Church 2007 B). Since the film screened only at midnight on Fridays and Saturdays at a single theater (Waverley), Klein, who owned the film, did not show it again till a festival in 1974 and then again in a single theater in Los Angeles in 1975. One scholar of avant-garde cinema views American spectatorship as closely tied to the country's "dominant ideology" which means that unusual and provocative films seldom find an audience, even among the smaller, art-house cinema crowd (Verrone 2012, 193). *The Holy Mountain* was so profoundly indulgent in terms of its surrealism and absurdism and so far removed from the realm of *El Topo's* easily identifiable Western genre that American audiences had trouble relating to it. Since Klein saw no financial return in distributing the film, he tried unsuccessfully to turn Jodorowsky toward a project that he thought would be a commercial success, a film version of *The Story of "O,"* a venture into soft-core pornography. He could not appreciate Jodorowsky's art-oriented film ethic and his devout anti-commercialism.

Academics have been more generous to the film than the early critics. For example, Robert Neustadt points out that "disoriented and fragmented subjects wandering in amorphous voids characterize the Jodorowskian quest for meaning" and that these wanderings are basically allegories and dramatized spiritual quests (Neustadt 1999, 83). Neustadt goes on to say that all of Jodorowsky's fictional quests are circular in that they end where they began. El Topo's progress from a black-clothed gunslinger to a brown-clothed monk indicates progression. In *The Holy Mountain* the circular progression is even more pronounced. The searchers, who abandon their previous lives as social mannequins for a spiritual quest, end up finding that the great sages they seek are nothing but mannequins like they were/are. Because Jodorowsky views social life as a parade of illusions we are forced to adopt, he offers to help us break free to a new state of understanding. Showing the audience the production side of the film at the very end is meant to destroy its suspension of disbelief. Cinema is just another illusion we live by.

The Brazilian academic Luis Garcia views the film as creating a surrealist "supra-reality," a combination of dream and reality as articulated by André Breton, the theorist of surrealism (Garcia, Luis. 2014, 37). Jodorowsky's extensive symbolism and juxtapositioning of contrary elements is the technique used to offer a "supra-reality." For example, the replay of the conquest of the New World using toads and chameleons to represent history is a supra-reality by using the symbolic meaning that culture gives certain animals to accentuate the nature of the conquest. It is more impactful than a historical reenactment using humans because the animals contribute to turning history into a dreamscape that mirrors our own consciousness and the workings of our subconscious. This conscious and subconscious dreamscape offers a parade of images—grotesque, comic, absurd, ridiculous, erotic, violent, horrific, and pastoral. Jodorowsky harnesses them for his storytelling.

Garcia explains that the techniques of cinema allow "a fusão numa mesma sequência fílmica do retrato de mundo consciente e do mundo dos sonhos das personagens, . . . / the fusion in the same filmic sequence of the portrait of the conscious world and the world of the character's dreams" (2014, 39). Because editing and montage allow the visual manipulation of time and space, cinema lends itself to this kind of surreal visualization. Garcia concludes that *The Holy Mountain* is the "most surreal of his films" (2014, 40). None of his later films achieved this level of "supra-reality." This may have been the cause of its box office failure. It was simply too far beyond the norm, especially in a feature-length film. As Jodorowsky said in a 1999 interview: "I was trying to make a film that would blow the mind" (Macnab 1999). He did so by marginalizing the typical narrative arc supported by a chronological presentation of events and in its place emphasizing the micro interruptions (the characterization, actions, costuming, and symbolism) he inserted into every scene. They were more than just distractions from the story; they became the essence of the film. For most cinemagoers this approach can be very disorienting.

While the film continues the religious tone begun in *El Topo*, it moves more toward ideas or techniques for transcending rational experience in order to intuitively unite with the divine. Even though most religious traditions have a mystical component, they are not part of their mainstream and are often reserved for special individuals. Jodorowsky may have been thinking that his film could emulate a mystical experience. While there is some anecdotal evidence of this happening, its achievement was most likely individual and sporadic.

The mysticism that Jodorowsky promotes is one that both references traditional religious rituals and blasphemes them (Breckenridge 2015, 15). In other words, Jodorowsky builds a symbolic structure that is imitative of well-known religions and their rituals, while at the same time subverting them with his own secular variations. Breckenridge concludes that *The Holy Mountain* does this to satirize the counterculture that it comes from (2015, 15). It is true that Jodorowsky seeks to challenge "all notions of spirituality" (Breckenridge 2015, 21). However, he does so in a mix of piety and irreverence that is not as satirical as Breckenridge claims. Jodorowsky's religio-sacrilegious obsession is viewed differently by the American scholar Jeremy Guida, who sees it as a pillar of Jodorowsky's "charismatic authority" (Guida 2015, 549). He asks:

> how could Jodorowsky's films produce such religious emotions? How else could he get away with such graphic and offensive images if there was not some deeper meaning behind it? Audiences returned, again and again, believing that Jodorowsky had not only produced their liminal experiences, but that he had also encoded some esoteric secret in the plethora of religious symbols. (Guida 2015, 549)

No doubt there were some who fetishized Jodorowsky as a guru masquerading as a filmmaker. In 1973 Jodorowsky most likely considered himself to be a filmmaker (he had just devoted seven years to making three films). But his evolving idea of the transformative/therapeutic power of cinema was pushing him in the direction of becoming a guru. The path to such status led through a process of "desacralizing," which meant subverting any and all sacred cows in his films (Santos 2017, 10).

Like most filmmakers, Jodorowsky has his own view of the film, a view that evolved over time. In a 2012 American interview about the film Jodorowsky said: "I believe in poetical revolution [. . .] In the consciousness." (Biesenbach 2012, 115). One of the key tools in his poetically visual arsenal is his emphasis on the symbolic meaning of colors in a culture. "Every color has a moral meaning," he says in the interview, "a philosophical meaning" (Biesenbach 2012, 115). For example, when he uses red in a film he wants the viewer to associate it with blood as the wellspring of life. *The Holy Mountain* is full of red colors and blood.

When the film became available in 2007, the *New York Times* reviewed it once more: "A scandal when first released, Mr. Jodorowsky's movie is a dazzling, rambling, often incoherent satire on consumerism, militarism and the exploitation of third world cultures by the West," writes the reviewer. "It unfurls like a hallucinogenic daydream, which is to be expected, considering that it's the follow-up to Mr. Jodorowsky's midnight movie 'El Topo'" (Steiz 2007). In 2007 the film was no longer a scandal. The times had changed. The reviewer had changed. The animal rights perspective was no longer present. As part of the reappraisal, the film critic for the British newspaper *The Guardian* baited his readers by writing: "Where else could you see a re-enactment of the conquest of Latin America with costumed frogs and chameleons? Or a geriatric hermaphrodite squirting milk from breasts that appear to be the heads of ocelots?" (Rose 2009). By the 2020s the film's bizarre imagery had taken on a patina of a curiosity, of a spirited, pre-digital theatricality that induces a detached curiosity rather than any kind of real mind alteration.

For Jodorowsky, the making of the film made him reflect on his use of women in his early films. In a 1989 interview with Roger Ebert at Cannes for the premiere of the final film in the trilogy, *Santa Sangre*, he says that making *The Holy Mountain* caused him to give up on filmmaking:

> After I finished "The Holy Mountain," I was so awake after six months of shooting, that I finally realized what I was doing in life, how I was hurting women. It affected my conscience. Then I stopped making pictures. I said, this is illusion. I need to work with reality, find myself, discover what I want to say, how to live, how to make a family . . . to live, you know? (Ebert 1989)

This explanation is at best an exaggeration, if not an outright lie, since he jumped into making *Dune* shortly thereafter, though his reflection on his view of women has a tinge of mea culpa. Because this film and *El Topo* were removed from circulation by Klein, Jodorowsky had to turn elsewhere for money to make another film, but his search led him into a no-man's land between the American and the European worlds. For a self-absorbed, charismatic, and volatile artist figure like Jodorowsky, escaping the clutches of his American producer/benefactor seemed like a gift from heaven. But it was not to be.

Conclusion

Jodorowsky worked best in an auteur framework, where his imagination and multidisciplinary art experience could fly off in all directions. Unbeknownst to him *The Holy Mountain* was to be his last auteur film for fifteen years. By losing his future funding and the distribution of his completed films because of his argument with Klein, he lost the ability to be an auteur. When next he became a director for hire on the ill-fated *Dune* project, he came up against a strong vision different from his own. *Dune* (1965) is a highly esteemed and extremely popular science-fiction novel by the American writer Frank Herbert, which won SF's preeminent Hugo and Nebula Awards. Some consider it the apex of twentieth-century science fiction writing. When one singular visionary like Jodorowsky has to adapt another singular visionary's work, conflict is inevitable.

His first three feature films were powered by his auteurism and his interpretation of North America's American and Mexican cultures. Living and working in Mexico and also in the United States exposed him to the rawness and vitality of "the New World" where land, space, and the Indigenous took precedence over the established historical identities of Europe, where cultural elites, intellectual and artistic theories, and the avant-garde were preeminent. When he took on the Dune project a year after *The Holy Mountain*, he did so based on his European connections. Taking on an American project with European funding forced him to straddle two worlds simultaneously. Could the alchemist make this unlikely combination work?

6

The Interregnum

Dune (1974–6), *Tusk* (1980), *The Rainbow Thief* (1990) plus Jodorowsky's comics/graphic novels

Klein's actions derailed Jodorowsky's trajectory as an auteur and pushed him toward being a director for hire. His first post-auteur project was adapting the American novel *Dune*. It was the first of three film projects on which he was primarily only a director, two of which came to fruition—*Tusk* in 1980 and *Rainbow Thief* in 1990. He did not appear in these films as an actor nor work in any other capacity the way he had done in his auteur films. Neither film found an audience and he later disavowed both.

The period between 1973 and his next auteur film, *Santa Sangre*, released in 1989, is a period in which he turned to graphic novels as his primary creative expression. He became known and admired for the graphic novel *L'Incal* (1980–88) as well as others. After *Santa Sangre* he also published fiction, plays, and nonfiction. This expansion into print gave him an opportunity to describe the development of his own psychoanalytical theories. His working in a range of genres and media showed his integrative powers as an artist and his ability to transfer ideas from one form of expression to another.

Dune (1974–6)

The sources of information about the failed Dune adaptation include the 90-minute 2013 documentary film made by Frank Pavich titled *Jodorowsky's Dune* and Ben Cobb's chapter on the project in his 2007 book. In turn, that chapter is dependent on an earlier 90-minute 1994 documentary *La Constellation Jodorowsky* plus a translation of Jodorowsky's "Dune: Le Film Que Vous Ne

Verrez Jamais (Dune: The Film You Will Never See)," a 16-page detachable insert from the 1985 issue of *L'Incal 4* in which Jodorowsky talks about what happened.

As a primary source of three hours of visual material in which the principals and commentators discuss, reminisce, and pontificate on the project and what it achieved or did not achieve, the Pavich documentary has serious limitations. Interviews are a form of oral history, which has its drawbacks because it is memory-based, performative, and often self-serving. Also the end result is dependent on editorial juxtaposing of sound bites that create a narrative flow which is constructed to make the film's point. Chronology is not always respected and various behind-the-scenes issues and conflicts are passed over. The goal of this documentary is a glorification and mythologizing of the project.

L'Incal 4's insert contains a narrative about the project written by Jodorowsky, who has a tendency to make exaggerated claims and focus the spotlight on himself. Because the discussion here is dependent on these narratives it should not be considered a definitive account of what really occurred. The documentaries that discuss the Dune project turn its failure into a powerful myth of Jodorowsky's genius, foresight, and successful protogenesis of a whole brood of great science-fiction films from *Star Wars* to *Alien*. This mythology is something that fits nicely with the wider myth of the importance of Dune in science-fiction literature. The longer it took to make a film based on the novel, the grander the myth became.

The 1965 novel by Frank Herbert was first optioned in 1971 by an American producer, who died shortly thereafter. Jodorowsky claims that he read the novel in one day while in New York, but whether in the 1965 English version or in a 1970 French translation is unknown (Jodorowsky 1985). Since the book is over 800 pages, this account is either a miracle of reading in a language in which one is not fluent or simply a quick skim or else pure fantasy. He then claims that he contacted Michel Seydoux, a 26-year-old French film distributor, who had distributed *The Holy Mountain* in Europe and who had shown an interest in making a film with him (Pavich 2013). Seydoux agreed to purchase the rights to the novel from the American company and have Jodorowsky direct the film (Jodorowsky 1985). Jodorowsky initiated the project because his relationship with Klein was over and yet he still wanted to make films, and because, as he says, "I just liked the story and needed to support my family" (Cobb 2007, 175). The spark between the novel and his own imagination seems to be the novel's grand cosmic scale, its religious allegory potential, and its male heroic arc. It is an American novel meant initially for an American audience. Jodorowsky was not an American. He had to go to France to find a sympathetic producer, which ought to have been a red flag. Eventually Hollywood would have to play a role and neither Seydoux nor Jodorowsky was part of the club.

Jodorowsky says he approached men who formed his "seven samurai" (Jodorowsky 1985). At this time the science-fiction genre, both its major writers and its film productions, was male-dominated, so it is not surprising that the talent he sought was male. Besides Seydoux, his creative crew consisted of H. R. Giger, the Swiss graphic artist, the pop rock group Pink Floyd, celebrities like the surrealist artist Salvador Dali and the rock star Mick Jagger, the French comic book artist Jean 'Moebius' Giraud, the American special effects expert Dan O'Bannon, and Christopher Foss, a well-known British comic book cover illustrator (Cobb 2007, 181). What is significant about this list is that it included creative people from both sides of the Atlantic. The budget was initially set at $9.5 million, of which Jodorowsky had spent a couple million by 1976. By then it had expanded into an estimated $15 million budget ($90 million in 2022 dollars). During those two years Jodorowsky, in conjunction with Moebius, produced a massive, tome-sized script that included concepts and artwork by Giger and Foss, as well as 3,000 individual sketches by Moebius. While the storyboard/script was very detailed in its storytelling, its vision could be interpreted as undermining the commercial success that Hollywood required. Seydoux could not raise the final $5 million from the American studios that he needed for the project to proceed. Although the film never did get made, the material that it generated was repurposed in Jodorowsky and Giraud's highly popular fantasy/science-fiction graphic novel series *L'Incal* (1980 on).

The project disappeared from the public consciousness until the appearance of Frank Pavich's award-winning documentary *Jodorowsky's Dune* (2013) almost four decades later. The film was awarded best documentary status at various film festivals and won the Audience Award at Sitges, the world's preeminent fantasy and science-fiction film festival. When the film premiered at Cannes, one American critic pointed out caustically that the whole point of the film was to make "the case for the overblown epic as a legendary lost masterpiece" (Dalton 2013). Because David Lynch did make a film version of Dune in 1984 that was panned by the critics and rejected by the public, Jodorowsky's earlier attempt to make a grand epic took on mythic proportions and added to his charismatic authority as a visual guru. Coinciding with the release of Jodorowsky's first film in twenty-three years, the autographical *The Dance of Reality* (2013), the documentary was a major factor in Jodorowsky's resurrection as a filmmaker.

Considering the mystique surrounding the "impossibility" of turning the novel into a successful film (at least until the fall of 2021 when Denis Villeneuve's version appeared to generally positive reviews), one could conclude that Jodorowsky's reputation as the filmmaker who brought genius to a classic of twentieth-century science fiction was justified. The rapidity with which Jodorowsky embraced the task, the orchestration of talent that he was able to achieve, and the mystical spirit with which he imbued his film concept added to the myth.

"I did not want to respect the novel," Jodorowsky states, "I wanted to re-create it" (Jodorowsky 1985). By re-creation he meant seeing it in a Jodorowskian way. What follows is Jodorowsky's enraged and enraptured poetic prose about his vision for the spaceships in the film:

> I do not want that man conquers space in the ships of NASA, these concentration camps of the spirit, these gigantic freezers vomiting imperialism, these slaughters of plundering and plunder, this arrogance of bronze and thirst, this eunuchoid science [. . .] I want magical entities, vibrating vehicles like fish of a timeless ocean. I want [. . .] womb-ships, [. . .] whore-ships driven by the sperm of passionate ejaculations. In an engine of flesh I want rockets complex and secret, hummingbird ornithopters, sipping the thousand-year-old nectar of dwarf stars. (Jodorowsky 1985)

In an English-language interview after the screening of the documentary *Jodorowsky's Dune* in the British Library, Jodorowsky makes the claim that he dictated the whole script to Moebius in four days (British Library 2014). While hard to believe, this claim points to the intensity of what Jodorowsky and Moebius were doing in creating the storyboards.

The *L'Incal* insert about the Dune project was published nearly a decade after the project ended, while the *La Constellation Jodorowsky* commentary added almost another decade to the previous one, and then *Jodorowsky's Dune* added a further two decades. This passage of time allows remembrance to move in certain pathways that may not always coincide with what truly happened or why. This allows *Jodorowsky's Dune* to celebrate Jodorowsky and the artists involved. It canonizes Jodorowsky as a creative genius martyred on the altar of Hollywood crassness. While singing the praises of what could have been, the film does not address the possibility that if it had been made and released, it could have been a flop, either because it was too esoteric for sci-fi audiences or because, if Hollywood had gotten involved, its commercial success would have countered

Jodorowsky's anti-commercialism. A hallucinatory science-fiction film may have worked or it may not have. After all those years, Seydoux admitted that the film Jodorowsky conceived contained a degree of madness (Pavich 2013).

Hollywood does not like madness, so when Jodorowsky says in the documentary film that he wanted the film's hero to be a prophet, a religious figure, a messiah, who dies a Christ-like death only to be resurrected in the consciousness of his followers, he is pushing against the calculations of the money men. Many years had to pass before these concepts found commercial success in *The Matrix* (1999). Jodorowsky presents his collaborators as spiritual warriors engaged in an epic battle to make the movie. Since the great prize of the planet, where the story is set, is a spice that expands consciousness and drives interstellar travel, this concept fits with Jodorowsky's own cinematic goals of mind-expansion. Jodorowsky says he wanted to add "spiritual meaning" to the novel (Pavich 2013). Not only was the film itself to be a religious allegory, but "every person who will work in this picture will be a spiritual warrior" (Pavich 2013). This emphasis on a religious epic is a continuation of the religious fixations in both *El Topo* and *The Holy Mountain*.

While preparing for filming, Jodorowsky continued the methods he had used in his earlier auteur films. He had a martial arts and weapons master train his twelve-year-old son Brontis, who was to play the lead. Brontis, who is fifty years old in the 2013 documentary, remembers how demanding the training was on him as a boy. Jodorowsky mentions that, when people criticized him for being so demanding of his young son, the answer he provides in the film is that "you need to sacrifice yourself" in order for others to change (Pavich 2013). He says, "I prepare my son exactly like Duke Leto [in the novel] prepare his son" (Pavich 2013). This mixing of fiction and reality is a technique that could be hard on any adult actor, but must have been exhausting for the juvenile Brontis, who had to live up to a fictional character's abilities. In the documentary he laments how tough it all was.

Besides the numerous sketches for the storyboard created by Moebius under Jodorowsky's direction, Chris Foss drew spaceships that were reflections of the natural world that Jodorowsky wanted—a pirate spaceship in the shape of a camouflaged fish, or a helicopter whose motion was powered by the motions of the wings of a hummingbird or a dragonfly. The costuming of the principal characters was extravagant, suited to a space opera in terms of its grandeur and excess. Jodorowsky even convinced the aging surrealist artist Salvador Dali to play the role of the evil emperor. Giger created the castle home of the Harikonnen evildoers in the shape of a bloated body. All these images were far beyond what the original novel contained.

"I was raping Frank Herbert, but with love," says Jodorowsky (Pavich 2013). According to Seydoux's account in the documentary, the studios refused to have Jodorowsky direct, which he considers a humiliation for Jodorowsky (Pavich 2013). Their decision simply showed that what Hollywood wanted (commercial success) was not what Jodorowsky wanted (creative license). After the film rights lapsed, the property was bought by the Italian producer Dino De Laurentis, who at this point was established in Hollywood, and he had David Lynch make a theatrical-release version in 1984 that was a box office and artistic failure.

Was Jodorowsky's version "ahead of its time" as some critics in Pavich's documentary suggest? Was it overly ambitious as Jodorowsky himself suggests rather bitterly at the end of the documentary? For something unrealized there can be no definitive answer, only speculation. What is important about the project's not being realized is that it was resurrected in one form or another in Jodorowsky's graphic novels from *L'Incal* to *Metabarons*. Jodorowsky says in the documentary that he is okay with this result because it validated what had been created and did not let it die. These graphic novels secured his and Moebius's following in a different but related medium and so kept his vision alive.

On October 22, 2021, Denis Villeneuve's long-anticipated film version of *Dune* was released on HBO Max streaming and theatrically around the globe. Villeneuve, a Quebec filmmaker who had migrated to Hollywood, was already known for two well-received sci-fi films, *Arrival* (2016) and *Blade Runner 2049* (2017), a sequel to the famous 1982 *Blade Runner* film. Hollywood decided his track record was sufficient for him to take on the task. Globally, the opening weekend box office was $220 million for a film whose production budget was $165 million (Outlaw 2021 and Weston 2021). The film was released in 2D, 3D, Imax Dolby, and 4D versions. In the forty-five intervening years since Jodorowsky attempted to make the film, so much had changed in filmmaking. There is now a greater emphasis on female roles, extensive use of CGI special effects, and the visual legacy of science-fiction films that came after 1975, all of which Villeneuve acknowledged in his version.

One result of the wide release of Villeneuve's *Dune* was the impact it had on the value of material from Jodorowsky's project. A month after the Villeneuve version was released, Christie's auction house sold a copy of the Jodorowsky storyboard tome for $3 million. Described as "a mythical object by sci-fi fans," the auction house first estimated its value at a mere $30,000 to $40,000, but it went for 100 times that amount, in part due to the renewed awareness of the Dune saga (Agence France-Presse 2021). Since Jodorowsky has his own copy, he can be considered well off. His failure has turned to gold. The alchemist reigns.

Villeneuve's version needs to be compared to Jodorowsky's because of its level of public recognition and its initial critical approval. *Variety* termed it "a majestically somber and grand-scale sci-fi trance-out" (Gleiberman 2021). *The Guardian* praised the film for its being an "altogether better behaved version . . . [that] dials down the crazy" and concludes that "Villeneuve is riding the sinewy worm of Herbert's sacred text with aplomb" (Kermode 2021). First of all, Villeneuve's film is dark, especially its interiors. They are gray concrete walls meant to imitate the stone castles of the medieval period. Its spaceships are equally gray-toned and monolithic in shape. There is little dialogue and the relations between the characters tend to be unemotional. The spirit of the film and its imagery is highly militaristic (the evil Baron Harkonnen is modeled on the Marlon Brando rogue colonel character in *Apocalypse Now*, a war epic about Vietnam). The film is driven by a thunderous score. All of this is to say that Jodorowsky's color-filled and nature-oriented scenario is very distant from this version. Where religion in Villeneuve's version is a mix of morose Catholicism, desert Islam, and pagan prophecy, Jodorowsky's approach was one of playful, psychedelic spirituality laced with joie-de-vivre. Although Villeneuve created a more conventional film version of the book, its two-and-a-half-hour "Part One" will likely be five hours in total when Part Two is made and released. And should there be a Part Three, the length of Jodorowsky's all-in-one film would have been comparable. Herbert wrote more Dune novels, which could turn into a seemingly never-ending proliferation of sequels and prequels. In fact *The Los Angeles Times* reports: "Along with the potential 'Dune' sequel, a spinoff series called 'Dune: Sisterhood' that will center on the Bene Gesserit order is already in development for HBO Max. And more projects may well be on the way" (Rottenberg 2021).

A year before the film itself was released, Jodorowsky was asked by *Indiewire* to comment on the trailer for the film that had been released by Warner Bros. His response reflects that, even after such a lengthy passage of time since he had faced off with Hollywood in the mid-1970s, he retains his essential critique:

> I saw the trailer. It's very well done [. . .] We can see that it is industrial cinema, that there is a lot of money, and that it was very expensive. But if it was very expensive, it must pay in proportion. And that is the problem: There [are] no

surprises. The form is identical to what is done everywhere. The lighting, the acting, everything is predictable. Industrial cinema is incompatible with auteur cinema. For the former, money comes before. For the second, it's the opposite, whatever the quality of a director, whether my friend Nicolas Winding Refn or Denis Villeneuve. Industrial cinema promotes entertainment, it is a show that is not intended to change humanity or society. (Sharf 2020)

Tusk (1980)

Jodorowsky wanted to continue being a filmmaker, which may be the reason why he ended up making *Tusk*, a children's story based on the work of a minor English novelist. Cobb claims he did this "after the failure of his cherished pirate adventure *Mr. Blood and Miss Bones*" (Cobb 2007, 191). The project is first mentioned in a *New York Times* article that says it is to be Jodorowsky's next film for ABKCO (Weiler 1973). *The Holy Mountain* was then premiering at Cannes and the break with Klein had not yet happened. One account claims that it would be "set and shot (in a boat!) on the streets of NYC" (Aruzuno 2009). The desire to make a film for young audiences seems strange considering his work up to that point, but maybe his fatherhood, including having his son Brontis, a boy of seven, act in *El Topo* was a stimulus. Since he had already envisioned a movie for children, *Tusk* may have been the consolation prize.

Of course, Jodorowsky was no longer in New York after 1974, having based himself in Paris to work on *Dune*. Because Seydoux had nothing to show for his producer efforts in that regard, Jodorowsky joined up with French producers Jean-Jacques Fourgeaud, Eric Rochet, and Sylvio Tabet of Films 21. They hired a screenwriter to adapt the 1930s story set in India about a girl and an elephant. With a script in hand they set off for India. Cobb says that Jodorowsky viewed the story as a paradigm equating British imperialism in India with the Spanish conquest of Mexico (Cobb 2007, 191). How a story of a girl and an elephant born on the same day could realize this metaphorical equating is difficult to envisage.

Cobb provides a "shot by shot" script and a description covering seventeen pages that provides little insight into a film that itself lacked insight into itself. If the film was meant for a child audience, then in the beginning its intercutting of scenes of the birth of a baby elephant and a human baby on a British-owned plantation in India is not appropriate. Yet the idea of a bond between a baby elephant and a little girl does fit a Disney context. For Jodorowsky, the white daughter of a white British plantation owner becoming impassioned about the plight of elephants, who symbolize India, is a way of melding the interspecies relationship. The girl is eventually sent off to boarding school while Tusk, the elephant, joins the others in their labor on the plantation. The two are reunited when she returns, but then Tusk escapes and is pursued by a local maharajah. Tusk is captured and blood is drawn from the elephant to be consumed by the hunting party—not exactly Disney or a scene suited to a child audience. Tusk escapes again and ends up derailing a train. In the midst of all this the girl is pursued by a gang. In the end Tusk is freed by his colonial master, who then rids himself of his colonial clothing and takes on Hindu attire and face markings. Cobb describes the concluding scene:

> Tusk, coloured a golden yellow from the festive powder, underlining his divinity, walks along and free through the plains. Morrison [the white plantation owner] is now indistinguishable from the chanting sadhus. (Cobb 2007, 210)

Mixing symbolism and condemnation of imperial politics with children's cinema proved to be a disaster. Of course, Jodorowsky blamed the producers for its poor showing and stated that if he had had more time to edit the film he could have made it into "a nice picture for children" (Cobb 2007, 210). Jodorowsky did not see the incompatibility between his own auteur style and children's cinema. It reflected a certain blindness to genre and audience. Jodorowsky had no connection to India. He had no understanding of its culture or cultures. Likewise, he had no experience of British colonialism in Indian history. Perhaps he felt that his knowledge of Spanish colonialism in Mexico gave him permission to equate it with what happened in India.

Jodorowsky's attraction to Herbert's *Dune* was plausible because he had experienced American culture for a few years and his own sense of the fantastical and the magical paralleled the science-fiction genre. His taking on the *Tusk* project was a director-for-hire job in which he had less control than on the Dune project. His taking on these off-the-shelf assignments inevitably led to disastrous results for the film and for himself. Filmmaking has to deal with the real world of actors, financiers, production staff, and so forth. It is not a manipulated fantasy like films themselves. Cobb is right to claim that *Tusk* has "to be his most misguided to date" (Cobb 2007, 191). The term "misguided" seems a propos, and yet Jodorowsky seemed not to have learned his lesson. He went on to repeat the director-for-hire experience a decade later with equally disastrous results.

The Rainbow Thief (1990)

After *Tusk's* failure Jodorowsky took up the practice of public Tarot card readings one day per week in Paris as well as other pursuits, including his graphic novel/comics collaboration, first with Moebius and then with Silvio Cadelo. These enterprises will be discussed later in this chapter. He did make an auteur film in 1989 titled *Santa Sangre* (*Holy Blood*), which is discussed in the next chapter. *The Rainbow Thief*, a film, was written by Berta Dominquez D., the wife of Hollywood and European film producer Alexander Salkind. Salkind made the first Superman movie in 1978, as well as films on Santa Claus and the Three Musketeers. His wife was a fan of Jodorowsky's earlier films, so she convinced Salkind to hire him as the director. The film was shot in Gdansk, Poland, and is officially an English-language British production. Although released in London and Paris in 1990, it never received an American release. It stars Peter O'Toole and Omar Sharif.

Cobb quotes Jodorowsky as saying that he agreed to direct the film because he "wanted to know what it was to have all the techniques and all the money to make a picture" (Cobb 2007, 247). This explanation seems like poor motivation for an auteur. He had just poured himself into *Santa Sangre*, so he may have just needed a break from himself, as well as a paycheck. The same scenario had played out after *The Holy Mountain* when he took on the Dune project. Jodorowsky was not allowed to deviate from the script and the film came in on budget.

The British Film Institute's *Sight and Sound* magazine characterized both *Tusk* and *The Rainbow Thief* as "impersonal films" meaning that they reflected another person's vision (Bitel 2016). In the case of *The Rainbow Thief* it was the producer and his scriptwriter wife that created the film. When Jodorowsky was asked by the British Film Institute in 2016 what he thought went wrong with both films he said:

> For me *Tusk* is a film as valuable as *El Topo*, only it is for children. What we have seen so far is an incomplete cut. But the producer, a crook like all filmmakers, declared bankruptcy, got the money in his pocket and fled, leaving the installation unfinished. I am still to this day fighting for the rights and the final cut, remastering and resubmission.
>
> *The Rainbow Thief* is something else. The film is not as flawed, has sequences that please me, but deep down it was an experience for me to get to know how the film industry works. I left disgusted with the experience. And what disgusted

me most was working with a *star* like Peter O'Toole—a little "god" of rotten vanity... I hated it to death and even today I still hate it. (Bitel 2016)

From these remarks it is obvious that Jodorowsky does not take responsibility for his mistaken belief that he could be a successful director for hire. In the history of cinema there are numerous directors who were not auteurs, some of whom have created a distinct film style. One only needs to think of Alfred Hitchcock to know that a non-auteur can be a significant director. Jodorowsky's failure to admit to himself that there is a basic incompatibility between making the kind of transformative films he was so good at making and directing mainstream material is a reflection of an oversize belief in himself and his ability.

The Comic Book Phase

In recent times there has been a significant correlation between the art forms of cinema and comic books. The phenomenon of Marvel Comics superhero figures migrating to the screen in non animated blockbuster films has become a staple of the last decade, thanks primarily to CGI software. Earlier animated film figures migrated from the screen into comic books because of the appeal of the characters. One scholar describes film and comics as "close cousins growing up in the same household. So it's not surprising that one sees a lot of cross-pollination here" (Aldama 2020, xii). Considering Jodorowsky's penchant for marvelous characters, fantastical costuming, and crazy scenarios, it is not surprising that he would turn to comics. In the 1960s he had already been cartooning for a newspaper in Mexico City and his meeting with the French-speaking Moebius on the Dune project showed him how the two could work together. What Jodorowsky had imagined for that film and what Moebius had then executed in the storyboard became the basis for a highly successful project. *L'Incal* was launched in 1980, continued for some years with further iterations as well.

L'Incal first appeared as *Une aventure de John Difool* (*The Affair of John Difool*) in *Métal Hurlant*, a French comics anthology originally launched in 1974 by Jean Giraud (Moebius) and three others, who styled themselves as the publishing house Les Humanoïdes Associés (Associated Humanoids). Their focus was science fiction and horror. In the United States the magazine was published as *Heavy Metal*. In the late 1980s a division of Marvel Comics published a three-volume version of *The Incal*. Many years later the original French firm moved to the United States as Humanoid Publishing and began reproducing the Incal saga. Not only was there the original series that had appeared almost annually in the 1980s, but it was also then followed by a prequel series that ran from 1988 to 1995 with Zoran Janjetov as the graphic artist. Then a sequel to the original was launched with Moebius in 2000, which was followed in 2008 to 2014 with a final series using José Ladrönn as the artist. On top of all this there were spinoff series related to the original universe of the Incal titled *Metabarons*, *The Technopriests*, and *Megalex*. In 2016 Humanoids published a digitally downloadable 112-page comic collection titled *The Jodoverse* with excerpts from all his major series, as a confirmation that over three and a half decades Jodorowsky had developed an international body of fans for his graphic novel space odyssey adventures.

It is not surprising that in November 2021 a press release from Humanoids, *L'Incal*'s publisher, announced that the series was scheduled to become a film (Leonte 2021). The director chosen for the project is Taika Waititi, a New Zealander of mixed Polynesian and Jewish descent best known for *Thor: Ragnarock* (2017) and *Jojo Rabbit* (2019). Jodorowsky was quoted in the media release as saying that he fully trusted the new director with his vision (Leonte 2021). In a YouTube video that accompanied the announcement Jodorowsky says he is "not in a condition to make this huge epic" and that he believes that Waititi is the kind of filmmaker who "wants to change the world" with his films, just as he had (Jodorowsky 2021). In the video, the 92-year-old Jodorowsky not only looks vigorous, but speaks with the same energy and commitment that he displayed in earlier videos such as the 2013 and 1994 documentaries. Because *The Incal* series remains a best-seller for the company and it is a major shareholder in Primer Entertainment, the production house for the film, there is a chance that it might get completed.

The series published by Humanoids were not the only ones Jodorowsky developed. During the same time period he worked on other series with artists Arno, Covial, Cadelo, and Bess. In total, his work is recognized as a valued part of the classic period of sci-fi graphic novels that proliferated in the late twentieth century. What Jodorowsky brought to his comic book narrative is the same kind of fantasy, spirituality, individual heroism against evil, and the future as a version of the present (and the past) that he first introduced in his films. Why did the genre work for him? It offered him a blank slate where the outrageous, the unbelievable, and the insane could be brought to life in a male-driven universe of fantastic adventures and captivating scenarios. In the graphic genre he could ride on his own comet through a universe of his own making. Although he could not draw that universe, he was its author. Comics are "one of the few remaining popular cultural arenas where creators are still relatively free to experiment with unorthodox subject matter" (Granholm 2015, 499). If anything, Jodorowsky was and remains unorthodox.

The academic study of comics has grown and *L'Incal* has attracted its share of attention. The period after 1980 is termed the "Dark Age" in comic book history because the themes and illustrations became darker and more adult-oriented in tone. What Jodorowsky was particularly good at was the creation of "transgeographies and posthumans" (Rosmaninho 2016, 111). His metropolis heroes like DiFool had occult powers that enabled them to survive the monstrous realities of a fearsome world. The French term for comics is "bandes dessinées" and Moebius is considered to be the artist who brought the genre into the modern age. One of the main theorists of the French comic book, Thierry Groensteen, presents the argument that narration is a supplement to the art because it is the art that appeals to the genre's audience. This may be valid in general terms, but it is problematic when applied to Jodorowsky and Moebius because it would subordinate the vision of the author to the talent of the artist. Jodorowsky's scripts for *L'Incal* should be considered 'programmatic' in that they provide the detailed storyline for the imagery. But the drawings and how they are distributed on the page would be within Moebius's purview. Since Jodorowsky was the narrative driver, the series is a reflection of his imaginative creation, including the main character John Difool, who is based on The Fool card in Tarot. Schematically it is a reflection of Moebius's art. That the two could work together to such a high degree of success indicates that their collaboration had an intrinsic unity of vision at its very core. Audiences may have loved the art, but the story and the settings Jodorowsky gave it were equally vital to the series' success.

Their unity of expression may very well come from their mutual rejection of the rational world around them in favor of a fantastic universe that is nevertheless vaguely rooted in a known world. For example, the *La Folle du Sacré-Coeur* (*The Mad Woman of Sacred Heart*) series that both of them collaborated on in the 1990s emphasizes the value of "prophetic qualities" when the protagonist is torn between rationalism and mystical visions (Lindstrom 2013, 131). Jodorowsky himself has said that "I decide to create a universe. In that universe I tell stories" (Neustadt 1996, 209). He considers his stories commentaries on the present: "I don't think it's the future. I think it is today" (Neustadt 1996, 211). An Italian study of the *L'Incal* series concludes that "Jodorowsky combines the grotesque and sci-fi dystopia in order to construct a satire of modern society, without renouncing a positive message and an ultimately utopian vision" [trans.] (Di Nobile 2016, 13). This is precisely what he did in his three auteur films from 1968 to 1973, in which he parodied society and offered journeys into eternity. That he should continue his attack on social corruption and hypocrisy, bourgeois hegemony, and militarism in his comic books indicates that his vision is deeply rooted, no matter which genre he uses for artistic expression. His imagination had found an expanding universe where it was free to grow without end. And yet in this environment of narrative freedom he found time and inspiration to make another auteur film. Sixteen years after *The Holy Mountain* he returned to Mexico, where he made *Santa Sangre*, his last auteur film for twenty-four years.

7

The Auteur Reborn

Santa Sangre (1989)

Jodorowsky was sixty years old when *Santa Sangre* (*Holy Blood*) was released in 1989. By that age most directors have their major work behind them and their future films are often judged to be lesser creations. One can still be creative in one's sixties but it becomes more difficult later on. Ingmar Bergman was thirty-nine when he made *The Seventh Seal*; fifty-four when he made *Cries and Whispers*; and sixty-four for *Fanny and Alexander*, after which his work declined. Alfred Hitchcock was thirty-six when he directed *39 Steps*; fifty-five when he directed *Dial M for Murder*; sixty-one when he made *Psycho*; and sixty-three when he made *The Birds*. The films he made after that were among his lesser ones. The great Japanese director Akira Kurosawa was forty when *Roshomon* was released; forty-four when *Seven Samurai* appeared; and sixty-five when *Dersu Uzala* came out. Using the age of these major directors as a gauge of achievement, one would be justified to think that *Santa Sangre* was a final moment of greatness. After all, Jodorowsky did not make another film for twenty-four years! Raising the issue of a director's age is not a reflection of ageism because Jodorowsky did go on to make excellent films when he was in his eighties; it is simply an observation on the normal trajectory of human creativity and its evaluation. *Santa Sangre* is the test case of whether he could be provocative at age sixty.

The three films *El Topo*, *The Holy Mountain*, and *Santa Sangre* are often viewed as a trilogy. Each of them was made in Mexico with its particular film industry structures, cultural ambience, and social history. Claudio Argento, the Italian producer of *Santa Sangre* is quoted as saying of Jodorowsky that "he is a crazy director for a crazy place like Mexico City" (Cobb 2007, 213). Mexico City was a "crazy" place for Argento because he was unfamiliar with it and he had never been engaged with Jodorowsky's street-oriented filmmaking technique. Complexity and confusion are part of most scenes because Jodorowsky's auteur vision is deeply rooted in the life and the people of public places. He drew his inspiration from their faces, their clothing, and their physiques. He found street life engaging. Perhaps he found its "reality," especially in Mexico, close to fantasy.

Cinema and its audiences had evolved in the sixteen years since he had released *The Holy Mountain*. Had Jodorowsky evolved as well? According to Cobb, he had because the film "reached a hitherto elusive mass audience" (Cobb 2007, 213). In other words, Cobb believes it was a commercial success. A low production budget definitely helps. Finding a large audience could be the result of Jodorowsky's toning down his content to be more accessible, or of audiences developing new tastes, or of the new technologies of film distribution (VHS and later DVD) giving the film wider circulation. While all these factors may have been at play, the real answer may lie in the film's popular genre, which is horror.

The producer of the film, Claudio Argento, had worked with his older brother Dario in making Italian horror films and decided to try something on his own (Cobb 2007, 213). It seems that Argento approached Jodorowsky with a story about a mental asylum resident written by his associate, Roberto Leoni. In the credits for the film there are three writers: Leoni, Argento, and Jodorowsky. According to Leoni, the film script was developed in the following way:

> Over time I developed a story that I told Claudio Argento because it was a time when we worked together. Claudio understood this story and indeed he even added to it things he thought and together we decided to present it to the director who seemed the most suitable to represent it, that is Alejandro Jodorowsky.
>
> Then, Alejandro developed this story with his imagination and his art, also telling me an episode that occurred in Mexico City which in some respects had similar characteristics and together we wrote the script by which he then made the film that we all know (translated from the Italian). (Leoni 2019)

The story Leoni is referring to is that of a Mexican serial killer of women named Gregorio "Goyo" Cárdenas Hernández. He spent decades in prison until his pardon in 1976 after which he became a lawyer and practiced that profession till his death in 1999. He was released without any memory of his crimes. Jodorowsky met him by chance in Mexico City and this serial killer's morality tale of redemption was blended with Leoni and Argento's script and became the plot of *Santa Sangre*. The film attributed Goyo's crimes to his upbringing and family, in particular the role of his mother. It also reflected Leoni's view that "I found Abel in what might have seemed Cain . . . this fact so ancestral and so mythical . . . is probably the origin of *Santa Sangre* because over time, I conceived a story in which even the worst demon actually can't forget he is an angel" (Leoni 2019).

Argento's take on the authorship of the film differed. He claimed that "*Santa Sangre* was really the first film for which I actually sat down in front of the typewriter. Although much of the plot was my idea, I think we all deserve credit" (Cobb 2007, 215). Both Leoni and Argento present themselves as the original writers, while Jodorowsky says "they did nothing," thereby giving himself most of the credit (Cobb 2007, 215). This kind of positioning over credits is not unusual in the film business because of the large number of people involved in a film's creation, but if this film is to be considered an auteur film of Jodorowsky's, he would have had to have a major role in the script, which becomes evident when taking into consideration its Mexican locale and characters.

To unravel the matter of authorship, one should begin with the *giallo* tradition in Italian horror cinema of which the Argento brothers were major players. Giallo films are a broad category that have come to be characterized as "spaghetti nightmares" that combine aspects of the horror genre and film noir's focus on criminality (Kannas 2019, 77). There is even a book titled *Spaghetti Nightmares* (1996) in which the Argentos are interviewed and from which Cobb drew Claudio's claims to authorship. In a giallo film the "killer's drive to commit murder is often inextricably linked to a past experience of violence and their stunted processing of this trauma furnishes them with a motive" (Kannas 2019, 78). This sounds very much like the concepts found in the film. However, the migration of the *mise-en-scène* to Mexico and a circus venue is surely Jodorowsky's. His auteur powers are fully realized in the film. It is fortunate that the source material fit his own philosophy of human psychology. Nevertheless, the film's roots in the Italian horror film genre contributed to its attracting a new audience outside the viewers that were attracted to *El Topo* and *The Holy Mountain*.

The film is an Italian–Mexican co-production that had a budget of $787,000 according to the Wikipedia entry on the film (1.9 million in 2022 dollars) Jodorowsky confirms the amount as "closer to $800,000" (Cobb 2007, 216). When compared to the budgets for *El Topo* and *The Holy Mountain*, *Santa Sangre* is definitely the lowest of the three, which is not unusual for the horror genre that tends to attract low budgets. That the films in the trilogy were funded in decreasing amounts reflects his problematic status as an auteur director to those for whom financial interest is paramount. It took some years for the Italian producer to find even this modest amount.

As mentioned earlier, one of the hallmarks of Jodorowsky's films is his casting of unknowns and street people. Not only does this allow him to spontaneously find people that may fit his vision, but also saves on costs. In this film he had Adán Jodorowsky play the young Fénix (the future murderer) and Axel Jodorowsky, the adult Fénix. Teo Jodorowsky plays a pimp, while Brontis Jodorowsky has a minor role as an orderly in the mental hospital. As well as his progeny, Jodorowsky included some professional Mexican actors and one American. The film was shot in both studio and street locations. The names selected for the characters were symbolically important. For example, Fénix is Spanish for phoenix, the bird that is reborn, which refers to Fénix's fate. In alchemy, the phoenix is associated with the final stage of the soul's development (Cobb 2007, 217). Then there is Orgo, the evil owner of the circus and Fénix's father. His name refers to orgasm, while his wife's name, Concha, is slang for vagina. Fénix's love interest is a deaf-mute named Alma, which is Spanish for soul. Using these names allows Jodorowsky to present his synopsis of the characters and their intrinsic role.

Because the horror film genre has developed numerous tropes and clichéd characters over the past century, one can imagine all kinds of sources or precursors for *Santa Sangre*. The story of a freed mental patient who goes on a killing spree is not unique. Nor are body-horror films such as those released by the Canadian David Cronenberg in the 1970s and 1980s, which Jodorowsky referenced in an interview in the second issue of *Eyeball: The European Sex and Horror Review* (Cobb 2007, 217). But Jodorowsky, as always, does not succumb to generic conventions because in this film he also injects "tender warmth" (Cobb 2007, 218). While there are fear-producing elements in the film, the emphasis is on empathy for a child trapped in an evil adult world. Since the story is set partially in a circus, a venue Jodorowsky knew from his youth, he acknowledges that the 1932 film *Freaks*, which dealt with the gruesome sideshows that often came with circus, was "my influence" (Cobb 2007, 219). In spite of having influences, Jodorowsky's film makes its own contribution to the genre and lifts it from the conventional to the surreal.

The film premiered at Cannes in May 1989 and then went on the festival circuit, winning three Best Film awards at fantasy film festivals in Paris, Brussels, and Madrid. As an Italian–Mexican co-production its next theatrical releases were in Italy in November of that year and then in the United States in April

1990. Mexico came a month later. The American release was limited, even though it was an English-language film. The *New York Times* reviewer saw the film at the Quad Theatre, an art-house cinema in Greenwich Village, which is the kind of venue where Jodorowsky's other films had flourished. Even though the film was shown at regular hours, the reviewer described it as "a 1960s-style midnight movie . . . intentionally tasteless, psychological, jokey and violent" (James 1990). The American box office is unknown, but it was probably minimal or modest at best. The film was rated NC-17, which meant no one under the age of eighteen was admitted. In 1991 Republic Pictures Home Video released a VHS version, whose package cover carried a Roger Ebert quote giving the film a top rating of four stars with a quote terming it "one of the best films of the year." A DVD version was released in 2004 (a Blu-ray version in 2011) by the American firm Severin Films, which went on to produce a 4K digital version for theatrical release in 2019. The film has been available in one format or another for the past thirty years. Since none of the earlier films were made available in the United States till 2007, *Santa Sangre* was Jodorowsky's sole representative for a long time.

The Film

His previous auteur films were structured on the theme of a physical journey that was meant to lead to enlightenment. The concept popularized by Joseph Campbell of the archetypal hero's journey gleaned from mythology is evident in his films. *Santa Sangre* deviates from that established trajectory by not having a physical journey present in the film. There is no alpha and omega arc. The antihero lives a tragic life that remains tragic at the end, even though he gains some insight. Campbell argues: "Whenever the human imagination gets going, it has to work in the field that myths have already covered. And it renders them in new ways" (Cousineau 1990, 179). In this film Jodorowsky renders the journey in a new way. He does so in the horror genre with its tradition of abnegation and hegemonic evil. Horror tends to happen in a singular space of entrapment (haunted house, spaceship, graveyard), which is why the protagonist in this film is generally enclosed in a room or a house, a stage or in his mind. The journey is primarily mental.

The opening scene includes two of his sons and his ex-wife in a scene with only four actors. Only Jodorowsky would dare to be so cheeky. Fénix (Alex

Jodorowsky) is naked and crouched on top of a bark-less tree trunk as if he were an animal in the zoo. The empty room is in a residence for the mentally deranged and he is approached by a doctor, an orderly (Brontis Jodorowsky), and a nurse played by Valérie Tremblay, his ex-wife. When they offer Fénix human food he refuses it, but then pounces on a raw fish as if he was a bird of prey. This act emphasizes his instinctual side, a creature formed by unconscious patterns of survival. The wild man image also connotes a certain innocence—of a creature unconscious of its appetites or their consequences. After he is zipped into a suit to make him presentable to human company, his face dissolves into that of an eagle, which flies to perch over the Circo Del Gringo, sporting an American flag. This shot denotes a flashback to Fénix's origins in the circus as the son of the circus's owner and brutish knife-thrower Orgo, and Concha, the leader of a religious cult. So begins the story of how Fénix became a mass murderer of women.

The circus as a setting is a new development for Jodorowsky, though he played with the idea in *The Holy Mountain*, where he had toads and chameleons reenact the conquest of Mexico in miniature. The circus setting is a venue rich with masked identities, amazing feats, ferocious animals, zany costumes, and a wild assortment of characters. These circus features suit the horror genre because they imply various kinds of death. The young Fénix is dressed in formal attire and sports a painted-on mustache. He is a child magician, who appears riding an elephant in a parade of characters—clowns, musicians, and a little person dressed as Aladdin from the *Arabian Nights*, who will soon take him on a magical journey. The carnival atmosphere abruptly stops when Fénix dismounts and speaks to his father Orgo, a loutish figure drinking in his car. Aladin (spelling of the character's name) takes Fénix to see the Tattooed Woman. Tattoos play a deep symbolic role in this film because they are marks of alternate identities. Fénix as an adult has his bird-of-prey/phoenix identity tattooed on his chest. The story of how that tattoo came about begins with his seeing the Tattooed Woman and Orgo together. While playing up to Orgo, the Tattooed Woman has been forcing her orphan ward to walk across a burning tightrope. The dichotomy of good and evil is now established with the drunk Orgo and the Tattooed Woman on one side, and Fénix, Aladin, and Alma, the deaf-mute, on the other. That evil is associated with a father and a mother figure is part of the Jodorowsky mythology that started with *Fando y Lis*. Jodorowsky amplifies the mother's seductive evil by having her tattoos contribute to the colors of a camouflage snake (biblical reference to Eve). Orgo begins throwing knives at her in an imitation of intercourse, which gives her masochistic pleasure. With Fénix watching this display, Jodorowsky is able to establish a child's revulsion at the primal act. But he is not the only viewer. Four sad-eyed clowns watch disheartened.

The figure of the Tattooed Woman may have been a staple of early circus "freak shows," but for Jodorowsky she represents a very powerful entity. A woman covered in tattoos is a provocative image. She has decided to change her outer appearance, an expression of self-determination, symbolic and magical powers, and audacious agency. He uses the same figure in his later autobiographical films, where the Tattooed Woman is a seductress and an all-powerful muse. For Jodorowsky, sexuality, creativity, fantasy identities, and empowerment are inextricably linked.

When Fénix meets the white-faced and white-dressed Alma, the Tattooed Woman's ward, he performs a magic trick—making an apple appear in his hand, which he then offers to her (it is now Adam not Eve that is the tempter in the Garden of Eden). With the magic apple in her hand she is now able to traverse the burning tightrope without injury. Followed by his clown protectors, who are carrying Aladin, Fénix rushes into the street to see a confrontation between Concha, his mother, and the police. He runs toward her crying "mama." As an adolescent he is still tied to her though he has begun in the previous scene to display the signs of budding maturity as a male. In these two scenes we have the basic theme of the film displayed—the struggle between love of mother and love of a mother-to-be.

Just as the Tattooed Woman represents rebellion against social norms, so Concha represents rebellion against religious conventions, whose representative is a monsignor/bishop, who arrives on the scene in a limousine. Concha is defending her heretical sect's temple from being demolished. It is dedicated to a saint and martyr that the Catholic Church does not recognize. She and all her followers are dressed in red robes, which to Jodorowsky represents the lifeblood of the body. This color stands in bold contrast to the regal purple robes of Church authority. On the one hand, there is the power of Rome and on the other hand, the power of the heretics.

The sanctuary is dedicated to a Saint Lirio, who Concha explains was a young girl raped and then mutilated and murdered by having her arms cut off. But her spilled blood continues to remain "alive" in a pool of blood, venerated by her followers. One of the adherents calls it "holy blood," the title of the film. The monsignor/bishop scoffs at this unauthorized piety and gives his support to the church's demolishment. As the building collapses, Concha, who says she will be martyred there, is embraced by Fénix. His affection and need for her encourages her to leave the site.

Saint Lirio's followers have a special sign on their robes, two versions of the letter "v" superimposed over each other. The letter could stand for "virgin," but it also looks like a mystical alchemic symbol. It also has an uncanny resemblance to the fish symbol used by early Christians to represent Jesus Christ. Of course, the reference to Lirio's amputated arms and the blood of the pool is a prefiguring of Fénix's turn from innocent child to bloody murderer. What is crucial at this point is the victory of male (Church) power over female (heretical) power, which is only temporary.

The next scene continues this representation of gender wars with the sexually provocative Tattooed Woman performing before a drunken Orgo. Concha interrupts this scene and threatens to kill the Tattooed Woman for seducing her husband. This sexually explicit scene is contrasted with Fénix and Alma's relationship when they are having an innocent Romeo and Juliet moment of mime. Jodorowsky next inserts a peculiar scene of the death and funeral procession of the circus's only elephant. Perhaps Jodorowsky places this scene here, right after the steamy sexual scene, as a way of referencing Freud's commentary on the link between Thanatos (death) and Eros (life). The life instinct is in a constant battle with the death instinct, and this may be Jodorowsky's cinematic way of expressing that idea.

The funeral procession is led by Orgo riding a horse while holding up the American flag. One can push the metaphor even further to say that he represents the American world as death-driven. The procession ends in the countryside. The boxed body of the elephant is dropped into a garbage-strewn ravine, where it is attacked by a mob of slum dwellers. They break into the "coffin" and begin dismembering and devouring pieces of the elephant. They act like human worms naturally devouring the corpse. A tearful Fénix, dressed in the red robe of his mother's sect, cries over what he sees, but his father says he must stop crying. He must stop being under his mother's sway and become a macho man like Orgo. A despondent Concha watches as Orgo takes away their son, removing him from her power and placing him under his control. He has Fénix forcibly tattooed on the chest with the same bird symbol that he has, indicating that the boy is on the road to manhood, however terrible that adulthood may be.

The tattoo that father and son share is that of the eagle that appeared at the beginning of the film, but Cobb insists on calling it a phoenix, a symbol of rebirth (Cobb 2007, 226). It represents both because it looks very similar to the American eagle, which would make sense considering his father is the owner of an American circus. But the concept of life after death that the phoenix represents in Egyptian mythology is also central to the plot of the film. Being marked by this tattoo means that he is being pushed to the dark male side. But then, dressed in the same shiny cowboy costume as his father, he meets Alma, now dressed in black, except for her whiteface, who touches the tattoo and mimes her hands into a bird that flies away, liberating Fénix from his imposed identity.

Next he and Alma appear in a magic act with Fénix as a young magician and she as his assistant. She enters a glass enclosure, which is then covered, and after he waves his hands the cover is pulled off to reveal his mother, Concha, whose character is now that of the "Queen of the Flying Trapeze." The equation between Alma and Concha is established in this transformative way as a prefiguring of the secret links that bind the characters in the film. Alma may represent innocence, but she is on the road to female maturity and the kind of power Concha displays. When Concha spies Orgo and the Tattooed Woman together, she grabs a bottle of acid which she throws over his genitals, castrating him. In response he pins her to his knife-throwing board and cuts off her arms, in imitation of what happened to Saint Lirio. The music turns hymn-like as Concha is martyred. Then Fénix watches his father cut his own throat over the loss of his manhood, while the silent Alma watches Fénix. Orgo's death has already been prefigured in the bloody death of the elephant, whose size and prominence Orgo emulates. The end result is that the distraught boy, who has just lost both his parents, is institutionalized. He and Alma are now united as orphans. This long flashback explains why Fénix is in an asylum. As the anguished young Fénix looks despairingly out of the rear window of the trailer in which he is trapped, we see Alma looking despairingly and longingly out of the rear window of the Tattooed Woman's painted VW van with a snake painted on it. They are mirrored souls yearning for each other and separated supposedly forever.

The martyred mother and the suicide of the father have imprinted themselves in Fénix's psyche, from which he must free himself in order to be whole. He is being pushed in a disastrous direction. While the dichotomies of evil and good, of love and lust, of father and mother are presented in an easily identifiable way in this inaugural act of the film, in the next act everything becomes murkier as Eros and Thanatos battle it out for his soul.

Flash forward back to Fénix as an institutionalized adult, who is taken out to see a movie with some residents with Down's Syndrome, but is waylaid by a sleazy character, who offers the boys cocaine and then takes them out on the street, dancing past a line of prostitutes. The Pimp character is played by another of Jodorowsky's sons—Teo, who a few years later was to die tragically. A catatonic Fénix is dragged along with the group. With his long hair, beard, and thin pale face he becomes a representation of Jesus and the other residents his disciples. Once the pimp has foisted off the boys on an obese prostitute, he goes dancing with the Tattooed Woman while Fénix watches with growing anger. The provocative dance has awoken his past emotions and energized him to escape the asylum for a stint in the real world. When he does, he sees his armless mother in the street. Mother and adult son are reunited and then disappear in a cloud of smoke, symbolizing a psychic bond more than a real one. She is dead after all. The killing spree he is about to embark on he does with the blessing and motivation of his mother.

The plot now moves to Alma, who reappears when her guardian, the Tattooed Woman, is used by the Pimp as a sex worker. Alma, now grown, is being dragged into the sex trade by her guardian, but she resists successfully and runs away. Now it is the Tattooed Woman's turn to be attacked when a mysterious hand throws a knife at her (reminiscent of Orgo's circus act) that strikes her in the stomach. The unseen attacker then continues with stabbing and slashing until she is dead. This gory murder is a perfect example of the slasher horror genre. Unbeknownst to the viewers, the assailant is none other than Fénix, who now has his first victim. Jodorowsky insisted on the brutality of the scene because "it's his obsession; he has to tear her to pieces in order to eradicate the problem" (Cobb 2007, 233). The Tattooed Woman was "a problem" for Fénix because of the way she treated Alma, but she was also a problem for Concha, whose husband she was seducing. The Tattooed Woman's violent death leaves Alma free, but also makes her vulnerable. After she discovers her guardian's savaged body she looks up at a picture of the young Fénix and Aladin from her circus days, at which point the film cuts to an adult Fénix, dressed as a magician as he is in the picture, walking down the street, where he meets Aladin, working as a shoeshiner. The figure of the shoeshiner was once common on Mexico City streets, a presence that symbolized class divisions and working-class poverty. Aladin maybe someone special in the circus, but he is a lowly figure on the street.

Together the two go into a theater that is advertising a show titled "Concha and Her Magic Hands." This is the midpoint of the film and we have reentered a circus-like, performative world, but one that is under his mother's control rather than the Circo Gringo that had been under his father's control. This shift in power captures one of the binaries that Jodorowsky emphasizes, that of mother and father. It also brings out the use of the family trinity that Jodorowsky had introduced in *El Topo*. In his view the family is a triangle of love, hatred, power, and neuroses in which the child is left burdened by the psychology of the parents. Jodorowsky eventually developed an approach he termed "metagenealogy" in which he offered a therapy for curing family obsessions. It is meant to free the individual from familial traps, legends, and imposed beliefs. The theory and practice of metagenealogy was first published in a Spanish edition in 2011, followed in 2014 with an English translation. This is several decades after *Santa Sangre* but the film is his first full cinematic expression of his theory of the family.

The strange, demented, or otherworldly consciousness generated in a child by a dysfunctional family is a staple of the horror genre, especially in American cinema. *The Exorcist* (1973), *The Shining* (1980), and *Pet Sematary* (1989) are some of the more famous ones from the period. Jodorowsky, however, subverts this trope by creating a genuine sympathy for the child turned insane adult. He has established the root cause of his mental illness in real happenings in his life. Metagenealogy explains Fénix's situation, while Jodorowsky's therapeutic practice called "psychomagic" offers a cure. The concept of psychomagic fits because it offers a prescription for liberation by "acting out" a provocative new identity that will cure the original ailment. The whole point of Fénix being a magician, first in boyhood and then when he transforms himself from a naked, beast-like creature trapped in an empty cell into a free-acting, fully dressed-up member of society, is to be an avatar of Jodorowsky's theory. By being his mother's hands and acting out her desires, he is trapped within her. Somehow he must be freed.

Fénix stands behind Concha moving his/her hands in mime motions, while she speaks about Adam and Eve and what happened. His silent motions and her words are not connected because they are a metaphor for the chasm between what he thinks is happening and what is really going on. The scene is presented in such a way as to expose Fénix as a failed conjurer, whose sleight of hand is there for all to see. This exposure is meant to question his value as a magician and the reason for his actions.

The absent hands theme continues when a stripper appears and tells Fénix that together she and he will create an act using his hands and her body that would be much better than the act of being his mother's hands. He agrees by reenacting his late father's knife-throwing tryst with the Tattooed Woman. Dressed in the same outfit as his father, he imitates his father's every move, but then his mother appears and insists that he kill the stripper because she is no different than the Tattooed Woman. She says that his hands and his arms are really hers. Unable to resist, he obeys. Jodorowsky makes it clear that Fénix's identity is ultimately under his mother's sway and not his father's. While he never succumbed psychologically to his father's efforts to make him be like himself, he was attracted to his mother's vengeful worldview. After the stripper's body is zipped up in a bunny suit she is laid to rest in a grave in the backyard of Concha's house. The scene is Dracula-like, as Fénix dressed in a black cape kneels over the open grave with its white-painted corpse, while a white ibis rises from the grave.

The next scene has Fénix having a nightmare. He awakes to find himself in bed with his mother. They are both dressed in the same silky white gowns, suggesting a non-incestuous relationship but nevertheless a twinning. They go down to breakfast during which the son's hands appear as the mother's as she eats and drinks. Jodorowsky now introduces the film *The Invisible Man* (1933), based on the 1897 science-fiction horror novel by H. G. Wells in which a scientist finds a way to make his face invisible but then is trapped without an identity because he cannot reverse the process. Fénix is enthralled by the replay of the movie on the television screen and so tries to make himself invisible to emulate the mad scientist but fails, at which point he claws at his face. All of this is a metaphor for Fénix not having his own identity and wanting desperately to escape his condition. At this point he sees himself as his mother.

Next we see him disguised in sunglasses, black hat, and coat going surreptitiously to a truck, where he purchases various chemicals. As he leaves, a truck goes by with the mannequin of a famous Mexican wrestler. This triggers a wrestling match between Fénix and a boa constrictor that comes out of his coat. The snake is Concha, his mother. Just as he is about to be strangled by the mother-snake it disappears. He has survived to fight another day. He goes to a theater where a wrestler named The Saint, advertised as the world's strongest woman, is taking on all sorts of challengers. Costumed like a saintly figure she is twice as tall as, and three times the bulk of, the other wrestlers. The Saint refers to a 1940s Mexican wrestler named "El Santo" (The Saint), who starred in horror genre movies such as "Santo versus the Zombies" and "Santo versus Frankenstein." There is also another allusion here—that of Concha's patron saint, St. Lirio the Armless. Armless human beings appear in his later films.

The wrestling motif pays homage to Mexican pop culture celebrities (The Saint was also a comic book superhero) and grounds the film in a world that Jodorowsky had experienced intensely in the 1960s. The imagined female Saint floors all the other wrestlers, and inevitably attracts Fénix's attention. He meets her in her dressing room and gives her a rose. She comes to his house dressed in black and white, the colors symbolizing the yin and yang of Tao philosophy—male and female. Then in a genuine Freudian slip Fénix leads him/her into the basement (his subconscious), where he has a mini-theater and where he says he will perform the ultimate magic trick—turning a skeleton into a flock of doves—reminiscent of the graveyard scene with the corpse of the stripper and the rising ibis. The corpse is in an Egyptian mummy box. Since his audience (The Saint) is a version of himself in bondage to his mother, this magic feat is all about his own transformation from subservient slave to liberated adult. But his power to liberate himself is cut short when he reopens the mummy case to find Concha dressed as an Egyptian queen in it. He cannot control his magician's hands when his "dead" mother orders him to kill The Saint. He uses a sword to slash The Saint from the back. Is he simply dispatching himself? Enter Alma, who has discovered where Concha and Fénix live. The dwelling is a version of the standard haunted house—ghoulish, dark, and empty with a life-size statue of St. Lirio. The house is a version of his own dark and ghoulish subconscious, the mind of a madman. Alma has to make her way through the labyrinth of Fénix's subconscious—the house's eerie hallways and rooms, where she comes across a body that we later learn is a life-size marionette of his dead mother.

Then we see Fénix lying over the body of The Saint, whom he has buried in a shallow grave just like the stripper's. As he stumbles around the graveyard, white naked women wearing lacy veils rise from numerous shallow graves to confront him. One of them leads a white horse with "tattoos" that identify it as belonging to the Tattooed Woman. They ask him why he is the killing these women. Recoiling, Fénix flees into his house of horrors (his mind), which sways like a ship in a storm. There he meets Alma and they raise their arms to each other and their hands touch. This act begins the ritual of liberation from his mother.

Concha appears, demanding that he kill Alma by cutting off her arms, just like his father did with her. This demand brings Fénix to the very core of the problem—his subconscious drives. Mesmerized, he drops Alma's hands, then walks toward Concha like an automaton, his arms outstretched. He picks up two knives from a table and advances on Alma, but this time he is able to assert himself. Instead of mutilating and killing Alma, he kills Concha. His hands are now his own. What Fénix needed was true love to free him from parental madness. Alma is pure of heart and willing to sacrifice herself on his behalf. That is why he sees her as his savior. She takes him to where she saw Concha's body to show him that his mother is truly dead, a lifeless marionette. The next scene has him pantomiming and singing with the marionette of his mother, which he then throws over a balcony, smashing its face. He then knocks over the figure of St. Lirio, stomping on it. Alma sets fire to both effigies, as well as the long red fingernails taken from his "motherly" hands. In this bonfire of haunting demons, Fénix is finally freed of his psychoses. He now knows that he is responsible for his murderous actions.

To signal his newfound manhood, Alma opens his shirt and pantomimes with her hands a bird rising from his chest, the phoenix/eagle tattoo referencing his rebirth from the wishes of his father. As his wordless muse she leads him to exit the front door of the house (the entrance of his subconscious) so that he can step out into the real world, where he is arrested for his murders. He raises his hands in a surrendering gesture to reality, free and happy at last. The film ends with a quote from the Psalms: "I stretch out my hands to thee: my soul thirsts for thee like a parched land . . . /Teach me the way I should go, for to thee I lift up my soul."

Critical Response

Jodorowsky characterized the film as "a sentimental picture" when it was released as a DVD version later in life (Cobb 2007, 245). This is a curious observation, which may contain a valuable insight. He may have meant that he had created a love story that was masked by the horror genre and that its essence was sentimentality. The sentimentality of a pure love story masked as a horror story allowed him to express his view of the psyche and its coming of age. The evil influence of the family can be overthrown. The film's positive resolution (victory over, or destruction of, evil) is also "sentimental" in that it tends to be truer in storytelling than in real life.

The film itself continues his established use of symbolic colors (red, white, and black), people with disabilities, sexual innuendo, and religious codes, but his incorporation of the tropes of the horror genre, plus direct references to psychotherapy, are something new. The horror genre itself is subverted by Jodorowsky who has said that he used "some echoes of horror films . . . *The Invisible Man . . . The Night of the Living Dead*," but that he overturned their generic conventions. "I am playing with horror," he stated, "and at the same time I am making anti-horror" (Jaworzyn 1990, 119). What this means is that he used the genre's traditional cloak of fear, tension, and dread to temporarily mask the inner beauty and humanity he was addressing. He was working through psychological obsession and oppression to achieve a final liberation. While Fénix is transformed, that is, freed to engage honestly with reality and his previous actions, the film itself is not really transformative for the audience because the generic conventions (haunted house, the souls of the dead rising from the grave, slasher murders, etc.) keep in place conventional norms. What distinguishes the film from the genre in general is its drawing on and illustrating the macabre (death) and lurid (blood) aspects of Mexican Catholic iconography inherited from the Spanish Catholic conquest. That Catholicism focuses on pain and suffering and heavenly intervention (miracles).

When the film had its theatrical release in 1989 and 1990 it was reviewed in the context of Jodorowsky's absence for many years. The widely syndicated American film reviewer Roger Ebert, who had viewed his earlier 1970s films as having socially redeeming values, continued defending him. Writing in 1990 when the film became available in the United States, Ebert called the film "a collision between Freud and Fellini" (Ebert 1990). "*Santa Sangre*" is a movie," Ebert writes, "in which the inner chambers of the soul are laid bare, in which desires become visible and walk into the room and challenge the yearner to possess them" (Ebert 1990). In a further review of the film in 2003, he wrote: "I believe more horror films should be made for adults, so that they are free to deal with true malevolence in the world" (Ebert 2003). What made the film an adult film rather than a teenager's distraction came in his concluding paragraph:

> The quality that Jodorowsky has above all is passionate sincerity . . . he has strong moral feelings. He has an instinctive sympathy for Fenix, who was born into a world of fanaticism and cruelty, and has tried, with the help of a deaf girl and a dwarf, to get back the soul that was warped by his father and trapped by his mother. Maybe one difference between great horror films and all the others is that the great ones do not celebrate evil, but challenge it. (Ebert 2003)

Ebert's identification of Jodorowsky as a filmmaker interested in a moral universe was not echoed by others. The reviewer for the *New York Times* did not take the film seriously, saying that it "resembles the lunatic reason[ing] of a dream," which makes it "eccentric" and it only works if the viewer is willing to play along with the idea of being inside the head of a madman's fantasy (James 1990). Jodorowsky's work usually leaves film reviewers divided between those that take his work seriously and those that either ridicule its excess or consider it unintelligible. This is not the case with academic commentary, which tends to consider his films worthy of attention.

David Church in his 2007 overview of Jodorowsky's films to that date emphasized the importance of Jodorowsky's own psychomagic theory to the film, quoting Jodorowsky himself on its meaning:

> Psycho-magic combines Jungian psychoanalysis with forms of superstition and mysticism (e.g., the Tarot) that speak to the subject's unconscious. This is based upon the belief in a "family unconscious," with past familial relationships (stretching several generations back) controlling all aspects of a person's current relationships and conceptions of the world. "If I want to understand myself," says Jodorowsky, "I have to understand my family tree, because I am permanently possessed, as in voodoo. Even when we cut ties with our family, we carry it. In our unconscious, the persons are always alive. The dead live with us. [. . .] Exploring the family tree means engaging in a fierce battle with the monster, like a nightmare." (Church 2007)

This description is a perfect fit with the character of Fénix, his origins, and his destiny. In contrast, the Peruvian academic José Carlos Cabrejo emphasizes the film's affiliation with other films in the horror genre, in particular with the slasher subgenre that developed about the same time. He says that "Alejandro Jodorowsky's entry into the chilling nooks and crannies of slasher movies is not surprising considering his proximity to the Theater of Cruelty . . . [trans]" (Cabrejo 2019, 123). He links what Jodorowsky was doing in Paris in the 1960s with this 1980s film. In a separate article focusing on slasher films, Cabrejo shows how Jodorowsky actually subverts that subgenre with Hindu and Buddhist religious thought. For example, the conclusion of the film reveals, according to Cabrejo, a Hindu state of "Maya" for Fénix in which all is revealed as illusion that has prevented the achievement of unity for the soul (Cabrejo 2019a, 171–2). That Cabrejo finds religious significance in the film outside of Mexican Catholicism indicates how Jodorowsky's imagery can be read in different ways. Church's psychomagic interpretation of the conclusion is as valid as Cabrejo's. One confirmation of this is Jodorowsky's 1990 comment that "this picture was like a subtle psychoanalysis for me. I was putting a lot of myself into it" (Jaworzyn 1990, 119). If Fénix is some version of Jodorowsky (the director does not appear in the film at all), then Fénix's transformation from a delusional character to a liberated one is an expression of the power of psychomagic as represented by

Alma, who, in turn, is a version of Jodorowsky as therapist, freeing himself from his own family bondage.

How does the film compare with his previous two auteur films? In each previous film in the trilogy, he constructed his narrative using the guise of a genre. For *El Topo*, it is the Western. For *The Holy Mountain*, it is sci-fi fantasy. For *Santa Sangre*, it is horror. Of the three films *The Holy Mountain* is closest to being a fully realized expression of his vision and sensibility as a filmmaker because the sci-fi fantasy genre allows for his religious symbolism to flourish. It is his greatest classic and his most transformative film for both actors and audience. *El Topo* is the most accessible and popular of the three because of its subversion of the Western genre and its dialogue with American culture and stereotypes. In contrast, *Santa Sangre* is the most compromised, and therefore the most conventional film of this trilogy because of its multiple writing credits and its deep engagement with the horror genre. With *Santa Sangre* Jodorowsky was able to complete a three-film cinematic statement that touched on all his spiritual and psychotherapeutic insights. After *Santa Sangre* he put his energy into writing. The writing served as the basis for his next three films, a trilogy that he made as an octogenarian.

The Birth of a Writer

After *Santa Sangre* and *The Rainbow Thief* Jodorowsky either intentionally or unintentionally turned his back on filmmaking. He became a writer of fiction and nonfiction, of poetry and plays, all the while deeply engaged in graphic novels. In the twenty years from 1990 to 2010 he produced over twenty comic book series, five novels, five books of poetry, six collections of essays, nine plays, four volumes of memoirs, plus other assorted nonfiction works on psychology, philosophy, and sociology that included major works on the Tarot plus his own psychoanalytical theories. Two of his autobiographical books became the basis for two future films that he made between 2012 and 2015. In those twenty years, he was averaging three publications per year, certainly a prodigious output. Of course, it would require a separate volume to discuss this productivity, but a general overview is both possible and necessary to contextualize these works in relation to his films.

Jodorowsky's writing has attracted scholarly attention, which offers explanations of the links between text and film. Robert Neustadt compared two of his novels, a play, and a comic book and concluded:

> Disoriented and fragmented subjects wandering in amorphous voids characterize the Jodorowskian quest for meaning. In spite of the salient differences, all four works elaborate pronouncedly circular narratives. All of these texts actualize and allegorize dramatic and spiritual quests. (Neustadt 1999, 83)

It is to be expected that an author's storytelling as expressed in one genre would also find a home in others. In particular, Jodorowsky's devotion to the Tarot and how he used it in his writing is also applicable to his films. Neustadt goes on to say: "One could read Jodorowsky's art as a re-presentation of the iconography that is represented on the [Tarot] cards. Jodorowsky's work . . . explicitly derives from, interprets and reconfigures specific tarot images" (Neustadt 1999, 122–3).

Jodorowsky's focus on the Tarot was most explicit in *The Holy Mountain* but it also found expression in the other films of the trilogy. One could say that during his absence from cinema the same preoccupations, the same enthusiasms, and the same visions found a home in other artistic forms. From the point of view of cinema, Jodorowsky's absence from the art form was a serious loss, but from the point of view of his volcanic personality and its continual eruption of ideas, metaphors, and narratives, this absence allowed him to propagate his ideas in other media. One academic rightly concluded: "His written body of work has been a diverse, abundant, and accurate reflection of his journey in search of the true self" (Martin 2009, 206). Jodorowsky made spiritual questing and self-understanding the central mode of human being. By writing, Jodorowsky linked his identity as an auteur with his identity as an author. Authorship offered him the creative control he craved and demanded. He had a special capacity to absorb ideas and practices from many sources and then transform them into something uniquely his own.

Jodorowsky's intense engagement with the human psyche was a deep well where he found endless inspiration. But he also liked the playful idea of magic tricks. He could combine the sublime and the ridiculous in equal measure. *Santa Sangre* is that kind of amalgam—a profound story told in a lowbrow genre. The image of the alchemist, who creates gold from base metal, is a fitting metaphor for a filmmaker who creates enrapturing films from the dross of ordinary human life. The building of narratives, whether in film or text, is an act that highlights the power of the interpretive moment. The philosopher Roland Barthes in his book *Camera Lucida* provided the world with the concept of a visual image's *punctum* (the part of the image that leaves a lasting impression on the viewers they are not conscious of initially). This concept is relevant to Jodorowsky's imagery because in spite of Jodorowsky's intention for a particular scene, there are always in that scene visual clues that have emerged from his subconscious and wait for our own subconscious to embrace them as meaningful. It is these "hidden" or "secret" elements that add richness and mystery to his films, allowing every viewer of an image's *punctum* to experience something different.

8

A Magical Childhood

La danza de realidad (*The Dance of Reality*, 2013)

The release of Jodorowsky's first film in twenty-three years was a minor *cause célèbre*. Film critics and journalists jumped on the event as newsworthy, resulting in an explosion of interviews, reviews, and commentaries. When *Santa Sangre* came out in 1989 the internet was still a curiosity, but when *La danza de la realidad* was released, its reception was driven by the internet universe, its social media, and digital publications. A film reviewer writing on the Roger Ebert website encapsulated the reaction when he wrote rhetorically: "Of all the possible cinematic trends of 2014, who could have possibly foreseen that the return to prominence of Alejandro Jodorowsky would be among them?" (Sobczynski 2014). Jodorowsky continued to surprise not only by releasing a new film after so many years, but also by incorporating elements of the musical genre into it, a first for him.

As word got out that Jodorowsky was back in business, the premiere of the film at Cannes on May 18, 2013, attracted more than its share of attention. *The Los Angeles Times* published an article based on an interview with Jodorowsky done via Skype. The journalist wrote:

> "The Dance of Reality" is among the most eagerly anticipated titles in this year's Director's Fortnight section at Cannes, which is also screening "Jodorowsky's Dune," a documentary by Frank Pavich about Jodorowsky's fabled, doomed attempt in the mid-1970s to turn Frank Herbert's classic science-fiction novel into a big-screen space opera. (Lim 2013)

The buzz about the return of Jodorowsky was aided by the simultaneous premiere of the documentary. Having a double-hitter that acknowledged his past work could only benefit Jodorowsky's return. Various observers and film critics were quick to link the documentary and the new feature film. When they were released in the United States the next year, the *New York Times* discussed the two in the same review:

> The Chilean-born filmmaker Alejandro Jodorowsky has recently been the subject of a revelatory documentary...—about a movie he never made... Since his heyday in the early '70s as a midnight cult-film pioneer with "El Topo" and "The Holy Mountain," Mr. Jodorowsky's semi-mythic status as a cinematic wild man outstripped his productivity as a director. So the arrival of a new feature—his first since 1990—would be grounds for excitement even if the movie in question, "The Dance of Reality," were not something very close to a masterpiece. (Scott 2014)

When the paragraph ends with the word "masterpiece," his former status as "a cinematic wild man" fades into obscurity.

The origins of *La danza de la realidad* film project are intimately linked to *Jodorowsky's Dune*. Jodorowsky was interviewed for the *New York Times* in his Paris home in March 2014 in time for the film's release in the United States in which he and others provide information on its beginning. Frank Pavich, the filmmaker of *Jodorowsky's Dune*, approached Jodorowsky in 2010 with his proposal to make a documentary about the aborted project. This led to Jodorowsky's reconnecting after many years with Michel Seydoux, the producer of the earlier project and eventually the new documentary (Benson 2014). Once the documentary was completed, Seydoux and Jodorowsky held a meeting in February 2011 in which "Jodorowsky proposed that Seydoux give him a million dollars to make his own film" (Benson 2014). Seydoux acquiesced because he felt that Jodorowsky needed "a second chance" (Benson 2014). That Jodorowsky then chose to make a film using his 2001 memoir (released in English translation in 2014) may be a reflection of his entering his eighties and coming to appreciate some kind of value in his own story. Just as Seydoux lost money on the Dune project, he also went on to lose money on this film. It cost closer to $3 million to make and it earned a modest half a million at the box office in its first year (boxofficemojo.com 2014).

In the Benson article, Jodorowsky states: "I had a son who died. That's where the fall of my ego started. That's when I had the terrible encounter with reality." Teo's drug overdose in 1995 spurred Jodorowsky's development of psychomagic therapy and he is quoted by Benson as saying to the crew: "This is not a film. This is the healing of my soul." This comment suggests that Jodorowsky saw the making of the film as a psychomagical act for himself as well as the family characters in the film. It involved his repairing the rupture with those he left behind when he went to France as a young man. He uses the film to transform his parents by giving them traits they never had, while maintaining his own posture of childhood innocence. The book lays the foundation of the film's approach. On the back cover of the English translation, Jodorowsky makes this statement:

> This book is an exercise in imaginary autography [writing about the self], although not in the sense of "fictitious," as all the characters, places and events are true, while allowing for the fact of the deep history of my life being a constant effort to expand the imagination and its limits in order to grasp its therapeutic and transformative potential.

Even this statement makes it difficult to distinguish the real from the fantastic. For example, his father's Don Quixote adventure to assassinate the reactionary ruler of Chile is an imagined projection of his father's revulsion against the ruler's ideology, which he must have expressed at home. The autobiographical book is over 400 pages long and contains photographs of himself and his family, giving it a patina of autobiographical authenticity. It contains sentences such as the following, which seem to present a genuine event (his desire for an unusual pair of shoes):

> My parents, used to having a strange child, asked me to be patient. That footwear could not be found in Topocilla's meager shoe store. [trans.] (Jodorowsky 2009, 19)

But then the story takes an apocryphal turn. Because Alejandro wanted a pair of red shoes, his mother had to obtain them from a town 100 kilometers away. He wears them to school, where he is made fun of by his fellow students, except for the teacher, who had early on claimed Alejandro had "a golden eye" because of the "oro" for gold and "ojo" for eye in his family name:

> The only one who applauded my taste was the good Mr. Toro. (Did my desire for red shoes come directly from the Tarot? In it, the Fool, the Emperor, the Hanged Man, and the Lovers all wear red shoes.) (Jodorowsky 2009, 19)

The Bull card in the Tarot references determination and constancy, so is "Mr. Toro" (Spanish for bull) a real name or just another symbolic element? The emphasis on the Tarot and his choices implies a certain destiny for himself, explaining that his unusual desire for shoes indicated that he was preordained to be ruled by, and rule, the Tarot. But, of course, we also know from his films that the color red represents lifeblood for the filmmaker. The color of the shoes could be a symbol of his anti-normative nature, but also that his choice of color is tied to his very life and its dance with reality. How much of the story is "real" and how much is a fanciful invention that simply prefigures his destiny is difficult to determine. In the film, the episode of the red shoes appears, but is totally transformed into a metaphor for life and death.

Chronologically linear narratives are usually detoured into the fabulous and the fantastic by Jodorowsky. Also, the book's genre of memoir is already suspect because that literary form itself is dependent on memory and what "revelations" the author chooses to make. While most readers of celebrity autobiography expect it to coalesce into an intelligible, recognizable persona of which they already have a public image, the author has his own goals. In all memoir writing, the real person becomes a character in a drama meant to make him or her of interest to the reader.

In his previous trilogy, he adopted *dramatis personae* that were projections of himself, in particular, as the seeker of enlightenment. In the 1960s, he was expressing a Buddhist philosophy of the self as illusionary, whose purpose was not individual identity but unity with the universal. His discovery of the importance of the Tarot, visually most evident in *The Holy Mountain* (1973), evolved into his own mastery of the practice. By the time *Santa Sangre* (1989) was released, his view of the self was leaning toward its being a distinct and identifiable entity. In the first trilogy he was happy to disguise himself in his fanciful characters, but in the second trilogy, of which this is the first film, he situated the narrative in a historically and geographically distinct self. He was no longer a metaphor but a person. This move from the universal to the specific meant that he had to apply his fabulist imagination to his own lived life. He gave that life both temporal continuity and psychological understanding according to the concepts that he had begun to espouse, promote, and practice.

Jodorowsky's presentation of himself in an unreal way transformed chronology, events, situations, and history into their opposites. He turned memoir into a three-ring circus where we witness strange and enchanting acts. Narya Schechtman, who specializes in narratives of the self, is explicit about the process that is involved in this kind of self-construction:

> We do not need to resort to a crude, literal reproduction of our physical and psychological histories, but can pick and choose the important elements, use sophisticated representational devices, and shape a story that can express what

we take to be the basic and essential information about our lives. (Schechtman 1996, 125)

Jodorowsky does just this by shaping a story about himself informed by his theatrical past and his unorthodox worldview. If his book on which the film is based begins as a work of creative nonfiction that evolves into what is currently referred to as autofiction (the narrative of the self describes real events in a nonnormative, nonlinear, and even obtuse and fantastical way), then how does he translate autofiction into a cinematic narrative? For one thing he does not replicate incidents as they are presented in the book. One example is his elevation of both his father and his mother to a state in which their fantasies, as he remembers them, are realized in a comic way. In the book (and to a certain degree in the film), his mother is presented as cold toward him, but he cast an opera singer in her role so that her lines could be sung operatically, because she may have dreamed of being one. Having her sing certainly softens her image. His father's hard-heartedness is balanced by having him attempt to achieve his desire to assassinate the dictator of Chile at the time. "My father was inhuman, I give humanity," he is quoted as telling an interviewer when the film came out. "To my mother I give dignity. Everything I gave to the characters of my genealogical tree . . . and then you have a past where all the characters are realized" (Benson 2014). By realization Jodorowsky means that he gave their dream life and their secret aspirations center stage in the film. What they dreamed of being and doing is given priority over who they were and what they did. By using this anti-historical but pro-imagination technique, he sought to redeem his parents by transforming them into their own fantasies. What is central to this act of redemption is that in looking backward into his past, he is able to create an unrealized future. Like a magician he is able to materialize for them what they could not realize for themselves. His parents are fictions in the film, not real people. As fictions they serve as exemplars of his psychomagical and metagenealogical theories. In psychomagic and psychogenealogy the patient is healed by "acting out" certain prescribed identities in order to repair the wounds left by psychological traumas, some of which are inherited from traumas experienced by previous generations, which have been left to fester in subsequent generations because they are unresolved. What happens to Jodorowsky's father as a politically motivated assassin is an example of this approach. The assassination is unrealized in the "real" way he may have intended (the dictator was never assassinated in real life). Instead, it becomes a symbolic killing of dictators in general.

The Dance of Reality is the demarcation point between Trilogy One and Trilogy Two. The latter begins with this film and is followed by *Endless Poetry* (2016) and *Psychomagic* (2019). This second trilogy focuses on the story of an individual self as opposed to a search for a universal self. Jodorowsky reversed direction in the second trilogy, from journeying forward into the future to one in which he travels backward into his own past. This new focus emerged from his writings and therapeutic practices during the twenty-three-year interregnum between Trilogy One (1968–89) and Trilogy Two (2013–19). While the first trilogy represented his individual spiritual journey through religions, philosophies, and therapies in search of enlightenment, the second trilogy represented a journey into self-understanding and personal identity.

The Autofictional Film as Visual Text

With a very modest budget Jodorowsky was working at a financial level below the average cost of each film in the first trilogy. He shot the film in Chile, the country that he had abandoned sixty years earlier and with which he had not maintained any meaningful relationship. As a result of having lived for sixty years as an expatriate, he could enter only the Chilean identity he knew during his childhood and youth.

The film begins with a sequence in which gold coins cascade downward accompanied by jazzy music reminiscent of the famous 1964 James Bond film *Goldfinger*. The reference to Midas and greed is established from the very first shot. The background color for the credits that run at the beginning of the film is red, to which is then added black and gold, as the coins fall. Red is Jodorowsky's signature color for blood and life, while he associates black with death and gold as a bridging color that belongs to both. The eighty-three-year-old Jodorowsky appears facing the camera head-on and begins a series of stern, didactic one-liners that are strung together to form a poem:

> Money is like blood,
> It gives life if it moves.
> Money is like Christ,
> It blesses you if you share it.
> Money is like Buddha,
> If you don't work,

You don't get it.
Money enlightens those that use it,
To open the flower of the world
And damns those who glorify it,
Confounding riches with the soul.

A break followed by a voice-over

There is no difference between money and conscience.
There is no difference between conscience and death.
There is no difference between death and wealth.

Jodorowsky's mantra about the right uses of money (sharing, opening up the flower of the world, that is for creativity) is contrasted with that about the wrong uses of money, primarily its accumulation for wealth and power. This dichotomy is embodied in the appearance of his father, Jaime Jodorowsky, played by Brontis Jodorowsky, who becomes the representative of the wrong usage of money, and young Alejandro, played by Jeremias Herskovits, who represents the creative usage of money. The opening scene is that of a circus, where a clown continues dropping gold coins, while an audience watches. He is clothed in black, gray, and brown and sports a white mask hiding his individual identity. A newspaper appears announcing the stock market crash of 1929, the year Alejandro was born. Blood is spattered over a headline that states 70 percent of Chileans are living in poverty. This is his time frame and mythological moment concerning money.

The next framing is space or geography, which appears in the next scene, where a long line of people, dressed in black and carrying black umbrellas sprinkled with dust, struggles down a boulder-strewn landscape devoid of any vegetation. This is the landscape of the northern Chilean desert region, where he was born. It extends from the Andes to the very shore of the Pacific Ocean. Then the film cuts to a scene with a small traveling troupe that operates the circus seen at the beginning. Into this set appears a stern Jaime dressed in a vaguely military outfit and Alejandro, who, like the boy in *Santa Sangre*, is dressed in the same cut of clothing as his father, though a brighter blue to distinguish him and perhaps suggest he is different. Alejandro sports golden locks that hang to his shoulders in an effeminate manner. Suddenly, the real Alejandro, now very much a senior, appears beside the boy and speaks for him, calling out that the family is "always outsiders, eternal outsiders." This is a reference to the family's Jewish identity as immigrants to Chile. Jodorowsky has now made two different appearances in the first few minutes of the film. The two appearances indicate to the audience that there are fundamental binary conflicts in the film (commerce vs. art, son vs. father). Likewise, the younger Alejandro's silence tells us that it is not he who is speaking but the elder Alejandro. In these introductory moments we have statements of Jodorowsky's philosophy, his early history and geography, and the ethnicity that defined him. We are also offered a succinct statement of the tense relationship between a father, who wants to make his son after himself, and a son that has a different destiny.

What follows visually confirms the conflict. Two clowns from the troupe approach Jaime and announce cheerfully that Jaime was once a member of their troupe and invite him to climb a vertical rope as he once had as a performer. A life in the circus signifies being an outsider to social norms. Jamie's former membership reinforces his state of being a stranger to mainstream Chilean society. Their asking about his store they call "The Grand Casa Ukraina" is a foreshadowing of his new occupation as a businessman, which is a step up in the world. In the circus upward mobility on the rope is simply a feat that is repeated over and over, and always includes a coming down. But in the real world upward mobility means a status of keeping people below you. Rope-climbing in a circus is a creative performance, while being a businessman involves an occupation with money, which Jodorowsky has always disdained. Jodorowsky wants his father's earlier occupation in the circus to be lauded, while his current occupation is soon to be denounced.

Jodorowsky's voice-over continues about his birthplace of Topocilla, which he terms "this lament of a town." Meanwhile, Alejandro runs home from the circus, where his buxom mother Sara, played by the Chilean opera singer Pamela Flores, sings out his name "Alejandrito" (Little Alejandro) and then adds a further identity to the boy, as her "dear father." This conflation of son and father is rejected by her son, who runs off. He has already run away from his domineering, macho father and now he is running away from his smothering, neurotic, and obsessive mother. He finds himself on the town's seashore, where he begins throwing stones into the water, something typically done by children, especially male ones. A strange character, who is a male but is denounced as an old woman by Alejandrito, demands that he stop attacking the sea, but the boy refuses. A tidal wave rises up to wash both of them away but they escape. The receding waters deposit a mass of fish on the shore, which attract a large flock of gulls. The gulls attack the boy as he stands amidst the fish, reminiscent of scenes from Alfred Hitchcock's horror thriller, *The Birds* (1963). Alejandro runs into the arms of the real Alejandro, who consoles him. This is the second time in the film that the two are entwined. Is this simply the sentimentalism of old age? Is this a sign of what he views as an innate feature of his personality—tenderness and caring? Or is it a symbol of unity between childhood and old age?

While the two actors remain silent, a voice-over by Jodorowsky asks:

"Should I suffer the anguish of the sardines or should I delight in the joy of the gulls?" This Zen koan is interrupted by a crowd of people rushing into the scene to fill their own baskets with fish. While they are harvesting the fish on the beach, the older Alejandro answers his own question by saying that life is "a web of suffering and pleasure." Meanwhile back at the Casa Ukraina, Jaime is so upset by a radio announcement by the local Chilean strongman Ibáñez that he will institute full employment that he pushes the radio into a toilet bowl and urinates on it. The urination is important because it is matched later on in the film when his wife, Sara, urinates on him in order to revive him from a death-like coma. In Jaime's case, the urination is a political act, while in Sara's case, it involves saving a human life. She succeeds, but his act of urination turns out to be only symbolic. It expresses but achieves nothing.

Alejandrito is presented in the next scene as a caring and kind soul when, by the door of the store, he scratches the back of a man who cannot do so himself since he has no hands, but his father rushes out, pushing the man away and calling him "a dirty cripple." In a total misunderstanding of Alejandrito's motivation, he accuses his son of homosexual tendencies because he touched a man's body. Sara intervenes to protect Alejandrito, claiming he is "holy." Jaime and the handless man get into a fight, calling each other names. What is ironic in this display of machismo by Jaime is the way it is framed by the shop window with its wares of women's lingerie. In his denunciation of his son he demands that Sara explain to him why she calls him both son and father. Sara sings out the story of her parents' flight from the anti-Semitism of Russia to Argentina and how her father, while lighting a lamp, fell into a barrel of water and drowned. When Alejandrito was born she considered him a reincarnation of her father because he had the same golden locks. Infuriated by this story, Jaime takes Alejandro to a barbershop to sever the connection on the maternal side and to make him masculine-looking. On the way he is confronted by a gang of amputees, their disabilities caused by mining accidents in operations owned by American corporations. They are pals of the man with whom he had just had an altercation, so Jaime struggles with them as they denounce him. He finally gets to the barbershop where two old barbers "cut off" the boy's hair, which they display as a wig that evaporates into thin air. The figures of the ancient barbers are reconstituted in the 2016 sequel to this film titled *Poesía sin fin* (*Endless Poetry*). They appear as ancient waiters, perhaps as a tribute to old age. In this way Jodorowsky makes retirees productive members of society, just as he is. They are a symbol of himself.

The "hair-cutting" scene is likewise vital to Jodorowsky's visual and symbolic lexicon. Little Alejandro undergoes an identity change from being Alejandrito, a Mama's boy, to being simply Alejandro, his father's son. Not only is his hair now short, but it is also his natural brown color rather than blond. The relationship between one's hair and one's identity are integral to Jodorowsky's conception of how the self can be transformed. It re-appears in *Endless Poetry*, when Jodorowsky appears at a crucial hair-cutting scene to complete the task the actor cannot. In this case, it is Adán Jodorowsky, playing Alejandro as a young man, cutting off the hair of his brother Brontis, who is playing the figure of Jaime, which he also played in this film. Shaving off one's hair is often associated with changed identities, for example, from being a lay person to becoming a monk.

Jaime brings the boy home, but Sara is appalled by her son's changed appearance and denounces them as murderers of her father and accuses them of making her an orphan. Of course, her conflation of son and father is tied to Jodorowsky's own theory of family trauma continuing through the generations. In this case Alejandro is cursed by his nameless grandfather's flight from anti-Semitism and then his later elemental death. Sara's continued recounting of the story is presented in a melodramatic way with appropriate operatic exaggeration. While she is singing, the story is acted out by a naked man carrying a torch. Full frontal male nudity is prominent at the start of this film. Later it is followed by full frontal female nudity.

Jaime then sets up a series of macho tests (in fact, tortures) for Alejandro to see if he is worthy of being called his son. There is a similarity to the tattooing of the eagle in *Santa Sangre*. The boy passes all three of them (tickling without laughing, being slapped and asking for more, and dental work without anesthetic). The number of tests (three) that he must endure is repeated soon afterward when the boy is taken to the seaside, where he meets a strange character named The Theosophist, who has esoteric symbols tattooed on his naked body. The role is played by Axel Jodorowsky, his second-eldest son (Brontis being the eldest and Adán the youngest).

Theosophy is a movement founded by Helena Blavatsky in the United States in the late nineteenth century. Its teachings claim that an ancient brotherhood of masters are keepers of a former wisdom that has been revealed through her and that one day it will eclipse all the religions in the world. The Theosophist tries to teach the boy how to meditate and then offers him medallions symbolizing the three religions of the Abrahamic tradition—Judaism, Christianity, and Islam. He says he should make a necklace of them to remind him that "a single god unites them." The link between the three monotheistic religions and the three tests that the boy has just endured to please his father emphasizes the importance of ternaries. The theme began as early as *Fando y Lis* when the two protagonists are guided to their death by father and mother figures. Threesomes are continued in *El Topo* and become the very foundation of symbolic meaning in *The Dance of Reality*.

In the next scene Jaime is shown caressing a nylon stocking, while mounting it on a display stand. This act arouses him, so he demands sex from his unwilling wife. Jaime is portrayed as someone more in love with the material objects in his store than his family. The father is both a materialist in the sense of someone attached to things, and a dialectic materialist, which is the ideology of the Marxist political movement to which he also belongs. He is the complete opposite of the spirituality embodied by the Theosophist to whom Alejandro is drawn. When Alejandro shows the three medallions he has been given to his father, his atheist father shouts "God does not exist" and he throws the medallions down the toilet, but the flush mechanism refuses to work. We have a replay of the impotence displayed in the scene of the radio and the urination. He demands that Alejandro choose between following him or the Theosophist. Alejandro says he will stay with his father. "What was I to do?" says Jodorowsky as he stands next to his childhood self.

The story moves over to an extensive account of Jaime's fate. First, he attends a communist cell meeting and then a meeting at the local fire hall, where he is a volunteer fireman. The group's mascot, a dog, has died and Jaime makes Alejandro the new mascot. An unhappy Alejandro resists being equated with a dog, but when Jaime gives him the red shoes from a black mannequin in the store window, Alejandro accepts the bribe. This is an imaginative take on the red shoe story in his written autobiography of the same name. The shoes only lead to tragedy because the empathetic boy gives the shoes to a shoeless shoeshine boy, who runs off, only to drown while climbing rocks in the shoes. Since red is the color of blood and life in Jodorowsky's symbolic universe, Alejandro's loss of the shoes renders him "lifeless." Jodorowsky signals this by having Alejandro prepare to throw himself off a cliff into the sea in order to die by suicide. But he is saved by the elder Jodorowsky dressed in a white suit, signifying he is his guardian angel. "You are not alone," Jodorowsky tells the boy, "you are with me." He concludes that we are only memories and that memories are only dreams. By "playing" himself in the film, the auteur is able to conflate reality with fantasy. It is really him, but it is a fictional him. If he interacted with his young self he did so only in his dreams or fantasies. By equating memories with dreams the deep separation between reality and fantasy, the conscious and the subconscious, is papered over. This act is the very essence of Jodorowsky's fabulism.

After he ends up showing fear during a parade honoring the late fire chief, Alejandro is deposed as a mascot. Jaime realizes he is not accepted as a legitimate firefighter because he is Jewish. Not being able to sustain the fantasy or illusion of fitting in, his world begins falling apart. He tries to compensate by bringing water to people dying of the plague, where he gets infected and is about to die until Sara in a moment of operatic prayer asks God to save him. She squats over her husband, urinates on his chest, and magically revives him. Her urination is a form of baptismal transformation, which makes Jaime a new person. He asks for forgiveness for his lack of faith and heads off to assassinate Ibáñez. The idea of urination as a form of healing water is associated with shamanistic practice. Likewise, Jaime is now "acting out" his assassination fantasies, which gives him a new purpose in life. Of course, all this has been dreamt up by Jodorowsky and has no basis in fact.

What follows is a series of tragi-comic attempts by Jaime to achieve his goal, all of which fail. Jodorowsky is using the classic figure of the delusional Don Quixote as his model. He has said that he wanted to use the film to redeem his father from his materialism and his stern machismo, but he does so in an ambiguous way. Turning him from a socialist realist character to a comic one is a form of redemption in Jodorowsky's world. Even so, he becomes sympathetic in the film only as a character when he turns into a penitent.

Meanwhile back at the Casa Sara proceeds to engage in a strange game with little Alejandro. She covers his naked body in black shoe polish, so he is in blackface (similar in appearance to the mannequin with the red shoes). Then she undresses and herself naked asks him to play hide and seek with her. The scene is a bit startling and Oedipal in tone. However, the older Alejandro (Jodorowsky) interrupts the scene with his appearance. While Alejandrito and Sara prance about, both totally blackened, he announces: "My mother dissolved into darkness and I never again was afraid of the night." The dance, in this case, is a dance in which he is freed from his mother since she became invisible. Since each of the characters started out white and then became dark (the round of night and day), their imitation of this cycle becomes a form of shamanistic healing.

The nudity in this scene is repeated in the next series of scenes when Alejandro is beaten up for being Jewish, comes home, and has his mother exorcise his identity in order to make him invisible, that is, undistinguished in the world and so unseen. He doesn't believe she can do this, but he is convinced when she enters the sailor's bar (where he was beaten up) completely naked and none of the denizens notice her. The extent of male and female nudity in the film is striking compared to his earlier films, where it tended to be momentary. The extended time frame exhibiting nudity in the film is a reflection of both the relaxed standards for cinema in the twenty-first century, and his own approach to the importance of nudity as an acknowledgment of our humanity. What is impressive is how both Pamela Flores, who plays Sara, and Brontis Jodorowsky, who plays Jaime and is tortured naked, are able to convey normality in their nude scenes. Equally impressive, and outside Hollywood standards, is a boy like Jeremias Herskovits having to act with a nude adult, Pamela Flores. Jodorowsky must have been very convincing and effective in having all three adapt to performative nudity as a natural condition.

Continuing her powerful magic Sara sends a message on a string of white balloons to Jaime that his family wants him back. The image is repeated in the next film as well. The message awakens Jaime, who is living in a shanty town, his hands clawed and paralyzed. His hair is long and scraggy and he looks pathetic, and yet the message causes him to embark on a penitential journey of return. He is now the prodigal father. Along the way he is attacked and ridiculed and even tortured after fighting off a parade of Nazis. He is inspired to be fearless by an old chairmaker named José, modeled after St. Joseph, who rehabilitates him and brings him back to normal life. The old man dies in a Pentecostal church where he has delivered the chairs that both he and Jaime have built.

When the prodigal father returns home, Sara tells him that he has modeled himself on tyrants like Stalin. He apologizes and when she hands him a gun he shoots portrait photos of Stalin, Ibáñez, and himself. When the images burn up, the Jodorowsky family of three re-appears as a unified whole, looking triumphant. Sara has applied the principle of psychomagic to cure her husband by having him kill idolatrous images rather than human beings. By doing so he becomes a new man. The family stands together on the stern of a purple-painted boat sailing from shore. It is piloted by someone in a black-and-white skeletal costume. The final scene in the film has Jodorowsky appearing next to

Mr. Death (the skeletal figure) and sliding behind him as his voice-over intones a poem about leaving the past and the painful burden of life, with only the wind remaining. As the voice-over presents this elegy, first we see black-and-white cutouts of the characters in the film watching the boat recede and then we see the boat itself disappear into white mist. The storied journey of life ends in the mists of time and the oblivion of death.

The scene is a repetition of Jaime's first leaving to assassinate the dictator when he takes a boat (the boat metaphor is a classic image of Odysseus's journey), but while Jaime's journey began and ended in tragi-comedy, this journey is plaintive, the voice-over reminding the audience that this is Jodorowsky's life as viewed from old age and the coming of death. The film began with a poem and ends with a poem.

Academic Commentary

The idea of Jodorowsky's first trilogy expressing his "charismatic authority" and his desire to produce "spiritual transformation" is less relevant in this later trilogy (Guida 2015, 550). A film about his past does not require charismatic authority. It does depict spiritual transformation but as a distant event, not as a desire for immediate implementation. Instead, the concept of magical transformation is more appropriate for the second trilogy. Magical transformation occurs when the filmmaker stages scenes that transform the character or the situation magically, that is, with full-blown fantasy. In *The Dance of Reality* childhood is presented in a dream-like state. Children spend much of their time in imaginary worlds commonly termed "play" and that is what Jodorowsky does. He plays *within* reality but he does so in an elevated sphere.

His earlier films were resplendent with religious symbolism and an adult consciousness searching for enlightenment. This is difficult to impose on a childhood narrative, but one way in which it can be transposed is through the concept of prophecy. Naomi Lindstrom has used the film *El Topo* plus *La Folle du Sacré-Coeur*, one of his graphic novels, as examples of the prophetic and apocalyptic nature of his work (Lindstrom 2013, 127–30). In *The Dance of Reality* Jodorowsky gives his father a fiery apocalypse, when the false political gods of politics are wiped out in an outburst of biblical violence. He also prefigures his father's future redemption from materialism, when he references Jaime's earlier self as a carnie. The past is connected to the future. The prophetic is expressed by his own appearance as an old man next to his young self, showing that he will live to a ripe old age with wisdom and poetry. Of course, the prophetic is easy to attain when you already know what the future holds, having lived it.

According to one view the film's main formal element is a series of "meta-performances" in which the protagonist is self-referential, especially in episodes that deal with his Jewish identity (Blanc-Hoang 2019). Jaime Jodorowsky, the father, tries to assimilate into Chilean society, but is always outed for being Jewish. It happens when he becomes a volunteer firefighter and also when he is a member of the Communist party. Little Alejandro also faces anti-Semitism, a theme omitted from the earlier trilogy. The tension in the film rests with the struggle between the family's visibility and invisibility around being Jewish. When his mother, Sara, takes little Alejandro to a bar, undresses, and nobody notices her, she believes she has proven how she can make her Jewishness invisible, that is, by showing that her body is no different from any other female body. But what is the most "meta" of the film is Jodorowsky's appearance in the film as he is—an old man, especially when he engages with his childhood self and offers solace and approval for little Alejandro's supposed misdemeanors.

Since he deals with his Jewish identity in this film, one ought to ask why he was circumspect about it in his earlier films. Perhaps his adult quest for universality in the human condition and his inclusion of a variety of religious traditions was a reflection of the state of his consciousness when he lived in Europe and Mexico. He saw himself as a universal entity that rejected assimilation into any society and he espoused a way to human equality that included all ethnic identities and all religious traditions. But that universal self-image could well have been a reaction to his experience of anti-Semitism in Chile in his childhood and youth. Only late in life did autobiographical reflections bring him back to the specificity of his upbringing and history in Chile

Jodorowsky's immigrant family experiences growing up in a hostile Chilean society ground his narrative in a sociocultural reality, while also allowing him to invent scenes and personalities that highlight this environment and its impact on him. One scholar of his family history novel *Donde mejor canta un pájaro* (1992/2001 2nd ed.) (*Where the Bird Sings Best* 2015 English trans) states:

> Jodorowsky also pushes his conception of memory to the limit . . . because it tests . . . rationality and order. Even though Jodorowsky narrates the life of his ancestors strictly following the order given by the family trees . . . the reader can hardly retain every link in the narrative chain and is carried away by the wonder

of stories whose perfect harmony dissolves into total anarchy. (Massman 2005, 136, translated from Spanish)

This observation is also applicable to *The Dance of Reality* in its cinematic form. For Jodorowsky memory is more an emotional state than a factual one. While grounded in historical events and family happenings, memory is a reflection of a present state of mind that reconstructs the past with contemporary elements.

The Peruvian academic José Carlos Cabrejo claims that temporality is a key feature of the film. He considers this film, more than any of his previous ones, to be "a fusion of the future, the past and the future" (Cabrejo 2019, 140). This emphasis on fusing elongated time spans so that there is little distinction between the three tenses fits with Jodorowsky's concept and use of memory. By fusing the tenses together he is able to express predestination. Cabrejo references Jodorowsky's book *Metagenealogía* (*Metagenealogy*) (Spanish edition 2011), which is subtitled in the Spanish edition as "The Family Tree as Art, Therapy and the Search for One's Essential Self" (trans.) and in the 2014 English edition as "Self-discovery Through Psychomagic and the Family Tree" in which Jodorowsky says that metagenealogy will free us from time consciousness (Cabrejo 2019, 140).

The film's treatment of time and childhood is turned into a living, ongoing present, so that Alejandro Junior and Alejandro Senior, when they appear in a scene together, are presented as sharing the same spirit and the same consciousness. Alejandro Senior may be the aging oak tree, but Alejandro Junior is an acorn with a certain destiny. These moments are highlighted in the film by a certain posing or static posturing of the two figures as if they were a tableau. This form of presentation takes them out of the historic flow of the film and puts them in a space in which time is irrelevant. In these static moments, Jodorowsky offers a magical healing of the past. Suffering, indignities, pain, and anguish are overcome. In other words, one's future self heals old scars. Jodorowsky's personal appearance in the film as an octogenarian is a fundamental statement of the unity of the self from early childhood to old age.

Understanding Jodorowsky's triangle of father, mother, and child as the basic geometry of human existence and consciousness is the first step in freeing oneself from that triangle. The process of developing a genuine selfhood beyond the inherited and imposed neuroses of the father and the mother comes from living a self-determining life. The family structure seeks to block genuineness and to channel identity by trying to make the child conform to parental wishes and aspirations. One has to wonder how Brontis Jodorowsky, who plays the disciplinarian and anti-cultural father figure, felt about acting out his own grandfather as conceived by his father? It must have rattled some chains in his psyche. Did he ever meet his grandfather? If not, what was it like to see or understand him only as a fantastic character in a film? Likewise, Adán Jodorowsky, who in the sequel plays his own father Alejandro as a young man, must also have had to deal with the implications of being both father and son. Acting in a role may not be of consequence for most actors, but when Jodorowsky makes family members act as other family members, he is definitely trying something personally challenging. Jodorowsky plays himself only as an old man. He stands above this psychological fray and leaves the heavy psychological lifting to his sons.

A major distinction between this film and his earlier ones is its highlighting the mutual love between child and parent. Academic commentary has omitted this subject, but it is important to the film and something new in his work. For example, in *El Topo*, the father–son relationship is didactic, strained, and eventually antagonistic, but in *The Dance of Reality* the mother–son relationship expresses a misguided nurturing in contrast to the father–son relationship, which is demanding and repressive. While *Fando y Lis* deals with the theme of love, the love it presents is lustful, sexual, and often lacking in tenderness. For Jodorowsky, to seek or create love in his own history is a departure, and a welcome one, from his earlier films. The apex of that love is his own tenderness toward his childhood self as if he was creating a spiritual self-parenting that he never had in real life. In this film he is a godfather to himself.

Journalistic Commentary

While academic commentary finds important references to certain themes in the film, journalistic commentary focuses on the excitement over the director's return and the narrative of a watchable and entertaining film. The audience for film reviewers and media journalists is a public interested in whether it was worth spending money on seeing the film, plus bits of gossip and production trivia. The *New York Times* review of 2014 speaks well of the film as something beautiful and coherent (Scott 2014). What is pleasing about the review is its description of Jodorowsky's appearance "as the protector of his younger self and as a kind of tutelary deity, infusing the story of his own life with a potent and implicitly political lesson" (Scott 2014). When the film was released in the United Kingdom, *The Guardian* reviewer wrote: "*The Dance of Reality* has more of a literary reflex than Jodorowsky's other films, a magic realist re-imagining . . . a touching and revealing testament" (Bradshaw 2015). The term "testament" fits with the previous reviewer's use of the term "deity." What Bradshaw may be alluding to in his review when he talks about Jodorowsky's "regret and sadness about his father" is that this film is actually an apologia for a broken relationship (Bradshaw 2015). There is a short distance between a cinematic prodigal father seeking forgiveness and Jodorowsky as a prodigal son seeking something similar through making the film.

The reviewer for Rogerebert.com noted how this film differed from his previous films: "[F]or arguably the first time in his career, Jodorowsky has found the confidence to communicate his ideas to audiences in a direct and unapologetically emotional manner" (Sobczynski 2014). The change in tonalities can be viewed as Jodorowsky's reaching a new level of maturity as a filmmaker in which the radicalism of his earlier auteur films is channeled into a more linear and accessible narrative. "Every one of my pictures is different—I die and I'm reborn with each one" is Jodorowsky's response (Lim 2013). That may be so, but *The Dance of Reality*, as the reviewers have remarked, marks a break with the first trilogy. It heralded a new phase in his life and his creativity as a filmmaker. He now seemed to want the film to be accessible and understood.

The film's novelty comes from several aspects that did not exist previously. This is the first time that he made a film embodied in his family's own history. Taking the family as a subject and then transforming its three main figures into personae in a mythological and allegorical story of redemption allows him to take audiences to "a higher realm" than simply the autobiographical (Melnyk 2017, 56). Facticity is subordinated to mythology. For example, there is in the film no mention of his real-life sister from whom he was estranged. In his universe of father-mother-child, siblings are irrelevant to the trauma that relationship imposes on each child. His family is situated historically and geographically in the film, but that outline is a palimpsest overwritten by the archetypal family.

Equally new is the emphasis on anti-Semitism as a scourge, which he and his family had to endure. It is a subject matter that did not come up in the earlier films. A third novel feature of this film is its downplaying of esoteric symbolism, which was so prominent in his earlier phase. This does not mean that the film is lacking in symbolic value, but only that its symbolism is not overpowering.

Finally, this is his first film in which the practice of psychomagic is so clearly presented through the figure of his mother, Sara. When she sings, she heals. Psychomagic is the ultimate healing power, while historical truth is nothing but a grotesque chimera.

Jodorowsky's approach to truth and individual psyche is captured in the way he attacks "chronology . . . with metaphors emanating from the collective subconscious" (Melnyk 2016, 65). Jodorowsky's visually hyperbolic universe found a new home in the biographic, where it proceeded to transform reality into archetypal myth. While retaining his usual trademarks (the disabled, mystical and mysterious characters, Tarot symbols) he moves from the stance of the earlier trilogy, where he seemed to be focused on changing human consciousness. Here he wants to show how the brutal underbelly of human existence could be healed for those who know how to free themselves from family oppression. In his next film he shows himself doing just that.

9

An Absurd Youth

Poesía sin fin (*Endless Poetry*, 2016)

Sequels rarely surpass, or even equal, the original. *Poesía sin fin* holds its own at a level at least equal to its predecessor. While the film has the same core characters (father, mother, and son) and some of the same performers, including Alejandro Jodorowsky himself, it moves the biographical story along from a time of childhood restriction to a time of youthful flowering. Small town life on the coast of Chile for a browbeaten young boy under the tutelage of a strict father is vastly different from life in the capital, Santiago, where the boy has turned into a young man full of energy, opinion, and talent.

The desire to make a sequel had several sources. It had its origins in Jodorowsky's intention, reported in various media, to make a quintet of films about his life. It was also a response to the flood of positive reviews and extensive media attention garnered by *The Dance of Reality*. The critics liked what he was doing. The times were now different and film production had new avenues of presentation, commentary, and funding. Both his autobiographical films came about at a time of internet dominance and the power of social media, but that hegemony had increased dramatically in the years between the first film in 2013 and the second in 2016. Now there were as many reviews and commentaries on popular websites as there were in traditional print media. The importance of the internet to his comeback is evident in the fact that Jodorowsky was able to establish his own film company to make *Endless Poetry* through the new social media mechanism of crowdfunding.

The idea had been proposed by one of his sons. On the crowdfunding website Kickstarter, he proclaimed that "all money should be transformed into poetry" (Kickstarter 2015). In exchange for the public's funds, he issued "Dinero Poético" (Poetic Money) with a goal of raising $350,000 (see http://ninipeony.com/portfolio/dinero-poetico/). On June 27, 2016, he tweeted, "Endless thanks for helping us make our film. May this Poetic money multiply in your life" (Jodorowsky 2016 Twitter). By June 14, 2016, he had raised $442,313 from 3,518 backers (Kickstarter 2016), which averaged about $125 per person. Of course, by then the film had been completed because it had already premiered at Cannes the previous month. There is poetic irony in this anti-money man creating his own currency. He also got money from the Chilean co-producer, Le Soleil Films, plus new money from Uplink Co. (Unijapan Bunkachocho), a Japanese film producer. The crowdfunding income went to Satori Films, Jodorowsky's own French company. This made the film a three-country and three-continent co-production. Jodorowsky was so pleased with the Kickstarter campaign that he started another crowdfunding campaign on another site, Indiegogo, to raise $150,000 for postproduction (Samuel 2015). Jodorowsky claimed that the budget for the film was $3 million (Bruder 2017). If that is really the case then the majority of the funds came from traditional sources, but what was exciting for him was that he had a following among "young people" whom he associated with social media. In a film website interview he said:

> Young people are not idiots. They need fun; they need the industrial movies because they're a lot of fun, but they also need art to give them some new way of living, to show to them life is not ugly. They want other things than drama and war in movies. They want a real spiritual search. [There] are a lot of young people who want that today. Thousands of them gave me money. Like me, they lost money for the pleasure of creating. (Bruder 2017)

In Jodorowsky's mind he was being resurrected as a filmmaker because, while he was now eighty-seven, his enthusiastic young followers gave him a sense of having conquered time and even aging. In the end the film's theatrical release earned half a million globally, so it was another money-loser for Jodorowsky, though there was DVD and streaming income later (boxofficemojo.com. 2017). In the United States its maximum release was a mere eighteen theaters (boxofficemojo.com 2017). He had been preaching from the start that he used money to create art, not to make more money. In the end, Satori Films (94 percent owned by Jodorowsky himself) declared bankruptcy after it was sued by one investor for the repayment of a $200,000 loan and his Chilean co-producer, Xavier Guerrero Yamamoto of Le Soleil Films, was also demanding over $800,000 from Satori (Ramanchandran 2020). In the end the only thing left was the poetry of his film.

The film is a worthy addition to Jodorowsky's body of work and received excellent reviews, which will be discussed in detail later. Jodorowsky gave an important interview about the film in the publicity handout for the film at the Cannes Directors' Fortnight, where it premiered on 14 May. In terms of raising money for the film, he recounted how he had saved a million dollars in the twenty-two years between 1990 and 2012 so that he could make two films. He said he would use half of that amount for the first film (*The Dance of Reality*) and the other half for the second film (Jodorowsky 2016a). For *Endless Poetry* the Mexican Moisés Cosío matched Jodorowsky's own half-million and that got the project moving, along with investments by the Chilean Xavier Guerrero Yamamoto. Michel Seydoux from his Dune days in the 1970s, who had funded *The Dance of Reality*, stayed away. However, Jodorowsky dedicated this new film to him in recognition of his support for the first film. One might consider the two films more like twins rather than as an original and a sequel because they use a number of the same main actors in both, their characters overlap, and Jodorowsky's personal presence is similar in both films.

In the publicity material for Cannes, Jodorowsky explains that both his autobiographical films are "a healing process" for himself (Jodorowsky 2016a). Since the two films are about himself, he went back to the places of his upbringing. By using the real locales in the films he believes that the films uplift those locales from the wretchedness that he assigns them in his memory. He terms it "a big cleanup" (Jodorowsky 2016a). By transforming his humble origins into places of significance he used cinema to heal/rehabilitate his family, including present members like his sons plus past members like his mother and father. He says:

> Then comes the healing of my family. I am in the film myself, at my present age, an old man, telling my story. I see myself telling it. The pivotal character of my father Jaime is played by my son Brontis. My son Adán plays me as a young man. Brontis plays his grandfather, a man he only knows through me and my trauma. Adán plays his own father. When Alejandro fights with Jaime, it's not only me fighting with my father, it's also Adán fighting with his big brother Brontis. (Jodorowsky 2016a)

Navigating these multiple identities turns the film into an exercise in psychodrama for its participants. That he was able to convince both Adán and Brontis, plus Pamela Flores, who plays his mother in the first film and his muse in the second film, to continue to recreate his life means they were willing to participate in whatever healing the film may have offered them.

Jodorowsky also maintains his determination to implicate the audience. "I want to make films that trigger a positive crisis within yourself," he says, "films able to make you face your essential self. Not your ego, not the personality created by your family, society, or culture. No, I want to reveal your sublime aspect" (Jodorowsky 2016a). So what possible crisis could a film like *Endless Poetry* precipitate in the audience? Jodorowsky creates surreal scenarios, outrageous situations, and unusual characters, and so the audience is pushed into strange and provocative territory. Jodorowsky is saying that the properties of cinema as a narrative device can be harnessed for therapeutic purposes if you make transformative cinema. Filmmaking allows him to confront his own demons and also allows him to hope that he is confronting those of his audience. After all, the family theme is relevant to everyone.

Jodorowsky is lucid about the way the film is to work as an act of poetry. By poetry he means "a way" of living and of "loving life" (Jodorowsky 2016a). Any creative act is poetic in his view, including the making of films. The Alejandro character is drawn to poetry in the film, not as an artistic endeavor to be put down on paper, but as a form of self-realization. In the film any poetry that comes from Alejandro is oral. It is always a performance. Jodorowsky says he appears in the film (and the previous one) not because he is a narcissist, but as someone who wants to talk "about oneself as profoundly as possible. That's what all poets do" (Jodorowsky 2016a). Talking, doing, performing is a theatrical interpretation of poetic being. For the audience to take the film as "a poem," one has to take into account certain attributes of poetry, including its tendency to speak metaphorically and to compress narrative to evoke the uncanny. An example would be Jodorowsky's portrayal of his father in the first autobiographical film in which he creates a personality and a chain of melodramatic events that have no basis in reality. Having a fantasy father was therapeutic for Jodorowsky and also poetic because it lifted the character from his mundane commercialism and political obsessions to a mythic presence. Likewise, the ending of *The Dance of Reality*, which has a strong family facing the future together as it heads off into the mists of time, is equally fanciful and therefore poetic. The title of the film, *Endless Poetry*, is his way of linking poetry and film in a creative whole.

The poetic quality of the film was not recognized immediately by reviewers and critics. The term never appears in the English-language reviews from Cannes (*Variety* and *Hollywood Reporter*). However, the more sophisticated mainstream American print media did play with the concept when the film was released in the United States in 2017. The *New York Times* recognized what Jodorowsky was trying to achieve when it wrote:

> For all of these characters, poetry is fundamentally a sensual undertaking, and Mr. Jodorowsky is a voracious poet of the flesh . . . Mr. Jodorowsky is a poet in the broadest sense, a restless artist whose temperament isn't wedded to any particular form. He seems to embrace cinema out of convenience. He can't beam his visions directly into your brain, or tattoo his words on your body, but this is the next best thing. (Scott 2017)

Likewise, the cerebral British print media used the term "poetry." Peter Bradshaw reviewing the film in *The Guardian* acknowledges that the writing of poetry or any kind of writing "is more or less absent from the film; Alejandro improvises lines of poetry on the spot, in conversation"(Bradshaw 2017). He finds the dialogue written by Jodorowsky to have a poetic quality. Considering the extensive poetic monologues in Jodorowsky's voice-over in *The Dance of Reality*, the poetic element in this new script is consistent with the first film.

E-zines, blogs, and websites do not carry the same cachet as these venerable newspapers, but they also are not afraid of the term "poetry." One example is the American music blog Glidemagazine.com whose reviewer wrote perceptively:

> His mission in life—in poetry—has been to crash the veil between our senses and the world, and between our *selves* and our senses, to achieve some kind of purity of absolute existence. Knowing this is the first step in experiencing any of Jodorowsky's works, be they written or seen. Trust nothing, least of all your brain, with its insistence on questioning meaning, and submit yourself fully to the sublimation of surreality. (Roberts 2017)

Another insightful example from the internet universe is provided by Slantmagazine.com. The highly regarded and widely read online magazine is based in New York. Its reviewer pointed out how a certain scene in the film, when Alejandro confronts a fascist parade, much as his father had in *The Dance of Reality*, he is tying his poetic walk in a straight line through the city of Santiago (a Dadaist poetic protest against social reality) with a reference to a military group nicknamed "La Linea Recta" (The Straight Line) that opposed the dictatorial desires of Ibáñez, the Chilean ruler in the 1930s and 1940s. He terms it "a visualization of the philosophy that would direct Jodorowsky's life from that point forward." (Smith 2017). The confrontation between poetic and political protest in his films results in a poetic rather than political triumph. Art may not be able to defeat politics every time, but it remains superior.

That Jodorowsky was able to include this bit of visual subtlety is an indication of the appeal of metaphor in his films. The film itself is resplendent with visual richness and color, the usual assortment of bizarre characters that he has dressed symbolically, and situations staged as dreamy nightmares. The continuation of his own story begins where the last film left off, when, as a ten-year old, he is living in Topocilla. In the previous film he established a basic paradigm for his film—the house/home/store interior as a place of neuroses, repression of the self, claustrophobia, and parental obsessiveness versus the external freedom of the street, its denizens, and nature (the waterfront). He rejects the ideology that glorifies the family and the home as a space of love, nurturing, and safety. He maintains the same binary paradigm in *Endless Poetry*, while adding the repressiveness of institutional life (the university) to interiority. He embraces the venerable metaphor of the sea, representing freedom and journeyed discovery in the first film, and he uses it again in this film.

The first scene in *Endless Poetry* shows the family from the first film saying goodbye to Topocilla. Again we have Jodorowsky's voice-over explaining in poetic language how he left his childhood home and landed on Matucana Street in Santiago. He stands on the empty street, its shuttered storefronts covered in graffiti. He is dressed in a black suit and he tells the audience the street is "now in decline," but when he was living there in the 1940s it was a vibrant working-class neighborhood. Suddenly the street is magically transformed with the unfurling of black-and-white representations of its 1940s streetscape to cover the current facades. Two black-clad figures, like stagehands, are the agents of the transformation as if they were changing sets. Their black clothing reflects Jodorowsky's, telling us that what we are about to see is theatrical. His presence during the changeover shows that he is in charge of his memories and that the link between the present and the past is embodied in him. It could also be that the run-down appearance of the street can be read as a metaphor for aging and physical decline.

Again he uses the motif of anonymous masked faces that he used in *The Dance of Reality* for the spectators watching a mugging and murder on the street. Young Alejandro, again played by Jeremias Herskovits, walks to his father's new store where a small person dressed like Hitler barks that the store makes war on high prices. Santiago is Topocilla all over again and Alejandro looks despondent. Sure enough, his father claims to discover two poor people stealing his wares, assaults the man and takes his wife out on the street, where he rips off her dress and humiliates her before the crowd. Sara, Alejandro's mother, played once more by Pamela Flores, sings operatically that Jaime (Brontis Jodorowsky) hasn't changed. He is still a bully. By using the same actors, dressed as the characters in the previous film, Jodorowsky provides narrative continuity to his story and affirms that their psychology supersedes physical or geographic change. Of course, since the redemption of his father in the previous film was pure fantasy, Jodorowsky had to revert to reality in order to call forth a new transformation. When Alejandro's maternal grandmother visits, she confirms the boy's negative judgment of the situation by saying the place stinks of "soot and excrement." Grandma appears as a patrician woman from the bourgeoisie, but that identity is undermined by her cradling a small black case shaped like a coffin, a memento of her late son, who died after choking on strawberry cake. In commemoration Sara presents her mother with a similar cake. Since Sara lamented her father's untimely death in the first film and her mother laments her son's untimely death, Jodorowsky has the pleasure of presenting us with the continuity of family neuroses that flow from generation to generation. The stage is now set for the great breakthrough by the young Alejandro.

It begins innocently enough when he is caught reading a love poem by García Lorca, the great Spanish poet who was killed by the fascist side in the Spanish Civil War in 1936. His father discovers this, denouncing Lorca as a homosexual because he was in the arts. He demands that Alejandro study to be a doctor. Then his mother takes the little coffin case from her mother and gives it to Alejandrito, revealing it to be her late brother's violin case and demanding that he study music in imitation of her brother. But Alejandrito burns it in the street, where a drunk prophesizes that "a naked virgin will illuminate your path." Again life outside the home/store is where freedom exists. The rebellion begins when Alejandro uncovers a typewriter and begins to write poetry.

The drunk's prophecy becomes the guiding light of the film, though in Jodorowsky's hands it takes a peculiar turn. One of the more delightful Jodorowskian exposés in the film is the next scene in which Jaime sits at a bare table with his pistol next to him, while he empties a paper bag full of cash, which he finds unpleasantly aromatic, so he disinfects it. The Freudian idea that excrement and money combine in the concept of "filthy lucre" is a regular theme for Jodorowsky, who shatters the scene with an earthquake that scatters the bills.

Writing poetry in secret is the start of his rebellion, which quickly turns violent when the family goes to visit relatives and Alejandro finds himself in the garden, where he chops down the "family tree." The act is meant to break the chain of family madness. But just before he does this, Jodorowsky exposes the corruption of the family, when one of the male relatives (dressed as a Hasid) at the poker table brings out a book labeled "The Torah" and puts it on the table.

It is filled with cigars. This bit of sacrilege condemns not only the family but also religion in general. Taking an axe and yelling "Fucking family," Alejandro begins the job of cutting off himself from this diseased entity. Confronted by the outraged family, he runs off into the street followed by his cousin, who praises him and takes him to a magical garden, where two sisters live—one a sculptor and the other a ballerina. The space is a dramatic contrast to the mercantile world of his father. He has entered the realm of art, where he is introduced as a poet and a great future artist. The ballerina is a stock Jodorowsky figure harking back to the tightrope walker in *Santa Sangre*. She is the initial figure of the bewitching muse, but she is not the last. She dances into view as a light and airy creature, ethereal in her footsteps. Her light being and her colorful costume are in stark contrast to the dark and dingy store his father runs. Jodorowsky insists that art is beautiful, while commerce is ugly. But there is an issue with the ballerina. She represents Alejandro's youthful, idealized, and erroneous fantasy of what a muse is. Once he actually embarks on a career in art he will find out that his muse is a tough taskmaster.

His gay cousin, who has led him to this enchanted place, tells young Alejandro that he loves him, but Alejandro gently lets him down. When the sculptor knocks on his door, the young Alejandro is gone. In his place is an older Alejandro, played by Adán Jodorowsky. We have jumped about a decade in his life. The adult Alejandro is invited to meet his brothers in art, who include an opera singer on a swing, a pianist who smashes a piano, and an artist who splatters paint on walls and on himself (the last two are both echoes of events in *Fando y Lis*). The landscape of his adolescent fantasies of art are now replaced by much more graphic and problematic characters. On being welcomed by this motley crew, he recites a lyric poem and proclaims, "I have sold my devil to the soul." This reversal of the saying signals that he has now reversed his life. From now on he is under the spell of the arts. Alejandro begins, as Jodorowsky himself did, with puppeteering, an art that holds a great deal of significance for him in his later role as a theater director and eventually a filmmaker. He also lived and worked as a young man in a theater troupe, ergo the artist's commune that is referenced here.

To display his artfulness Jodorowsky puts on a Punch and Judy-style puppet show with lines from a poem by his literary idol the Chilean Nicanor Parra, titled *The Viper*, which recounts the poet's struggle with his poetic muse. The Punch puppet is Parra, while the Judy puppet is a naked buxom creation who prefigures the muse he is about to meet at the Café Iris, a mysterious place where strange events happen after midnight. When he gets there at the bewitching hour, the café is filled with sleepy denizens and ancient waiters moving in slow motion. He is in a dream. Enter a large, loutish, foul-mouthed, angry female with long red hair, who stomps about in her boots yelling at the occupants before sitting down to smoke a cigar and guzzle beer. Unbeknownst to the innocent Alejandro, she is to be his poetic muse (played by Pamela Flores) and the opposite of his fantasy of a muse, the ballerina. She is identified as the poet, Stella Diaz, and the innocent Alejandro falls for her, believing she will lead him to poetic ecstasy. They leave together. On the street they pass a mime theater called "Les Enfants du Paradis" (Children of Paradise), where he performs a mime, one of his later arts, and professes his love for her. She scorns him, states that he is a virgin, and then sends him away to meet her the next night back at the Café Iris.

When he shows up at midnight she is not there. As he waits for her to appear, he gets progressively more and more drunk until she comes in on the arm of Nicanor Parra, his idol. In a drunken stupor he comes over to their table, denounces Parra as a nobody, and identifies Stella with the poem *The Viper*. A muse is not an angel, Jodorowsky is saying, but, rather, a brutal, demanding, loutish creature without manners or refinement. He is associating his poetry with the underbelly of life, its violence, pain, and ugliness. After Parra throws Alejandro into her arms, Stella carves his initial "A" into her left hand and he tastes her blood, thereby binding them together forever. She takes him to her place, where she blindfolds him. Blindfolded, he shows his poetic power by naming the garments she is removing even though he cannot see. When she lies naked on the bed sideways, she reveals a series of skulls tattooed up her spine. In this way Eros (love) and Thanatos (death) are united as he consummates their relationship.

Using a sudden jump to Pamela Flores, now as his mother Sara back at home, Jodorowsky creates an Oedipal symbol of mother and lover, which he himself acknowledged in the media material for the premiere of the film at Cannes. When he is asked about the same actress playing both mother and muse, he responds:

> Yes, that's important. Psychoanalytically, Alejandro elides his mother into his mistress. It's an Oedipal shift. He's fascinated because he sees his mother as he's never seen her before. (Sartori Films 2016)

Since his mother is the artistic one (an opera singer in both films), he now can see her and, therefore, art in a sexual way. He steals some money from his father's stash of cash to give Stella. Together they head back to the Café Iris. On the way she asks him how he would define poetry and he responds: "It's the luminous excrement of a toad that's swallowed a firefly." This definition of the poet's relationship to his poetic muse or inspiration amuses her. The definition represents his view that art involves both light and darkness, beauty and ugliness, the enlightened and the befouled. But the Café Iris is closed for a funeral, so they go to a dive inhabited by a rough bunch of cutthroats, who want to sodomize him. Stella saves him by fighting them off, but as they flee he suddenly begins to reject her. Upon finding his cousin Ricardo hanging from a tree, a death by suicide that Alejandro explains was caused by his being forced into becoming an architect, which he did not want, the two split up. Alejandro needs a reprieve from Stella so that he can find himself.

For forty days and forty nights he paints the faces of puppets because he says he has lost his true face. This period of self-examination and exploration references the forty days and forty nights that Jesus wandered in the desert seeking his true mission. It is generally considered a time of fasting and prayer, which is why he rejects the food he is brought. Jodorowsky is saying that the search for the true self is a religious quest. Jodorowsky's religious allusions, which are prominent in his films since *El Topo*, are part of what the famous literary critic and thinker Northrop Frye termed "The Great Code" of biblical references and allusions deeply engrained in Western literature. Jodorowsky carries this over to the visual realm of cinema. Among the major filmmakers of the past century, who were not making explicitly biblically themed films, Jodorowsky is one of the most frequent users of biblical allusion. One might even say his films are manifestations of biblical allegory and that his metaphors are drawn from both the Torah and the New Testament. For example, the concept of "forty days and forty nights" is the length of time it rained to create the great flood that swept the world away and have Noah save the creatures of the earth (Gen. 6:9–9:17).

When he returns to the Café Iris Alejandro finds Stella transformed. She has cut her red hair short and, like a religious acolyte, is dressed all in white rather than the jumble of colors covering her before. Alejandro calls her previous costume her chaos. She tells him she has found her hero and is pregnant. Now it is her turn to turn away from him. In departing, she gives him a box with the remainder of the red hair she had cut off. Upset by this (Jodorowsky uses red as a symbol of life), Alejandro burns her hair reciting a poem/prayer as if it were a sacrifice or an offering. Hair cutting is one of those fundamental symbols of religious purification and transformation (ergo her white robes) that Jodorowsky draws on regularly. It appeared in *The Dance of Reality* when his father Jaime cut off Alejandro's blond locks and it will reappear at the end of this film when Jaime has his hair shaved off by Alejandro and Jodorowsky himself! We are now half-way through the film and Stella's transformation signals that Alejandro has transformed himself as well. He is no longer the naïve young poet. He is ready to be a true artist.

The three major colors that Jodorowsky uses in the film—red for life, white for purity, and black for death—are repeated over and over again. For example, Ricardo, his gay cousin, wears a white suit indicating his pure intentions. And the grand finale of the film is resplendent with black and red-clad participants holding up a white-clad angelic Alejandro. The power of this color-based symbolism is evident in the sexual exchange that Alejandro has with his muse. It is a bit of a violent affair with his tousling her red hair intensely. Since red is the color of love and life, the scene portrays the poet's engagement with life and the struggle that it involves. It is neither pretty nor polite. But since Stella Diaz has a tattoo of black skulls on her spine, life also involves death. Jodorowsky is intoning the Freudian concept of human instincts being driven by the opposing life force of Eros and the death drive of Thanatos. They are united in every person's psyche and they are in constant conflict, producing turmoil and disruption. Jodorowsky represents that conflict metaphorically through color symbolism and the actions associated with each color.

Alejandro finally finds himself most fulfilled when he is a puppeteer. Jodorowsky wants us to know that the concept of poetry is applicable to all the arts. It is his generic term for artistic creativity. So when he says he is "a poet" he is not referring to books of poetry which he has written, but to his total creative effort. His initial choice of the art of puppeteering links puppets, which are humanoid figures, with humans. Changing humans is not a typical artistic goal. In the film, his desire to transform people occurs when he gifts two of his puppets to a famous artist, played by the modernist Syrian poet Ali Ahmad Said Esber (penname: Adunis/Adonis), and his girlfriend. The artist offers him his studio because he says he is going to Paris. Alejandro is thrilled and throws a party to celebrate. People in all kinds of costumes appear and he has performances enacted, including the reading of a poem by a poet he admires. He tracks down the poet and together the two of them walk through Santiago in a straight line because poetry/art can overcome anything. The march of the two poets is contrasted with the seated figures of the poet's parents, frozen in time, caught up watching the daily affairs of "The Cold War." Art moves life forward, but politics and power stifle.

The walk of the two poets represents a change that characterizes this film. It emphasizes duality over the triad of father, mother, and son that was the consuming metaphor of the first autobiographical film. In this story of liberation from the family, we have Alejandro and his muse, followed by the repetition of the two-puppet relationship (Punch and Judy/André and Luz), and now the pair of poets defying the physical universe. This duality symbolizes the natural progression from family to creating the duos that become the basis of future families. The poets, upon completion of their journey of triumph, proclaim that "poetry is an act." They then appear on stage together to prove their point. First, they recite a poem denouncing poetry and, opening the guitar cases beside them, begin throwing raw meat and eggs at the audience. The scene is a tribute to the "happenings" and provocative Panic events that he was later to excel in.

"Poetry" as a term encompassing all art must include acts of desecration that are central to the Dadaist and Surrealist tradition. Desecration is actually a form of transformation, when an original identity is overturned. The sacred is desacralized. The duo go to a statue of the Nobel Laureate Pablo Neruda, Chile's most famous poet, which they paint over so that Neruda is "invisible." Performing this poetic act, Alejandro proclaims, is a suitable tribute to "the nobodies of this dreamless city," who are people that are invisible. This scene offers Jodorowsky's sense of youthful escapade, while commenting on the discrepancies between Neruda's privilege and his communist politics. The film successfully blends the enthusiasm of youth with the wisdom of old age by creating fantasy events such as this that serve to prefigure later events in his life. For example, when he gifts the two puppets of themselves to André and Luz, he is making a leap into the future. While having no last name, André is made to look like an aged André Breton, the great surrealist, whom he admired and met in Paris after he departed Chile. Jodorowsky was disappointed by Breton, who was well past his prime in the 1950s, and this disappointment and criticism is inserted into the scene, when the dour André character recognizes Alejandro's talent and leaves him his empty studio, which Jodorowsky immediately fills. The aged Breton seems almost dead, while the young Alejandro is filled with life as he dances around the studio. André's studio space is a metaphor for the emptiness of the surrealism he was to find in Paris.

There is an alternate reading of this scene that is more radical. It would probably appeal to Jodorowsky more than the previous one. Let us say that subconsciously Jodorowsky has recreated in the relationship of the old man André, whose name begins with an "A" like Alejandro's and Luz, the youthful beauty, a mirror of his own relationship with Pascale Montandon-Jodorowsky. She is Jodorowsky's wife, although four decades younger. That Adunis (born 1930) and Alejandro (born 1929) are of similar age adds to this interpretation, as does their life and longtime friendship (as of 2022 both men were still living in Paris). In this interpretation, Adunis/André/Alejandro is a kind of mirror of Jodorowsky as he stands, an old man with a suitcase symbolizing a life of journeying, of being an exile, a wanderer. This self-referencing is a way of conflating his and Adunis's Paris present with their Paris past, which in the film is still in the future. This time-shifting is just the kind of game that Jodorowsky enjoys.

In the next scene an American woman, speaking in English, proffers libations from a cauldron over an open fire (read: witch or oracle). She reads Alejandro's tarot in concert with a naked young man, an oracle. Since Jodorowsky is well known for saying that Tarot readings are about who one is at that moment, rather than a prophecy about one's future, her use of Tarot in this way makes her suspect. Again Jodorowsky is playing games because he inserts cards that point to his real future, since they have already happened. The first card that Alejandro draws is The Devil, which the young man says indicates he will discover his dark side and live a creative life. The second card is The Star that means he will go from "woman to woman" but eventually find his ideal partner (read: Pascale Montandon). Alejandro sits down and is joined by Jodorowsky, who hovers over him from behind. This scene imitates similar ones in *The Dance of Reality*. Jodorowsky tells him: "I am the man you will be. You are the man I was." Alejandro is uncertain and worried when he thinks of the future, but Jodorowsky pushes him off the seat and tells him to "Live!"

Alejandro's first encounter is with a woman, who is suicidal because she thinks his poet friend, Enrique, no longer loves her because she is a little person. He consoles her and convinces her to live. But then Enrique appears and denounces her for making love to Alejandro. The story segues to Alejandro meeting a clown from the circus in Topocilla, who invites him to perform, which he does. The performance ends with his being body-surfed by the audience, which will be repeated in a much more colorful and dramatic way at the end of the film. The image of Alejandro being carried aloft by people is a reference to the energy of audiences that people in the performing arts need for their art to be validated. Eventually, the little person and her little person suitor, the two poets, and others from the art commune rendezvous at the Café Iris, where they share a kiss of peace. Suddenly, Jaime and Sarah arrive in their bed clothes to announce the family home has burned down and that they are going to a hotel. Alejandro responds with joy! His family is now homeless, which he thinks is a good thing because for him home was a prison, but more importantly he is now free to pursue the arts without the burden of family. They all go to the burned-out premises, where Alejandro dances a victory dance and goes inside, where he inspects the remains. Since the house was his former residence it contains objects from his life, including the Pinocchio cartoon portrait that hung in his bedroom. The image now lies on the ground. The reference in the caricature is to a "Jewish" nose because he was called "Pinocchio," an anti-Semitic term thrown at him by boys in Topocilla.

When he exits the charred house he is carrying his mother's girdle, which he attaches to a bouquet of heart-shaped red balloons that a clown gives him. He then sends it aloft, signaling the final break with his childhood and his family. His friends tell him to celebrate by going to the carnival, where he is carried aloft by a vast crowd of red-costumed devils. He is dressed in white, with an angel's wings. The devils meet another vast crowd of black-and-white skeletons. They intermingle so that Death (black and white) and Life (red) dance together. Costuming, music, dance, and confetti recreate a carnival atmosphere that is visually arresting and one of the signature scenes of the film.

But Alejandro is unhappy. He appears with a white face as a white-clad clown, when he is joined by Jodorowsky with a cane, who sits next to his youthful self. The old man tells Alejandro not to worry about the future and the death of everything. "Old age is not a humiliation," he says, "You detach yourself from everything—from sex, wealth, fame, even yourself." He tells Alejandro that death involves turning into a butterfly, a beam of pure light, which the next scene mimics with the red devils and the black skeletons carrying Alejandro's white-clad, angelic figure aloft.

One would think that this would be a fitting conclusion to the film, as the present (Jodorowsky) and the past (Alejandro) are united. But it is not. First, Alejandro meets his former idol, Nicanor, who now teaches at the university. Alejandro says he will not accept a bourgeois lifestyle such as university teaching and, instead, will break free from establishment norms. Second, he finds himself confronting an Ibáñez fascist parade and shouting "Death to Ibáñez" but is ignored. This is Jodorowsky's commentary on the relationship between politics and the arts, and how cultural practice cannot stop history. He then sings goodbye to his artistic friends and heads to a dock by the sea, where he meets his father. Jaime begs him not to go to Paris, but Alejandro denounces him for his lifetime of insensitivity and his lack of affection while he was growing up.

The two wrestle and fight and Alejandro defeats his father, another symbol of his newfound maturity. This imagined violence sets the stage for Jodorowsky's personal appearance in a purple suit. The color is important because it is one that he associates with therapeutic and ritual power, which will become even more evident in the next film. He insists that father and son (in this case, the two actor brothers) embrace affectionately. They do. Then Jodorowsky gives Alejandro an electric shaver to cut off Jaime's hair, which, in the DVD version, he does. In the theatrical release Alejandro stops half-way, unable to complete the task, and so Jodorowsky takes over. The bald Jaime is now a transformed figure and kisses his son farewell, something he probably did not do in real life.

In this scene Jodorowsky continues the transformation of his father that he began in *The Dance of Reality*. For the second time, Jaime becomes a new man. This imaginary reconciliation is framed by Jodorowsky by telling Alejandro that "You went to France and never saw him again." They not only have to kiss and make up for this great rupture in the past, but Jodorowsky also says to Jaime, "I forgive you Jaime." The scene is poignant and powerful as Jodorowsky speaks in a deep, emotional way, his face pained. Whether this is Jodorowsky "acting" to express the moment, or an "acting out" by Jodorowsky of a lifetime of pain, I cannot say. Most likely it is both. The forgiveness comes out of Jodorowsky's acknowledging that it was his father's cold-hearted meanness that drove him in an opposite direction—to love life.

The film ends with a repeat of a scene first used at the end of *The Dance of Reality*. The penultimate scene has Sara walking down a promenade of cardboard cutouts of characters in the film, the same way the young Alejandro did in the earlier film. She is singing a farewell. The final scene has Alejandro standing at the stern of a small tug, which is painted purple like Jodorowsky's dockside dress, indicating that the boat is both a symbol of himself and a powerful expression of change and transformation. A black skeleton figure with white wings stands behind and over him. As the boat sails backward into the mists, Jodorowsky intones a poem, much like he intoned a poem at the beginning and end of *The Dance of Reality*. He recites:

> I have learnt to love
> I have learnt to create
> I have learnt to live.

This mantra is about his present as an old man and the three things he did well. Alejandro has yet to learn all this because he is only starting out on the adventure of an expatriate's life. Jodorowsky is telling us that this is yet to happen—love, creativity, and life. The boat disappears into the white mist like it did in the previous film. Copying aspects of the beginning and end of the previous film is Jodorowsky's way of telling us that this is a fabled narrative, a "once upon a time" story that has more of the morality tale than historical fact.

The film is touching in its conclusion. It begins with rebellion against the family and ends with a post-historic reconciliation. Using cinema to create an imaginary moment of reconciliation is something worthy of Jodorowsky's engagement with art. Jaime Jodorowsky (1901–2001) was twenty-eight when Alejandro was born and Alejandro was seventy-two when his father died. That he never saw his father from the time he left Chile in 1953 till his father's death must have left a psychological scar on Jodorowsky that he tried to heal with this film when he was eighty-seven and conscious of death. In a 2015 interview in *Paris Review* that was not published till 2018, Jodorowsky talked about the film and the English-language edition of *Where the Bird Sings Best*, his fanciful family history that had just been released. In the interview he explains why he ended the film this way:

> I waited until I could forgive them. It took me a long time to forgive them. If your parents haven't fulfilled what they were supposed to, you have a right not to love them, not to see them. You have the right to free yourself and have your own life. But even if you live your own life, all of this will remain inside of you. You have to come to terms with what you carry inside of you, make it yours, absorb it. In the film I'm making right now, I thank my father for all that he gave me. Everything he gave me is everything he didn't give me. Thanks to him, I was able to discover mysticism, because my father never gave me that. I was able to discover humanity, because my father never gave me humaneness. Thanks to my mother who didn't know how to love me, I finally discovered how to love a woman. It took me seventy years to find the love of my life! If I am born into this body, I have to self-actualize. It has taken me awhile, but I'm getting there. (Kan 2018)

In making this film Jodorowsky transformed himself from a prodigal to a repentant son, even a loving one. The film is both a statement of himself as a good father because he is there for Alejandro, whenever the boy and the young man are at a crossroads, and an act of expiation for his lifelong rift with his father and mother. There has been no sequel, no third installment, which may indicate that what was most important to Jodorowsky was said in this film.

Academic Commentary

The film has garnered its share of critical insights and analysis. Although not an academic, Martin Kudláč, a film critic based in Slovakia, wrote a thoughtful and insightful commentary for the film's launch at the Locarno Film Festival in August 2016 that was re-published in *ScreenAnarchy.com*. He pointed out how the film was a mix of psychomagic therapy and metagenealogy and that it had a therapeutic purpose. In this case, it was meant to heal the rift between Jodorowsky and his late parents. He joined other critics such as the American film scholar Adam Breckenridge who considered the film Jodorowsky's "most restrained work" and most accessible, because in Kudláč's words, "the thick coat of esotericism" in which he had cloaked his earlier films had been reduced (Kudláč 2017 and Breckenridge 2017). Only his essential color symbolism, his religious allusions, and his surreal characterization were carried over.

José Carlos Cabrejo has published both a book and an article that include a discussion of the film. In the article he talks about the themes of transfiguration and punishment (Cabrejo 2020, 78). This would include the punishment inflicted on Jaime by Alejandro kicking him and then his transfiguration when he has his head shaved and kisses Alejandro for the first time. In the book he has a chapter titled "La danza de la poesía" [The Dance of Poetry] in which he discusses both films together. He paraphrases Jodorowsky speaking via a video appearance at a Montréal film festival screening of the first film that links the concept of poetry with the concept of cinema:

> [T]here is no difference between poetry and cinema, between being naked in body and being naked in soul, given that in body and soul is the fullness of poetry. (Cabrejo 2019, 139)

He appears naked in the video as an embodiment of this idea. This suggests that he sees himself and the creative energy in him as being one with the film, which would support the point made previously that the film is an act of personal healing and reparation. Cabrejo also associates "nostalgic emotion" with the film (2019a, 150). When he argues that the use of the black-and-white cardboard cutouts is an expression of nostalgia, he may be associating their "color" and static nature with a remembered past. The cutouts look sad and therefore lack the idealization of the past usually associated with the concept of nostalgia (Cabrejo 2019b, 164). What would be more accurate would be to see them as figures from the past in the same way that the Santiago streetscape from 2015 was transformed by black-and-white sets to emphasize their past and documentary identity.

Cabrejo also makes a great deal of the concepts of *animus* (male consciousness) and *anima* (female consciousness) that he sees Jodorowsky imprinting on the characters of his mother and his father in both films. While this is a traditional opposition, a binary characterization with the male being "hard" and the female being "soft," Jodorowsky rejects both his parents, meaning he favors a unified characterization that is more in line with the thinking of the psychologist Carl Jung that both are aspects of each human being. Throughout the chapter Cabrejo refers to Jodorowsky as a "demiurge," which is a term from early Greek thought that signifies a divinity that created the physical world. This designation is valid in terms of auteur filmmaking. In spite of the numerous people and their creative abilities involved in making a feature film, the auteur remains the pivotal creative visionary, especially in an autofiction such as this one.

Henri-Simon Blanc-Hoang in an article on Jodorowsky's Jewish identity in *The Dance of Reality* identifies the formal device of "meta-performance," by which he means Jodorowsky acting as himself in the film (which he also does in *Endless Poetry*). Jodorowsky does so, according to Blanc-Hoang, so as "to shed light on and raise awareness of political issues and social challenges," in particular the impact of his Jewish identity on his growing up in the Chilean context of the 1930s and 1940s (Blanc-Hoang 2019). While in the earlier film, Blanc-Hoang argues, the Jodorowsky family was unable to escape anti-Semitism in spite of their attempts to fit in using various roles, in *Endless Poetry* there is "no anti-Semitic incident" as such (Blanc-Hoang 2019). It is true that Alejandro is accepted into the circle of artistic types, where he becomes a puppeteer (or in Cabrejo's terms "a demiurge") whose only identity is the neutral concept of poet. But the presence of the Pinocchio portrait in the burnt-out remains of the family home signifies that his Jewish identity remains, even if he is no longer experiencing anti-Semitism. The house-burning is a purification rite in Jodorowsky's symbolic universe that matches the tree-cutting earlier in the film, but it does not mean the end of his Jewishness.

My own interpretation of the film in several earlier articles (2016 and 2018) no longer has the depth of insight that writing this book has given me, but they still convey a certain analysis worth repeating. First, my claim that his new films "lack the raw, Mexican-infused power of his early classics like *El Topo*" continues to be valid and has been confirmed by others critics (Melnyk 2016, 64). The key word is "Mexican-infused" because the two autobiographical films were made in Chile and are meant to reflect the Chilean world he knew. They incorporate his later philosophies and artistic practices. They are also devoid of the future-oriented intensity of the earlier auteur films, where questing was the main metaphor. My observation that the film's "surreal aspects" are essential to its transformative, life-changing nature refers to the dual structure of the two films (Melnyk 2016, 66). That structure maintains a foundational linear narrative interrupted by surreal and meta-performative interjections. What we have is a conventional consciousness assaulted and overtaken by a dream-state. These events of dream-states transform the past, allowing reconciliation and forgiveness to actually occur, especially for Jodorowsky himself.

I point out that "self-exile is different from an exile that involves being driven or forced out by others," and that self-exile is a concept rich with meaning for Jodorowsky (Melnyk 2018, 69). "He is telling us [as he exiles himself from Chile in the film] that we are exiled from our true selves," I write, "and that the self that has been hidden must be revealed" (Melnyk 2018, 69). The film is an act of self-revelation that can occur only when the creative part of the self is allowed to embrace the past in a non-historical, non-memorialized way, which means making it fabled and magical. Presenting the past as a fantasy allows the past to receive an allegorical healing, which, in turn, allows what Jodorowsky terms "the soul" to find rest. In my 2018 article, I retell how portraying his own father in *Endless Poetry* caused a real-life transformation in Adán Jodorowsky:

> [He] went into the Atacama Desert of Chile after the film was made, where he cut off his hair and buried it in the sand, signifying that he wanted to be a new man, just like the film proclaimed. He took back his birth name and re-adopted his father's last name, while previously he had created an alternate performer's name for himself in order to be free of the Jodorowsky myth. (Melnyk 2018, 68)

This reconciliation with his own father parallels what happened in the penultimate scene on the dock in the film when his father reconciles with his father. Acting in that scene led to a fundamental change in his own life. Both Jodorowsky's own reconciliation with this father and his son's transformation suggest that *Endless Poetry* is Jodorowsky's most transformative film, at least for himself and for members of his family.

10

The Therapist on Film

Psychomagic, A Healing Art (2019)

The critical success of his two autobiofictional films raised expectations that there would be a third installment. Since the second installment came out in 2016, it was reasonable to expect the third one in 2019. Instead, he released the documentary *Psychomagic, A Healing Art*. Feature-length documentaries had come into their own in the twenty-first century. Jodorowsky was simply contributing to this trend. The documentary mode tends to be much less costly than a narrative film (the participants are not paid the way actors are and the use of sound stages is not common). The equivalent in television are reality shows. Jodorowsky could make his film at a relatively low cost. The financial factor was probably significant, but it may also have included other factors such as the unwillingness or suitability of family actors to participate in another film. Having worked through his need for family reconciliation in *Endless Poetry* he may have felt that there would be nothing transformative in the next installment.

It needs to be said that this documentary and his autobiofictional films are related. They both purport to deal with the real world, whether present or past. *Psychomagic* moves beyond the indirect application of his therapies in his feature films to a direct, hands-on exercise. The film shows him practicing psychomagical and metagenealogical therapies with real subjects. Making a film displaying his work gave him an opportunity to reach a global audience quickly and easily. Although internet streaming services create the possibility of global access, the audience for this film remains limited. Jodorowsky is not a household name in psychotherapy. As the film's director, writer, main performer and editor, he continues his auteur approach. The film belongs to his body of personal work. The film was produced by his own company, Satori Films (the word "satori" means "sudden enlightenment," which is the ultimate goal of Zen Buddhist practice). Xavier Guerrero Yamamoto, his Chilean producer from *Endless*

Poetry, is listed as a producer, while his wife Pascale Montandon-Jodorowsky is listed as director of cinematography and his son Adán is responsible for the music. The project raised money through crowdfunding like the previous film. By the spring of 2018 Jodorowsky had raised almost $200,000 from several thousand contributors (ulule.com/jorodowsky). In a ten-minute YouTube fundraising pitch for this film, which is included on the crowdfunding website, Jodorowsky stated that any monies left over could be used for "Essential Trip," the name he had given to the sequel to *Endless Poetry*. As of 2022, three years after *Psychomagic*, there is no indication of this sequel going into production. That he was still dreaming of a new installment in the autobiographical series at that point is a positive sign. He indicated it would be the final episode of a "trilogy," where originally it had been a suite of five films. It would seem he had become aware of his waning power to overcome all the hurdles, from writing to raising funds to working intensely with a cast and crew that a filmmaker faces when making an auteur film. Until this projected film appears, *Psychomagic* will remain the final film in his autobiographical series. If it does ever see the light of day, then *Psychomagic* will be moved aside. It will have held the spot temporarily.

The film was first shown in Lyon, France, in September 2019. It did get screened at a few film festivals in 2020. ABKCO Films, his US distributor, launched the film on a streaming service, Alamo on Demand, in August 2020 and then added the film to its 4K restoration box set of Blu-ray discs along with three of his other films. The film can be streamed through Amazon and Apple TV. The film's sporadic theatrical release, very limited circulation on the festival circuit, and its availability primarily on streaming services, did not preclude it from getting some critical response. The reviewer for the Rogerebert.com website concluded his assessment with a phrase worthy of a circus barker: "It's ridiculous, it's unbelievable, it's bullshit—it's Jodo!" (Abrams 2020). Nevertheless the reviewer found that the strange rituals that Jodorowsky creates for his "patients" make the film "amusing and engaging." The *New York Times* reviewer treats the film with a bit more seriousness when he writes that Jodorowsky is contrasting the scientific claims of Freud for psychotherapy with his own magical techniques that resemble performance art. The reviewer cannot take psychomagic seriously as a therapy since psychotherapy in general has been discredited and is no longer in vogue (Kenny 2020). A more extensive review on Indiewire.com describes the film as a "mesmerizing summation of his unusual career ambition, a dream-like chronicle of human suffering for which Jodorowsky offers a wild solution on par with his craziest filmmaking conceits" (Kohn 2020). Linking Jodorowsky's feature films with this documentary recognizes the continuity between the two genres when practiced by the same filmmaker. Some of the episodes in the film are certainly reminiscent of scenes in the feature films, which he actually puts into the documentary to preface each episode. For example, a man attaches a photo of his father to balloons and watches them fly away, which is similar to the scene in *Endless Poetry*, where Alejandro lets his mother's girdle fly away in the same way. Another is a scene with a man putting images of his family on pumpkins and smashing them. In *The Dance of Reality* Jaime shoots at images of his political mentors seeking to obliterate the dictatorial demon inside himself. Kohn's conclusion that "his filmmaking has always walked a fine line between the ridiculous and sublime" is valid both for this film and for all his others (Kohn 2020).

Slantmagazine.com's reviewer thought that the film "could easily stand as a fitting encapsulation of the themes of suffering and transcendence that have run throughout his entire career" (Wilkins 2020). But others consider the film no better than an infomercial. One reviewer unkindly wrote:

> It's selling a product, a cult of personality around a man whose enduring career has rested on occasionally reminding people he's still around, still being wild, still making movies that play well in art cinemas and then vanish into the ether. (Dossey 2020)

Whether the film is a legitimate documentary or an infomercial for Jodorowsky and his therapeutic ideas is not the crucial issue. Its critical reception (there has been no academic response to date) is a repetition of the range of critiques from ridicule to acclaim that his feature films generated when they first appeared—no change here. The crucial question is whether the documentary displays any new cinematic approaches that were not there previously in his films. Did he have the power to innovate in 2019, when he was ninety, or was the film simply a rehash of his past work?

Jodorowsky on the Film

Jodorowsky presented his own view of the film in several interviews in which he tried to answer those who considered the work nothing but self-promotion. Nofilmschool.com interviewed the filmmaker and his wife when the film debuted in the United States. In the interview, Jodorowsky explains that his therapy is free and he charges no fee:

> Psychoanalysis is a science, Psychomagic is an art. But my initial goal was to heal psychological problems within myself. We are not doctors, and Psychomagic is not an industry that asks you to pay a lot of money to heal yourself. I do this for free . . . I devote my life to it without treating it as a business. It comes from a passion to create something new. (Weinstein 2020)

Jodorowsky explains his therapeutic technique in this way:

> I met with each person once beforehand to map out their genealogical tree. . . . Then, based on what kind of family you have, I decide what Psychomagic act I will assign to the person. From there, we prepared for the act and decided which things would be important for each person—like wearing a costume, for instance. (Weinstein 2020)

Jodorowsky also eschews the term "documentary" to describe the film:

> The film is not a documentary. Documentaries speak about reality, but they show what has happened in the past. As we made this picture, we were not showing things of the past. We were making it right then and there. We wanted the audience to feel real emotions because so many movies essentially create fake emotions with actors—theatrical emotions. But here, we're showing absolute reality. (Weinstein 2020)

Since he uses clips from his earlier narrative films and clips from pre-2018 psychomagical events, he confirms that these techniques had already been exposed in his narrative films and that he had been engaged in psychomagic for some time. Wrapping the documentary in a historical cloak is his way of giving the subject temporal and autobiographical depth. Jodorowsky claims that his use of psychomagic goes back fifty years when in *El Topo* he had little Alejandro (Brontis) bury his mother's photo. This was a psychomagic act because it changed Brontis's life and his own (Weinstein 2020). Pascale Montandon-Jodorowsky, who is part of the interview, reiterated the pscyhomagic element in his earlier films:

> There is not much difference between Alejandro's older movies and this one. In all of his movies, there is a journey between dreams and reality, but everything in them is truthful. As Alejandro said, you can see Psychomagic in *El Topo*, too. And at the end of *Endless Poetry*, you see him perform a Psychomagic act: He's healing himself by speaking to his father through his sons. (Weinstein 2020)

In another online interview, Jodorowsky boldly stated: "Psychomagic is the sum of everything I have been and everything I have worked on" (Amorosi 2020). Psychomagic is part of all his auteur films, beginning with *El Topo*, because they contain acts of psychological healing. One could legitimately conclude that while this film shows Jodorowsky creating psychomagic acts for others to perform, his earlier auteur films are vehicles for his own and his family's personal psychomagic acts of liberation.

The Film Itself

Does this film add to the overall validity of his work or does it detract from it? Is it a fitting capstone to his film career or a deviation? What, if anything, is novel about it? These are difficult questions to answer because the film's genre deviates from the other films. One approach that may allow insight into the film's value is to consider *Psychomagic* an exalted form of "home movie." It captures Jodorowsky working at home and often in his Paris milieu. He used his wife, who is not a cinematographer by training, for some of the cinematography, which gives some of the film an amateur feel, appropriate to a home-made movie. The cinematic quality of the film was pieced together in postproduction. A scene-by-scene description and analysis allows us to formulate a judgment about his approach and situate the film in his body of work.

The film begins with Jodorowsky explaining how psychomagic differs from psychoanalysis. Psychoanalysis is about talking, while psychomagic is about acting he says. In psychoanalysis the therapist does not touch the patient, while in psychomagic, touch is fundamental. Jodorowsky is a great believer in the healing power of human physical contact, such as hugging. Jodorowsky is sitting in a garden in a ratty old suit with a dark purple shirt. He is "reading" from a red notebook as if he were a professor lecturing to his students. The color red is his iconic color of life, so the notebook serves as a metaphor for a book of life. The purple shirt mimics the purple in a video that he says marked the birth of psychomagic many years earlier. In that video two brothers wrestle as Jodorowsky massages them. They have been in competition for their mother's affection. As the wrestling ends, the mother figure, whether real or not, appears wearing white and soothes them. So she and Jodorowsky become what he calls "the mother and father of psychomagic." The brothers are wearing purple, as is Jodorowsky, so his wearing a purple shirt now links him to that scene, which ends in a kind of gentle ballet signifying the torment is over and that they are reconciled. The color purple is also prominent in scenes of change and transformation in the previous film, *Endless Poetry*.

This example of the "first" psychomagic act is followed by a clip from a 2006 Spanish television episode in which Jodorowsky explains his method as being "anti-surrealist" because his approach is to infiltrate reality with the language of dreams rather than having dreams turned into art the way Dali, the preeminent surrealist, did. Jodorowsky does not want dreams to be represented. He wants them realized. What is particularly interesting in this anti-surrealist claim is that it parallels his earlier claim about psychomagic being distinct from psychotherapy. It seems that Jodorowsky has to claim originality for his therapy in order to validate it in his own mind. Copying others (all the while referencing them) is something he abhors. His stance must always be that of an originator.

Then the film screens an episode from *The Dance of Reality* in which the young Alejandro and his mother are covered in black paint, while they are dancing around. This episode from the film purports to show a psychomagic action because it led Jodorowsky as a boy to stop being afraid of the dark. How painting one's naked body in black paint and dancing with his similarly unclad and painted mother would lead to a loss of this phobia is not explained. It's all magic. Unless of course, this loss of a fear of darkness is a metaphorical statement in which darkness stands for something else like sexuality. Jodorowsky claims the film clip represents something real from his childhood, but what kind of "reality?" Since the scene is total fantasy, using it in a documentary ends up equating psychomagic with the artifice of theatrically. Jodorowsky thinks that representing the stopping of his childhood fear of the dark is a legitimate representation of a truth.

Jodorowsky's attempt to put his therapeutic practice on par with that of Freud fails because psychoanalysis has had and continues to have numerous practitioners, while those practicing psychomagic are likely few apart from Jodorowsky himself. Since psychomagic is not a business model that earns an income, its appeal is limited. Centering the practice in Jodorowsky over so many years suggests that it is dependent on the master himself. Other practitioners of the art do not appear in the film. Documenting Jodorowsky's proficiency in psychomagic practice begins with his first "patient," a man with a serious father-complex. Of course, Jodorowsky's own autobiographical films express the same emotions and denunciations of his own father, so this patient is a perfect substitute for himself. This is Jodorowsky's way of linking his own story to that of others. The man is suicidal after being abused by his father, so he is taken to Spain by Jodorowsky and his team, where Jodorowsky smashes dishes he has placed on his chest and rubs black pieces of wire representing worms or snakes in the same place, after which the nameless man throws them off. Then Jodorowsky has him buried in a shallow grave with only his face exposed, which he covers with a glass pot with holes for breathing. The shallow grave is an image that appears in his other films, beginning with *Fando y Lis*. Then Jodorowsky spreads some offal over the site, which attracts vultures that fight over the food. They are chased off. The ritual is highly shamanistic. The man rises and is then baptized with milk, whose white color signifies purification. He then dresses in new clothing and represents himself as a new person freed from his obsession. He sends a color photocopy of his father attached to balloons into the sky, while Jodorowsky inserts a clip of Alejandro sending his mother's girdle aloft in the same manner. The man tells us he is now able to love.

The second episode is titled "Birth Massage." It begins with a scene from *Fando y Lis* in which Lis is lying naked on a pile of animal skulls. The scene suggests that the next patient is dealing with a death wish of some sort, an attraction to lifelessness and negativity. A young woman explains she is afraid of having a child and giving birth because of her poor relationship with her mother. Against melodic background music she is stripped of her clothes by two therapists, both of whom are wearing white. She is then manipulated into a series of fetal positions and ends up lying in a sheet next to the seated body of the female therapist, who is gray-haired and is clearly acting as a nurturing body to this "baby" girl. Using a colored cloth rope representing an umbilical cord, the "mother" cuts the cord and sets her free. First she is supported by the "father and mother" therapists but then she walks free. The next shot has her dressed and announcing she is free of anger toward her mother. The transition from nakedness to normal dress marks a rebirth into a new adulthood. The rebirthing is reminiscent of a similar scene in which Jodorowsky is born again as a baby in *The Holy Mountain*. The episode ends with her showing off her pregnant state, indicating the therapy had helped her to overcome her anxiety.

The third episode is titled "Couple in Crisis" and deals with two people who are going through a difficult time in their relationship. The man undergoes a similar naked experience with the two therapists because he still feels a child within himself. While the man may feel liberated after his therapy, the woman decides she wants out of the relationship. In order to ease the transition to the breakup, Jodorowsky has them perform a psychomagic act of both of them walking together down Paris streets, dragging a long chain, signifying their being chained to each other. This act is prefigured by showing a scene from *Tusk* of the elephant dragging a chain. At the end they hug and walk away from each other. This is the least effective episode so far. It does not convey the reasons for one partner seeking an end to the relationship, though there is a great deal of attempted explanation by each of them. What is different about this episode is that the normal trajectory from anger to love in the previous episodes is replaced with an anger to separation trajectory.

The fourth episode is titled "An Australian in Paris Angry Against His Family." A man who is angry at his family for the way it has ignored him puts out three pumpkins on a backstreet, places a photo of his father, mother, and sister on each of them and using a red sledgehammer, smashes them. Is the red sledgehammer a symbol of life because of its color or a symbol of violence? The pumpkins are clearly their heads, but does smashing them free him because doing so releases his anger? And what about the choice of a back alley full of graffiti? Does it signify the decay in his mind caused by family dynamics? The metaphoric structure of psychomagic with each element chosen by Jodorowsky to signify something else is his way of directing the sufferer to enter the zone of internal pain in order not to carry out his deepest desires in reality. The man then puts some pieces of shattered pumpkin into a box that he mails home to the family. The episode is introduced by a scene from *Endless Poetry* in which Alejandro is chopping down the family tree. The man's conclusion after this act is to say "I feel a little bit free." The act did not rid him completely of his angst.

The fifth episode is about menstruation and it also begins with a scene from *Endless Poetry* in which the Small Woman asks Alejandro if he will have sex with her even though it is her period. Of course, Alejandro agrees. The film cuts to Jodorowsky in a 2006 television presentation in which he advises women to use their menstrual blood to paint self-portraits and then display the art publicly as a celebration of the "creativity of their period." A group of naked women do just that, but the main focus of the episode is a female cellist, who, while playing the cello, speaks of her approaching Jodorowsky about making her cello more female to her. He tells her to paint the back of her cello with her menstrual blood over a period of nine months and then clean it off at a public concert. She narrates that when she had done this she felt she had reconciled with the cultural attribution to certain instruments being more "male" than others and that her cello was now "female." She had given "birth" to a new cello.

The sixth episode concerns a Mexican woman, whose fiancé had committed suicide before their marriage. The woman then left Mexico for eight years, and returned with Jodorowsky in order to overcome her unwarranted feelings of somehow being responsible for his jumping out of the apartment balcony. Jodorowsky has her return to the apartment building, then don a wedding dress and go through a cemetery, ending up at its chapel, where her wedding dress is buried in a crypt. She then proceeds to skydive like her late fiancé had done many times. He had used the same farewell phrase when he committed suicide as he had used when he left her to go skydiving. After skydiving and burying her wedding dress, she says she is free of guilt about his suicide.

The seventh episode is about Jodorowsky's psychomagic healing of a middle-aged stutterer. After interviewing the man, Jodorowsky explains to him how his stuttering is associated with his family tree and how he has been kept at the level of a child. He needs to grow up in order to overcome his affliction. The man first dresses up in a boy's sailor outfit and then goes on carnival rides as if he were a child. Jodorowsky claims this frees him from his childishness. Now the adult has to be set free as well. This involves Jodorowsky holding the man's testicles, telling him that this is where his strength is, and having him yell out sentences and math tables—all without stuttering. The psychological block that caused his stuttering is being lifted. The man then strips (nakedness is an integral part of any Jodorowskian transformation because it involves the removal of the old and the donning of the new), paints his genitals, and is covered in gold paint. Now as the golden boy (wearing golden shorts), he goes out to stroll in public. This act is necessary because he had told Jodorowsky that he always felt that people had viewed him as a child because he stuttered. He thanks Jodorowsky for curing him of his affliction.

The eighth episode involves an old woman, who feels she has failed in her life and has lost empathy for others. She is depressed and worn out. He holds her hand and offers her an action that he says will help her overcome her psychological ailment. He gives her a bottle of water and together they go to a large tree in a park nearby and he has her pour the water onto the roots of the tree. He tells her that for twenty-one days she must take the full bottle of water on walks in the street and use it to perform "acts of giving." What happens afterward we do not know since the episode ends with her hugging Jodorowsky on the steps of her home.

The ninth episode involves a singer who has father issues, especially in regard to his father's philandering when he was a performer. The son feels that he has repressed his sexual desires in order to support his mother in reaction to his father's actions. He composes and performs a song about this issue as he plays the piano in an empty theater. Eventually he dresses in his father's favorite costume and strolls down the street singing and is joined by another voice (his father's?) so that each echoes the other. The episode ends with the man singing a dirge and then attacking the keyboard with frenzied fingerboarding, after which he declares: "I feel light, I'm a new man."

The concluding section of the film is titled "Social Psychomagic" and involves film or video clips from an earlier period of his psychomagic practice. The first is a scene from 2008 of him with a female cancer patient in a theater in Santiago, Chile. He asks the audience to project their desire for her healing by stretching out their arms toward her, which they do. Ten years later the survivor is interviewed for the documentary. She says she felt the energy projected on her for days afterward and that she came to realize that "healing comes from the inside." This is probably the most disturbing clip in the whole film since it involves a medical condition and the way it is presented in the film hints that psychomagic at least contributed to her "cure." This is an unfortunate presumption because it turns Jodorowsky from a psychological healer to a physical one, which is a problematic claim.

The second clip concerns a gay couple who, while standing in a public space surrounded by people, have their clothing cut up and removed from their bodies. Then they are dressed in new suits. A religious-like procession carrying a wood closet ends in a bonfire, where the closet is turned to ashes, signifying their coming out of the closet. The only notable aspect of this short clip is the clear reference to having to be stripped ritually and then ritually reclothed, meaning that they are now new people, dressed in a way that reflects their true selves. The transformation in clothing signifies a transformation of the person. It is a device that Jodorowsky uses frequently.

The final clip in the film, titled "Walk of the Dead, Mexico City, 2011" harnesses "social" or collective energy for his psychomagic ceremonies as he did in the previous two clips. This one engages hundreds of participants, much like the scenes of dancing devils and skeletons in *Endless Poetry*, in order to make a statement of public power. The clip is preceded by a scene from *The Holy Mountain*, with the firing squad executing young people from whose chests fly live birds, signifying the liberation of the soul. The 2011 event was a public march to denounce the drug wars in Mexico and commemorate the tens of thousands of its victims. Beginning in front of the Palacio Bellas Artes in central Mexico City, the march of people with skeleton masks and skeleton images on their faces, heads out chanting "Psychomagic against violence." Jodorowsky is one of the leaders and he is wearing a skull mask and a purple scarf. The march ends at a square, where a mariachi band leads the marchers in singing a song in which a mother mourns the death of her son. The skull faces are associated with Mexico's most famous day, the Day of the Dead. Jodorowsky was able to utilize this folk art in his protest against all the killing involved in that war.

Jodorowsky's taking psychomagic to the streets in a collective demonstration is a step-up. The demonstration becomes, like the psychomagic acts performed by individuals, a catharsis for the participants and a public display of Jodorowsky's social and political values. But what is important for his creative legacy is the color purple that he wore at this 2011 event because he used the color in a very early example of psychomagic when he and the wrestling brothers all wore purple. In the recent 2018 episodes he is also wearing a purple shirt. He clearly associates that color with being a master and with spiritual leadership.

The film ends and the viewer may be left wondering what the point of the film is. Is it meant to confirm the validity of psychomagic as a therapy? Is it meant to document a practice? Or is it simply an autobiographical statement about who he is in the same way that the previous two films are? Psychomagic acts in his feature films could be dismissed because of their fictional and surreal aspects. The documentary grounds the practice in the real world. The film is his way of preserving his theory for posterity. Yet, its association with just one practitioner—the ever-present Jodorowsky—diminishes its value as a serious, far-reaching therapeutic method. Only by documenting its widespread use could the film have heralded psychomagic as a worthy addition to psychotherapeutic treatments.

Is the film a convincing explanation of psychomagic? As a documentary, it is middling at best. Jodorowsky is not a maker of documentary films. As described earlier, the film has the feel of a home movie, albeit at a higher level than most. The film does have its moments of intensity, but the technique he presents remains questionable and unproven in the long run. Psychomagic is very much tied to his personal capacity to intervene and prescribe. Movements led by a cult-like leader seldom survive for long unless they are heavily institutionalized through a growing number of followers and a new cadre of erstwhile leaders. This has not developed.

Assessment

By making himself so prominent in this film in comparison to the earlier autobiofictional films, he comes across as a personality with a large ego. He made the film about himself. It is not as if someone outside his world recognized the importance of what he was doing and so decided to make a documentary about it. This is particularly true of the "social psychomagic" clips in which he appears in the role of a showman performing psychomagic by prompting audience participation. Today one could imagine that kind of personality appearing on numerous high-profile American television shows whose hosts would use the episode for entertainment purposes, while the promoter would use the broadcast to attract all sorts of celebrity figures who wanted to be cured of whatever psychological ailments they felt they had. Unfortunately, the film doesn't add anything significant to Jodorowsky's stature as a filmmaker and most likely he never intended that it should. His using clips from his earlier feature films is a sign of where his true stature lies. Their artistry stands in stark contrast to the real-world characters who applied to be part of his film and display nothing but subservience to the master. They appear as puppets manipulated by a puppeteer. While Jodorowsky has every right to create a permanent record of psychomagic as he practices it, the record he has created is more entertainment than science. As he has often said, he is an artist. Psychomagic is one of his artful works.

While the film deviates from his body of narrative films, it fits with the autobiographical drive that generated *The Dance of Reality* and *Endless Poetry*. However, the viewing public would have been better off seeing a third installment of the original series concept, which would have been about his life in Paris in the 1950s and Mexico in the 1960s. By substituting a documentary for a narrative film, he lost an opportunity to engage his full imagination. Instead, he has produced something minor in the same way a great novelist is remembered for one or more works of fiction rather than the writing of a nonfiction memoir.

11

Jodorowsky Redux

Evaluating the Art of a Fabulist

In 2022 Jodorowsky turned ninety-three. Any future cinematic work by him would be an exceptional achievement. What he has created to date leaves a rich trove for viewers and critics alike. That some of his best work was completed when he was an octogenarian is unusual. It indicates that Jodorowsky is an artist of immense energy. Because his film work was limited in the earlier period, his imagination retained a reservoir of imagery and narratives that came into play many years later. His work in graphic novels and comics, plus the large body of writing that occupied his attention between 1990 and 2012, kept him focused on the mythic and the fantastic. He was able to draw on all of this when he was in his eighties.

Jodorowsky is foremost a fabulist. By a fabulist I mean a person for whom the world is primarily fabled. Its reality is mythic, archetypal, fantastic, and dreamlike. The fable tradition is ancient. It started with the use of animal characters in narratives that were meant to teach a moral. So it is not surprising that Jodorowsky has been described as a moralist. A development of the term "fable" is the word "fabula," which refers to an early form of drama. For Jodorowsky storytelling needs to be dramatized for it to have power. The more recent term "fabulation" involves the use of allegorical and surreal effects to convey a story's message, which is certainly applicable to Jodorowsky. Jodorowsky's fabulations theatricalize, moralize, and allegorize human life. The fabulist sees truth as residing in myths. Human psychology uses myths to understand the self and the world. That is why his memoirist films are works of enchanting fictionalization, on par with his earlier narrative films. Facts, chronology, and realism are anathema to great storytellers like Jodorowsky, who "dresses up" every word and image.

Margaret Visser writes elegantly about the relationship of story and dream, which is the foundation of Jodorowsky's approach to cinema:

> Nightly, in our dreams, we create structures intricately patterned, rich with fantasy, and peopled with vivid characters who embody emotional intensity, meaning, and design. Not only do we contrive and conjure up our own dramatic creations, but we act in them as well, suffering and discovering through the vicissitudes of the story. We are, at the same time, the audience at the spectacle: as our own dreams unfold, we watch and listen, spellbound. (Visser 2002, 30–1)

Jodorowsky is both participant and spectator in his dreamy films. By being both a player and a watcher, he turns his films into transformative experiences for him and others involved. While we all dream, very few of us make dream-like films. Feature-length narrative cinema is an expensive art. It is not only costly, but also complicated to produce, involving many interlocking and sometimes contradictory parts and players. Once Jodorowsky had experienced the animus of the business side of filmmaking in the 1970s, he took a long time to return to his auteur roots.

If I hadn't seen *The Dance of Reality* and *Endless Poetry*, I would never have taken up the challenge of writing this book. The films were a discovery, a revelation that their filmmaker was undervalued. He needed a new appraisal. When I told my brother, the composer and pianist Lubomyr Melnyk, that I was writing a book on Jodorowsky's films, he was genuinely excited and pleased. He told me that his seeing *The Holy Mountain* inspired him to create "Continuous Music," his signature technique, which he has been composing and performing ever since. There is a mystical quality to his music and trance-like performances. It is as if Jodorowsky's film had freed a deep inner power in my brother to create original music. My brother's story provides a clue to the value of Jodorowsky's cinema. For creative people it can be life-changing and inspirational. Jodorowsky mentions one such figure—Marilyn Manson, the American pop singer and musician, who called him "to tell me that my films, especially *The Holy Mountain,* had inspired him so much" that he wrote a script titled *Holy Wood* that he wanted him to direct (Jodorowsky 2005, 237). The script was an attack on Hollywood and was never made. It can be argued that the impact of his films on the artistic personality is his cinematic legacy.

The Spaniard Buñuel and the Italian Fellini were two contemporaries of Jodorowsky, whose films most closely resembled his. Their bodies of work are more extensive than his (twenty films for Buñuel; thirty films for Fellini). Their narrative style, while using surreal, absurdist imagery and political satire, tends to have more conventional narratives than his. Jodorowsky trumped them in his intense use of religious symbolism, his featuring of nonprofessional actors and family members, his emphasis on personas with unusual deformities or injuries, and his underlying spirit of circus-like zaniness. While they are now part of the pantheon of great twentieth-century filmmakers, Jodorowsky is still awaiting his turn. Jodorowsky's filmmaking consists of two intense periods (1968–73 plus 1989 and 2013–19) that resulted in two trilogies, broken up by a long hiatus, which was due to having his earlier films removed from circulation. During this break, he engaged in other artistic pursuits, like writing and comic books, which neither Buñuel nor Fellini did. Buñuel worked more or less regularly as a filmmaker in a thirty-year period from 1947 to 1977, as well as making films prior to the Second World War. Fellini likewise worked regularly as a director in cinema in the four decades between 1950 and 1990. Their body of work is substantive as well as distinctive. All of which is to say that the limited body of work produced by Jodorowsky makes him a special case as a filmmaker, whose status in the canon needs to be approached with care and an openness to seeing him in a singular light. Let's begin with the concept of his being a maker of cult films.

    The popular label of "cult" filmmaker did have validity fifty years ago when Jodorowsky made *El Topo*. It is no longer valid. Jodorowsky's work has moved beyond that label into an arena where he deserves to be redefined. Jodorowsky wanted his films to transform both actors and viewers. He also desired a level of engagement with his films that would result in a new personality for those who made it and those who viewed it. This was especially true of his early films like *El Topo* and *The Holy Mountain* in which the primary performers had to go through religious-like gestalt experiences such as fasting and taking hallucinogens. He had the performers do this in order to strip them of their normative modes of thinking and being so that they could better convey the message of the film. In his later two autobiographical films and his psychomagic documentary, the transformative impulse continued. There are several aspects of his specific filmmaking technique that contributed to making his films transformative. First, he usually did only one take of a shot in order to capture human spontaneity and to reduce the chance of artificiality. Second, he used amateurs and street people as actors in order to provide a genuine humanness to the film. Using "real" people shifted the film away from celebrity actors and their performances. Third, he undercut conventional beauty by using unconventional body shapes and sizes, both clothed and naked. He despised Hollywood's dependence on physically attractive male and female stars.

How transformative his films were for audiences is difficult to determine. Anecdotally they made an impact on figures like John Lennon and Marilyn Manson. As for the general public who saw his films, there is no record of their impact. Jodorowsky says certain of his films were personally transformative for him. Both Brontis and Adán Jodorowsky indicate that acting in their father's films had an impact on them in terms of identity. Because of my writing this book, a new and positive relationship came about between my brother and myself, a connection that had been lacking for decades. From my experience I can see how transformative Jodorowsky's cinema can be—if not for everyone, at least for some.

Jodorowsky contributed three elements to cinema. The first is his making each of his films totally *theatrical* in the sense of emphasizing performativity and illusion. His engagement with the Panic Movement in France and then his one-off theatrical happenings in Mexico taught him the value of provocation and absurdist juxtapositioning as a tool of psychic liberation. He transferred that sensibility to cinema. The viewer of his films is constantly aware of how these films favor the unusual and the transgressive, but in a way that seems highly performed. Realism was his enemy.

The second aspect is his making each of his films highly *poetic* in the sense of impregnating his images with a surfeit of symbolic references, metaphors, and allegories. His films cannot be separated from the powerful and symbolic use of color and costuming. Nothing is what it seems on the surface because it is always representative or symbolic of something else. In this way the viewer enters a kind of hall of mirrors, where reflections play off each other, in order to confuse what is real and what is not. Not only are the characters unrealistic in their demeanor and dress, they are also always standing in for something. They are never themselves in the ordinary sense of the term. The normal grounding that most narrative films have in a recognizable place, landscape, or character is subverted in his films, so that the world becomes a living poem filled with allusion and reflection. The viewer floats in a hallucinatory dreamscape.

Third, he made his films fundamentally *spiritual* by incorporating religious references from a variety of faith traditions, sometimes in a sacrilegious way. But even as he featured these elements, he subverted them by having the theatrical, the poetic, and the spiritual elements costumed and situated in a carnival atmosphere. In this way they could not be taken at face value. He introduced comic touches, as well as bizarre and even silly ones, in order to point out the artificiality of his creation. In the end he made clear that we as humans prefer living in fantasy. Our conscious life is a mixed-up dream full of repressed subconscious traumas that direct and reign over the human psyche.

Only if we connect with Jodorowsky's films on a subconscious level can we truly appreciate their transformative potential. Traditionally associated with the chaotic content of dreams filled with confusion and frustrated desires, the subconscious is a powerful force in our daily actions and thoughts. The surrealists that Jodorowsky initially admired were focused on the power of dreams. They were following early-twentieth-century Freudian and Jungian ideas about human psychology that were popular at that time. Carl Jung considered dreams and mythology as the narrative expression of the subconscious. In his description of what a dream is, one can see a reflection of Jodorowsky's approach to film narrative:

> The dream is a fragment of involuntary psychic activity . . . Of all psychic phenomena the dream presents perhaps the largest number of "irrational" factors. . . . Usually a dream is a strange and disconcerting product distinguished by . . . lack of logic, questionable morality, uncouth form, and apparent absurdity or nonsense. (Jung 1974, 68)

Jodorowsky did not take a "scientific" interest in the phenomenon the way Jung did. Rather, he saw himself as an artist using artifice to replicate the qualities of dreams in a cinematic dreamscape. He took archetypes found in fable and religion, and then embedded them in his films.

The figure of the male hero in quest of truth and enlightenment is aligned with his own life. As an auteur he created out of his own intense imagination and the specifics of his own life and its distinctness. While he did create female personas, acting as muses or sorcerers, these were most often antagonistic foils to the quester and the search. His films should be viewed as highly personal expressions close to his own male psyche. That is why he had so little interest in the commercial potential of his films, always preferring to see them as works of art, whose meaning was mysterious, multifaceted, and open-ended. The fact that so many of his films involve gurus or spiritual masters of one sort or another indicate how obsessed he was with first learning from masters and then becoming a master himself. Whatever spiritual journey he happened to be on when he made a particular film, found its way into the film.

While his early films continue to be watchable, they are products of their time. The reaction of a twenty-first-century audience to *El Topo* is much different from that of a similar demographic in 1970. For the latter the film was an experiment in psychedelic art, while for the former it is a curiosity from the past that can be read as a postmodern fable. His later autobiographical films are more accessible to the current generation because they display a filmmaking maturity that carries humor and fewer demands on the audience. Nostalgia rather than revolution reigns.

While making a contribution to cinema through his films' theatricality, poetic qualities, and their spirituality, can his work be considered canonical? To use a religious metaphor, one might rephrase the question by asking how a heretical filmmaker might be considered canonical? His *sui generis* personality with its profound anti-commercialism created works of art that stood outside the cinematic mainstream, so he might not really care if they are heralded or ignored. He operated as "a transcontinental artist working in two languages, three countries and three continents" (Melnyk 2018, 59). His combination of an expatriate identity with other national cultures and their artistic movements in South America, North America, and Europe resulted in a worldview that centered very much on self-development and self-preservation. When one is a stranger and the other through most of one's working life, the only constant is one's self and one's identity as the alien. His working in different places and cultures encouraged a syncretism that he was attracted to because it showed the diversity of human cultures. He can be considered a cinema revolutionary because of the transformative demand he has made of his films. He wanted his films to be different, to be provocative, and to stand outside established boundaries. They are.

Just as his therapeutic practices synthesized aspects from such diverse sources as shamanism and Freud, his cinema synthesized aesthetic movements as diverse as surrealism and folk art. This synthesizing gave his films the feel of distinct creations because the mix was very much his own. Since no one else has ever made or been able to copy a Jodorowsky film, one can rightly say that his films defy imitation. The reason for this lies in his intense personal belief in transformation. One would have to be a clone of Jodorowsky's personal history to copy his narrative structure and style. His originality as a filmmaker is rooted in his project of transformation.

If we measure the time spent by Jodorowsky on his various artistic pursuits, we can gauge their importance to him in a quantifiable (though not a qualitative) way. He spent twenty years working as a theater director (1948–68). He devoted some part of forty to fifty years to writing, starting with a play in 1948 and ending with a graphic novel/comic book in 2018. He spent less than fifteen years in cinema production. He spent the least amount of time in his life making films. And yet, his films are what he is best known for and for which he has a global audience. Why is this so?

First, his films carry a distinct stamp. While he was influenced by and has been compared to filmmakers such as Fellini and Buñuel, his work remains original. While situating his work in relationship to theirs helps define its content to some degree, it also carries a note of subordination. He remains "like" the others rather than his own person. This approach detracts from his achievement in filmmaking. Second, his films attracted media coverage that gave him a certain stature among cinéphiles. Third, his work in non-film art forms (other than comic books and graphic works) never attracted the kind of critical attention his films have. His work in theater, other than the Panic Movement in France, did not advance the art form in any significant way. Likewise, his books, while voluminous, were not critically heralded. His therapeutic works represent an outlier philosophy that is not taken seriously in psychology circles. As for his fame in the world of comic books and graphic novels, it is associated with a cult status shared with fans of his highly regarded illustrators and artists. His films are his greatest legacy.

Jodorowsky was a victim of two colliding forces—one external and the other internal. The external force was the structure of the film industry, in particular the lack of ownership of their art among its creative agents, who had no control over its dissemination. That control rested with business elements such as corporations, who could, as was the case with ABKCO Films, remove his films from circulation for decades. The internal force was auteurism. His non-auteur films were failures artistically, while his auteur films shone with genuine illumination. When the power of others collided with that of the self, his film career got sidetracked. If he could not make his own films, he made poor films or no films at all. This requirement to create only from within himself turned out to be a limitation, but one necessary for his growth as a filmmaker. His auteur films are an expression of the richness of his imagination, which fueled his creative agenda and infused his films with their idiosyncratic view of the human condition. While he allowed himself to be fully expressive of his art in his films, there was a cost to doing this. After his experience trying to sell *Endless Poetry* to distributors, he denounced the "Hollywood colonialization" of the industry in an interview attached to the film's DVD. He complained that the German distributor offered his company, Satori Films, a mere $20,000 for the German distribution rights, while the film cost $3 million to make. "How can an auteur cinema live?" he asks rhetorically. The uncompromising filmmaker is left standing outside the system in search of a small, yet appreciative audience.

His engagement with other artistic forms and his limited film production has lessened his importance in the eyes of film academics. Like all academics they prefer creativity to be linked to a single art form. Jodorowsky's commitment to artistic eclecticism has worked to keep him out of the upper echelons of auteur filmmakers. This book has attempted to show the connection between his various artistic creations and his films in order to highlight their interconnectivity and mutual inspiration. Because of academic commitment to disciplinary boundaries, the orthodox differentiation between various art forms and a narrow view of who has a legitimate right to comment on cinema, a written project that fully integrates all his creative work has yet to be accomplished. I can only speculate, but I suspect that when such a project of integration is completed, the world will discover an artistic master, whose unorthodoxy and eclecticism exhibit a surprising degree of unity.

The Man and His Words

Jodorowsky has given innumerable interviews in the span of his long career. Filmmakers, especially unusual ones with outlier personalities, develop followings of journalists and bloggers striving to channel him through the art of interviewing. Often seeking explanations for his imagery and his symbolism, interviewers get repeat answers from the master. The result is the manufacturing of a persona, some of which is authentic and some of which is inauthentic, inaccurate, and fanciful. One might say that Jodorowsky has imagined himself for his public in a way that corresponds with his films and their content. He presents these films as an extension of himself, as wondrous works of art and a form of holistic healing. The man we get from these interviews tends to be consistent from interview to interview, remaining both revealing and obtuse, while always intense and self-assured.

Jodorowsky is attracted to the interview because he can control its narrative and project the kind of persona that he thinks is proper. In researching his interviews, one can get swamped by their sheer number and repetitive content.

He offers answers that he considers to be definitive, but they are often open-ended and inconclusive. What he does convey is having had a magical life filled with deep emotions and great struggles. "I will continue making movies until I die, until my last moment, that's what I will be doing" is a statement he made in 2017, which is a typical example of his exaggeration and bravado (Bruder 2017). It seems very much an aspirational goal than a realistic one considering the complexity of getting a feature film made, the amount of creative energy and insight needed to produce a first-class script, and the physical challenges facing a nonagenarian working in numerous locations and on various sets. In an interview available as an extra on the DVD of *Endless Poetry*, he says that in spite of his old body aching, he gets "creative ecstasy" from making films.

Even if he never makes another film he does leave a cinematic legacy with a full and complete arc. Beginning with his early period (*Fando y Lis*) in the late 1960s, followed by his classical period from 1970 to 1990 (*El Topo, La montaña sagrada, Santa Sangre*), and concluding with his late period from 2013 to 2019 (*La danza de la realidad, Poesía sin fin, Psychomagic, A Healing Art*), he has evolved and matured as a filmmaker from the wildness and symbol-drenched surrealism of his classical period to the narrative power and emotional trauma of the late period. His legacy is one that has not been imitated by other filmmakers because his films are completely rooted in his personality and ideas. There is no one else like Jodorowsky, which makes his films original. They are complex narratives with a rich visual presentation.

Jodorowsky Has the Last Word

Excerpts from quotes in some of his numerous interviews serve as a tribute to the deeply rooted continuity in his thinking. They offer insight into a singular creative and intellectual journey that was very much his own. He deserves the last word using a few snippets, constructed into a kind of prose-poem with dates and sources.

Healing and Cinema

I think an artist can heal people. Art can do it. (Cobb 2007, 273)

Mime and Cinema

Mime deals with expression and movement in space; if you know mime you know exactly how to shoot a film. It was thanks to mime that I could make movies without having had any training. (Macnab 1999)

Money and Cinema

With *The Holy Mountain* I was trying to be totally honest. I had no dreams of making money or becoming famous . . . Films were like poetry to me, and I always used to say that I asked of movies what hippies ask of drugs. I was trying to make a film that would blow the mind. (Macnab 1999)

Movies are a commercial industry . . . Today a picture has value if it makes a lot of money. Myself, I declare I want to make a picture to lose money. Really! I want to lose money . . . Why's that? Because it is not the finality of art to make money." (Rose 2009)

Religion and Cinema

At the time I made *El Topo* I was meditating with a Buddhist Zen Monk and in *The Holy Mountain* I was very influenced by the Kabbala, Tantra . . . I was asking the picture the same of the religious act, the sacred books. [I thought that] cinema could be a way. The sacred way . . . . (Cobb 2007, 269)

Theater and Cinema

Theater is an urban ritual. Film is a global ritual. Theater is a momentary ritual in the present. Film lasts for a long time. It persists, leaves a trace. Theater happens for a city. Film happens for the planet. The world of theater is limited because of live actors. But film has everything. It's the most complete form of art that exists. (Kan 2018)

Theory and Cinema

There was an accident and it resonated with me: approaching the scene, witnessing this body transformed by the street car, seeing the reactions of the onlookers from different angles, then interacting with this man in a personal way. It stayed with me for some time. When I began to think of films I realized that I did not want to make compositions as much as I wanted to create accidents. I wanted to shoot the accidents and respond to them in their moment. (Nardone 2020, 5–6)

Wisdom and Cinema

Everything is constantly changing. So when a human being remains unchanged, like a rock, clinging to what he or she is throughout an entire lifetime, it's a tragedy. A human being has to be fluid, changing, expanding, developing, and at any given moment, has to ask, why am I suffering? Why does this bother me? Why am I searching for something? Why do I hate such and such thing? Why can't I forgive and why can't I liberate myself from this? All of my work is that, it's the development of a character who slowly but surely expands, self-actualizes, and reaches a higher spiritual level. My characters obtain wisdom. To arrive at such wisdom is to arrive at the joy of living. (Kan 2018)

On Aging and Cinema

I am alive and still making movies because of what's inside me. What else am I to do? It's a big, big joy to do what I do. Inside, I am ageless. I will continue making movies until I die. Until my last moment, that's what I will be doing. (Bruder 2017)

The Auteur Filmography of Alejandro Jodorowsky

***La Cravate* (*The Severed Heads*, 1957).** Color. 20 minutes. Starring: Denise Brossot, Rolande Polya, Alexandre Jodorowsky, Gaul Gilbert; Created by Saul Gilbert, Alejandre Jodorowsky, Ruth Michelly. Music: Edgar Bischoff.
    Viewable on YouTube: https://www.youtube.com/watch?v=H1rhIqZDs2Q
    In 2021 ABKCO Films released the film as an extra feature on both the Blu-ray and DVD discs of their 4K restoration of *Fando y Lis*.

***Teatro sin fin* (*Endless Theater*, 1965).** Director: Alejandro Jodorowsky. A collage of black-and-white film footage from the May 1965 Panic Movement four-hour performance of the play "Sacramental Melodrama." Black and white. 18 minutes with music and the original stage sound.

***Fando y Lis* (*Fando and Lis*, 1968).** Black and white. 96 minutes Spanish with English subtitles. Producers: Moshes and Samuel Rosenberg; Director: Alejandro Jodorowsky; Screenplay by Fernando Arrabal and Alejandro Jodorowsky; Cinematography: Reynoso y Corkidi; Music: Pepe Avila, Hector Morelli, and Mario Losua; Distribution: Cannon Releasing Corporation: 1970 theatrical release with English subtitles (82 minutes). In 1999 Fontana Films, an Australian company, released the film on DVD with a director's commentary. It was released again on DVD in 2007 by ABKCO Films in the full 96-minute version. The 2007 DVD version also includes the following: feature commentary by Alejandro Jodorowsky and on-camera interview; original theatrical trailer; and Louis Mouchet's interview with Jodorowsky from his 1994 documentary *La Constellation Jodorowsky*. *Fando and Lis* received a 4K digital restoration in 2016 and was released by ABKCO Films in March 2021 on a Blu-ray disc with the addition of his 1957 film, *Le Cravate*. Extra features include audio commentary by Alejandro Jodorowsky, "Jodorowsky Remembers *Fando y Lis*"; new interview filmed in Paris; newly filmed introduction with Richard Peña, Professor of Film Studies at Columbia University; *La Constellation Jodorowsky*, Louis Mouchet's feature-length documentary on the work of Alejandro Jodorowsky with appearances by Marcel Marceau, Peter Gabriel, Jean Giraud, and others; original trailer; image gallery.

El Topo (*The Mole*) (1970). Color. 124 min. 1:33:1 aspect ratio. In Spanish with English subtitles. Producers: Moshes and Saul Rosenberg, Roberto Viskin; Director: Alejandro Jodorowsky; Screenplay: Alejandro Jodorowsky; Cinematography: Rafael Corkidi; Editor: Frederico Landeros; Music: Alejandro Jodorowsky. The film was released in 2007 on DVD by ABKCO Films with extra features. In 2021 ABKCO Films released a 4K restoration of the film in both its original 1:33 aspect ratio and a 1.84:1 widescreen version. The bonus features include audio commentary by Alejandro Jodorowsky, "Jodorowsky Remembers El Topo"; a new interview filmed in Paris; newly filmed introduction with Richard Peña, Professor of Film Studies at Columbia University; a new interview with Brontis Jodorowsky, "The Father of Midnight Movies"; an archival interview with Jodorowsky filmed in 2007; original trailer; image gallery.

The Holy Mountain (*La montaña sacral*, 1973). Color. 113 minutes Executive Producer: Allen Klein; Producers: Robert Taicher, Roberto Viskin; Director: Alejandro Jodorowsky; Writer: Alejandro Jodorowsky; Cinematography: Rafael Corkidi; Music: Don Cherry, Ronald Frangipane, Alejandro Jodorowsky; Distribution: ABKCO Films. ABKCO released a DVD version in 2007 that included Jodorowsky's commentary on the Tarot and some deleted scenes plus a page from the script. The text on the DVD box claims the DVD has an "on-camera interview with Alejandro Jodorowsky," which it does not. There was a Blu-ray version released in 2011 and again in 2021. The 2021 Blu-ray contains an audio commentary by Alejandro Jodorowsky, "Jodorowsky remembers *The Holy Mountain*"; a new interview filmed in Paris; a newly filmed introduction with Richard Peña, Professor of Film Studies at Columbia University; an interview with Pablo Leder, reminiscing about his roles in *El Topo* and *The Holy Mountain*; "The A to Z of *The Holy Mountain*," a new video essay by writer Ben Cobb; plus previously available (2007 DVD) deleted scenes with director's commentary; a short film in which Jodorowsky explains the secrets of the Tarot; original trailer; image gallery.

Santa Sangre (*Holy Blood*) (1989). Color. 123 minutes. English. Producers: Claudio Argento, René Cardona Jr., Angelo Iacono, Anuar Badin; Director: Alejandro Jodorowsky; Writers: Claudio Argento, Alejandro Jodorowsky, Roberto

Leoni; Cinematography: Daniele Nannuzzi; Editor: Mauro Bonanni; Music: Simon Boswell; Distributors: Mainline Pictures and Expanded Entertainment. Issued in a VHS English-language version in 1990 by Republic Pictures Home Video, followed by a DVD and Blu-ray version in 2011 by Severin Films. This release had of extra material, including a Jodorowsky commentary/interview. The same firm then did a 4K restoration with material from the 2011 release that includes an audio commentary/interview with Alejandro Jodorowsky and journalist Alan Jones, "New Blood—Alejandro Jodorowsky on the restoration of *Santa Sangre*"; deleted scenes with optional director's commentary; theatrical trailer. Also included was a separate disc with the following: *Forget Everything You Have Ever Seen: The World of Santa Sangre*, a 96-minute documentary directed by David Gregory with Alejandro Jodorowsky, actors Axel Jodorowsky, Blanca Guerra, Thelma Tixou, Sabrina Dennison, Adán Jodorowsky, Elenka Tapia, Teo Tapia, Roberto Leoni, Simon Boswell, Sergio Arau and Greg Day; "Like A Phoenix," an interview with producer Claudio Argento; "Holy Blood," an interview with cinematographer Danielle Nannuzzi; "Mexican Magic," an interview with executive producer Angelo Iacono; "The Language of Editing," an interview with editor Mauro Bonanni; "Innocence in Horror," an interview with screenwriter Roberto Leoni; clips from the Santa Sangre thirtieth anniversary celebration at the Morbido Festival, Mexico City; "Goyo Cárdenas Spree Killer," a documentary on the real-life inspiration for *Santa Sangre*; Jodorowsky 2003 Interview; Jodorowsky on Stage Q & A; " Echeck," a short by Adán Jodorowsky; Simon Boswell interview with Jodorowsky; "Close Your Eyes," a Simon Boswell Music Video.

La dansa de la realidad (*The Dance of Reality*, 2013). Color. 133 minutes. Spanish. Producers: Michel Seydoux, Alejandro Jodorowsky and Moises Cosio; Executive Producer: Xavier Guerrero Yamamoto; Director: Alejandro Jodorowsky; Writer: Alejandro Jodorowsky; Cinematography: Jean-Marie Dreujou; Editor: Maryline Monthieux; Music: Adán Jodorowsky and Jon Handelsman; Costume Design: Pascale Montandon-Jodorowsky; Production Companies: Caméra One (France) and Le Soleil Films (Chile); Distribution: Pathé and ABKCO Films. Released on DVD, Blu-ray, and digitally in 2014 by ABKCO Films. The discs contain three extra features: Alejandro Jodorowsky discussing the film, under the title "What is Reality?"; Brontis Jodorowsky discussing playing his grandfather, under the title "My Father's Father"; Pascale Montandon-Jodorowsky discussing costume design, under the title "Art of the Costume."

***Poesía sin fin* (*Endless Poetry*, 2016)**. Color. 128 minutes. Spanish and English, 35 mm. Producer: Xavier Guerrero Yamamoto; Executive Producers: Alejandro Jodorowsky et al. (12 others!); Director: Alejandro Jodorowsky; Writer: Alejandro Jodorowsky; Cinematography: Christopher Doyle; Editor: Maryline Monthieux; Music: Adán Jodorowsky; Production Design: Alejandro Jodorowsky; Costume Design: Pascale Montandon-Jodorowsky; Production Companies: Satori Films (France), Le Soleil Films y Le Pacte (Chile); Distributor: ABKCO Films. DVD and Blu-ray release 2016 (123 minutes) by ABKCO Films in Spanish with English subtitles. Extra features on the DVD include "On the Set of *Endless Poetry*," which includes various scenes and how they were shot; "Conversations between Takes" that include Alejandro Jodorowsky defending auteur cinema; Adán Jodorowsky talking about life on the set; Alejandro Jodorowsky and Xavier Guerrero Yamamoto talking about the film's release; "Alejandro Jodorowsky and the Seagulls," a short of Jodorowsky feeding seagulls from the window of a seaside hotel in Nice. All three films are attributed to Pascale Montandon-Jodorowsky.

***Psychomagic, A Healing Art* (2019)**. Color. 104 minutes. 35 mm. Spanish, French, and Spanish with English subtitles. Producers: Guy Avivi and Xavier Guerrero Yamamoto; Director: Alejandro Jodorowsky; Writer: Alejandro Jodorowsky; Music: Adán Jodorowsky; Cinematography: Pascale Montandon-Jodorowsky; Editors: Alejandro Jodorowsky and Maryline Monthieux; Production Company: Satori Films; Distributor: ABKCO Films. Released in the United States on Alamo on Demand streaming services (August 1, 2020) and on Blu-ray by ABKCO films in the 4K Restoration Collection (August 26, 2020). The film is also available individually on DVD and Blu-ray and on various other streaming services like Amazon.com and Apple TV.

Filmography (Other)

La Constellation Jodorowsky (1994) is a documentary directed by Louis Mouchet with interviews with Alejandro Jodorowsky, Jean "Moebius" Giraud, Fernando Arrabal, Peter Gabriel, and Marcel Marceau in French and Spanish. Released by Neovision and available on Vimeo.

https://vimeo.com/ondemand/jodorowsky. Accessed May 28, 2021. Also available on 2021 Blu-ray version of *Fando y Lis* (ABKCO Films).

***Jodorowsky's Dune* (2013)** is a documentary by Frank Pavich which contains interviews with Jodorowsky, Michel Seydoux, H. R. Giger, Chris Foss, Nicolas Winding Refn, Amanda Lear, and Richard Stanley. It is distributed by Sony Pictures Classics. The film is 90 minutes. You are able to stream *Jodorowsky's Dune* by renting or purchasing on Google Play, Vudu, Amazon Instant Video, and iTunes. https://www.youtube.com/watch?v=BNGzBhWwmEE

Bibliography

Abrams, Simon. 2020. "Psychomagic: A Healing Art." August 7. https://www.rogerebert.com/reviews/psychomagic-a-healing-art-movie-review-2020. Accessed January 24, 2022.

Agar, Chris. 2021. "How Much Dune Cost to Make (& How Much It Needs for Box Office Success)." *Screenrant.com*. October 29. https://screenrant.com/dune-movie-2021-budget-cost-box-office-breakeven/. Accessed February 8, 2022.

Agence France-Presse. 2021. "Film Storyboards for Doomed 1970s Version of Dune Sell for Euros 2.7 m." *The Guardian*. November 22. https://www.theguardian.com/film/2021/nov/22/film-storyboards-for-doomed-1970s-version-of-dune-sell-for-266m. Accessed November 24, 2021.

Aldama, Frederick Luis. 2020. "Our Republic of Comics: An Introduction." In Frederick Luis Aldama, ed. *The Oxford Handbook of Comic Book Studies*. Oxford: Oxford University Press. xi–xxiii.

Amorosi, A. D. 2020. "In Conversation: Alejandro Jodorowsky on the Intersection of Art and Healing." *Floodmagazine.com*. October 15. https://floodmagazine.com/81478/in-conversation-alejandro-jodorowsky-psychomagic/. Accessed January 24, 2022.

Aruzuno, Lee. 2009. "Jodorowsky's Dune And The Greatest Films Ever Made." *The Quietus.com*. October 16. https://thequietus.com/articles/02992-jodorowsky-s-dune-and-the-greatest-films-never-made?page=1. Accessed August 20, 2022.

Barber, Nicholas. 2019. "Is Jodorowsky's Dune the Greatest Film Never Made? A New Film of the Classic Sci-fi Novel Is Due in 2020, But Will It Match up to Alejandro Jodorowsky's Surreal and Legendary Vision?" March 14. https://www.bbc.com/culture/article/20190312-is-jodorowskys-dune-the-greatest-film-never-made?ocid=ww.social.link.email. Accessed October 4, 2021.

Barthes, Roland. 1991. *Camera Lucida: Reflections on Photography*. New York: Hill and Wang.

Benson, Eric. 2014. "The Psychomagical Realism of Alejandro Jodorowsky." *New York Times*. March 14. https://www.nytimes.com/2014/03/16/magazine/the-psychomagical-realism-of-alejandro-jodorowsky.html. Accessed December 1, 2021.

Biesenbach, Klaus. 2012. "Alejandro Jodorowsky." *Interview* 42 (2): 114–15.

Bitel, Anton. 2016. "Alejandro Jodorowsky: Pulling Rusty Brains Out of Burrows to Dimensions Never Imagined." *Sight and Sound*. May 14. https://www2.bfi.org.uk/news-opinion/sight-sound-magazine/interviews/alejandro-jodorowsky-pulling-rusty-brains-out-burrows. Accessed October 27, 2021.

Blanc-Hoang, Henri-Simon. 2019. "Meta-performance and Jewish Identity in Alejandro Jodorowsky's *The Dance of Reality*." *Postscript* 38 (2/3): 70–5. https://www.proquest.com/docview/2350105352/fulltext/DD15DACBD73C4CE8PQ/1?accountid=9838. Accessed January 13, 2022.

Boxofficemojo.com. 2014. "The Dance of Reality." https://www.boxofficemojo.com/title/tt2301592.

Boxofficemojo.com. 2017. "Endless Poetry." https://www.boxofficemojo.com/release/rl3825436161/weekend/. Accessed January 3, 2022.

Boxofficemojo.com. 2022. "Dune." https://www.boxofficemojo.com/title/tt1160419/. Accessed February 8, 2022.

Bradshaw, Peter. 2015. "The Dance of Reality Review—My Father the Hero." *The Guardian*. August 20. https://www.theguardian.com/film/2015/aug20/the-dance-of-reality-review-my-father-the-hero. Accessed December 21, 2021.

Bradshaw, Peter. 2017. "Endless Poetry Review—Jodorowsky's Shocking Thrill Ride Into His Past." January 5. *The Guardian*. https://www.theguardian.com/culture/2017/jan/05/endless-poetry-review-jodorowskys-shocking-thrill-ride-into-his-past. Accessed August 22, 2022.

Bradshaw, Peter. 2020. "El Topo Review—Jodorowsky's Weird World of Occult Psychedelia." *The Guardian*. January 9. https://www.theguardian.com/film/2020/jan/09/el-topo-review-alejandro-jodorowsky. Accessed May 15, 2021.

Breckenridge, Adam. 2015. "A Path Less Traveled: Rethinking Spirituality in the Films of Alejandro Jodorowsky." *Journal of Religion & Film* 19 (2): 1–24. https://digitalcommons.unomaha.edu/jrf/vol19/iss2/. Accessed October 4, 2021.

Breckenridge, Adam. 2017. "Endless Poetry (2017)," directed by Alejandro Jodorowsky. *Journal of Religion and Film* 21 (2). https://digitalcommons.unomaha.edu/cgi/viewcontent.cgi?article=1932&context=jrf. Accessed January 2, 2022.

British Library. 2014. "Alejandro Jodorowsky: Film, Comics and Conversation." Interview video. 80 min. https://www.youtube.com/watch?v=sJHdOxgS-Vg. Accessed October 10, 2021.

Buder, Emily. 2017. "'Endless Poetry': Why Alejandro Jodorowsky Thinks You Should 'Make Movies to Lose Money.'" *Nofilmschool.com*. July 11. https://nofilmschool.com/2017/07/alejandro-jodorowsky-interview-endless-poetry. Accessed January 3, 2022.

Burgos, Fernando. 1984. "Modernidad y neovanguardia hispanoamericanas." *Revista de Estudios Hispánicos* 18 (2): 207–21. https://www.proquest.com/docview/1300116571/fulltextPDF/115187A58E434818PQ/1?accountid=9838.

Cabrejo Cobián, José Carlos. 2019a. *Jodorowsky: el cine viaje*. Lima: Universidad de Lima.

Cabrejo Cobián, José Carlos. 2019b. "Budismo, hinduismo y la mutación del subgénero de terror *slasher* en la película *Santa sangre* de Alejandro Jodorowsky." *Diseminaciones: Revista de Investigación y Crítica en Humanidades y Ciencias*

Sociales 2 (4): 157–74. https://revistas.uaq.mx/index.php/diseminaciones/article/view/21. Accessed November 18, 2021.

Cabrejo, José Carlos. 2020. "Sobre las etiquetas de género en tres películas de Jodorowsky: Poesía sin fin, La danza de la realidad y Fando y Lis." *Ventana indiscrete* 23: 76–8. https://revistas.ulima.edu.pe/index.php/Ventana_indiscreta/article/view/4850. Accessed August 22, 2022.

Canby, Vincent. 1971. "Is El Topo a Con?" *New York Times* 23: May D1. https://www.nytimes.com/1971/05/23/archives/is-el-topo-a-con-is-el-topo-a-con.html. Accessed December 1, 2021.

Cannes. 1973. https://web.archive.org/web/20160304194014/http://www.festival-cannes.fr/en/archives/1973/juryLongFilm.html. Accessed September 27, 2021.

Cerdán, Josetxo and Miguel Fernández Labayen. 2009. "Arty Exploitation, Cool Cult, and the Cinema of Alejandro Jodorowsky." In Victoria Ruétalo and Dolores Tierney, eds. *Lasploitation, Exploitation Cinemas, and Latin America*. New York and London: Routledge. 102–14.

Christies. 2019. https://www.christies.com/lot/lot-moebius-6236976/. Accessed June 21, 2021.

Church, David. 2007a. "Review of Ben Cobb, Anarchy and Alchemy: The Films of Alejandro Jodorowsky." *Journal of Surrealism and the Americas* 1 (1): 68–71.

Church, David. 2007b. "Alejandro Jodorowsky." *Senses of Cinema No. 42*. February. https://www.sensesofcinema.com/2007/great-directors/jodorowsky/. Accessed September 29, 2021.

Church, David. 2011. "Freakery, Cult Films, and the Problem of Ambivalence." *Journal of Film and Video* 63 (1): 3–17. https://muse.jhu.edu/article/414644. Accessed August 2, 2021.

Cobb, Ben. 2007. *Anarchy and Alchemy: The Films of Alejandro Jodorowsky*. Creation Books.

Cousineau, Phil. 1990. *The Hero's Journey: Joseph Campbell on His Life and Work*. San Francisco: HarperSanFrancisco.

Dalton, Stephen. 2013. "Cannes Film Review: Jodorowsky's Dune." May 19. https://www.hollywoodreporter.com/news/general-news/jodorowskys-dune-cannes-review-525204/. Accessed August 22, 2021.

Di Nobile, Antonella. 2016. "Il folle, l'androgino e l'ibrido: elementi grotteschi e carnevaleschi ne *L'Incal* di Jodorowsky e Moebius." *Between* 12: 1–13. https://www.betweenjournal.it/. Accessed December 5, 2021.

Dollar, Steve. 2014. "Reality is Relative." *The Washington Post*. 22 May. E12.

Dossey, Evan. 2020. "Psychomagic, a Healing Art." *midwestfilmjournal.com*. https://midwestfilmjournal.com/2020/08/07/psychomagic-a-healing-art/. Accessed January 14, 2022.

Ebert, Roger. 1972. "El Topo." https://www.rogerebert.com/reviews/el-topo-1972. Accessed July 27, 2021.

Ebert, Roger. 1989. "Interview with Alejandro Jodorowsky." https://www.rogerebert.com/interviews/interview-with-alexandro-jodorowsky-1989. Accessed September 30, 2021.

Ebert, Roger. 1990 "Santa Sangre." June 27. https://www.rogerebert.com/reviews/santa-sangre-1990. Accessed November 17, 2021.

Ebert, Roger. 2003. "Santa Sangre." August 31. https://www.rogerebert.com/reviews/great-movie-santa-sangre-1989. Accessed November 17, 2021.

Evans, Neil. 2014. "Filmmaker Retrospective: The Surreal Cinema of Alejandro Jodorowsky." *Taste of Cinema*. September 12, 2014. http://www.tasteofcinema.com/2014/filmmaker-retrospective-the-surreal-cinema-of-alejandro-jodorowsky/2/. Accessed November 10, 2021.

Galarza, Brenda Arriaga. 2006. "Criticas Extrínsecas: Pelicula La Montaña Sagrada de Alejandro Jodorowsky." MA Thesis. Universidad Autónoma de Neuvo León. http://eprints.uanl.mx/20380/1/1020152060.pdf. Accessed September 7, 2021.

Garcia, Estevão. 2012. "Le Mexique d'Alejandro Jodorowsky dans *La Montagne sacrée*." Translated into French by Sylvie Debs from the Portuguese. *Les Cinémas d'Amérique latine*. 20: 4–23. https://doi.org/10.4000/cinelatino.412. Accessed September 8, 2021.

Garcia, Luis Eduardo Veloso. 2014. "Caracteristicas surrealistas no filme a montanha sagrada, de Alejandro Jodorowsky." *ArReDia* 3 (5): 35–46. https://ojs.ufgd.edu.br/index.php/arredia/article/view/2604/2055. Accessed October 2, 2021.

Gleiberman, Owen. 2021. "'Dune' Review: Spectacular and Engrossing . . . Until It Isn't." *Variety*. September 3. https://variety.com/2021/film/reviews/dune-review-spectacular-and-engrossing-until-it-isnt-1235051928/. Accessed October 26, 2021.

Granholm, Kennet. 2015. "The Occult and Comics" in Christopher Partridge, ed. *The Occult World*. Oxford: Routledge. 499–508. https://www.academia.edu/11761144/The_Occult_and_Comics?auto=citations&from=cover_page. Accessed October 29, 2021.

Greenfield, Robert. 1972. "Alejandro Jodorowsky's Magic Mountain: On Location with Director Alexandro Jodorowsky, the Creator of 'El Topo,' for His New Film 'The Holy Mountain.'" *Rolling Stone*. June 22. https://www.rollingstone.com/movies/movie-news/jodorowskys-magic-mountain-on-location-with-the-creator-of-el-topo-231419/. Accessed September 1, 2021.

Groensteen, Thierry. 2014. "Narration as Supplement: An Archaeology of Infra-Narrative Foundations of Comics." (orig. pub. 1988). In Ann Miller and Bart Beaty, eds. *The French Comics Theory Reader*. Leuven: Leuven University Press. 163–81.

Guida, Jeremy. 2015. "Media Review: Producing and Explaining Charisma: A Case Study of the Films of Alejandro Jodorowsky." *Journal of the American Academy of Religion* 83 (2): 537–53.

Hoberman, J. 1983. "*El Topo*: Through the Wasteland of the Counterculture." In J. Hoberman and Jonathan Rosenbaum, eds. *Midnight Movies*. New York: Harper & Row. 77–109.

Houdassine, Ismaël. 2014. "La réalite se transforme, au fur et á mesure que le récit se dirige dans un univers composé de mirages et de reveries." *Séquences: La revue de cinema No. 289.* mars–avril, 32–3. https://www.erudit.org/fr/. Accessed August 31, 2021.

IMDB. 2013. "Dance of Reality." https://www.imdb.com/title/tt2301592/.

James, Caryn. 1990. "A Family That Could Drive You Crazy." *The New York Times.* April 20. Section C, 12. https://www.nytimes.com/1990/04/20/movies/review-film-a-family-that-could-drive-you-crazy.html. Accessed November 8, 2021.

Jaworzyn, Stefan. 1990. "The Rat Will Improvise—Alejandro Jodorowsky." *Monthly Film Bulletin* 57 (675): 117. https://www.proquest.com/docview/1305836474?accountid=9838&parentSessionId=ef6vHN1gscxdXd3vTk61nvAegsaGPyEF%2Fae%2BDaHvwAs%3D&pq-origsite=primo. Accessed February 17, 2022.

Jodorowsky, Alejandro. 1971. *El Topo: A Book of the Film.* New York: Douglas/Links.

Jodorowsky, Alejandro. 1985. "Dune: Le Film Que Vous Ne Verrez Jamais." *Métal Hurlant* No.107. Paris: Les humanoïdes associés (16-page detachable supplement) and "Dune: The Film You Will Never See." http://www.duneinfo.com/unseen/jodorowsky. Accessed October 7, 2021.

Jodorowsky, Alejandro. 1990. *Santa Sangre.* VHS. Republic Pictures Home Video.

Jodorowsky, Alejandro. 2007a. *El Topo.* DVD. ABKCO Films.

Jodorowsky, Alejandro. 2007b. *Fando y Lis.* El Topo DVD. ABKCO Films.

Jodorowsky, Alejandro. 2007c. *The Holy Mountain.* DVD. ABKCO Films.

Jodorowsky, Alejandro. 2008. *The Spiritual Journey of Alejandro Jodorowsky.* Translated by Joseph Rowe. Rochester: Park Street Press.

Jodorowsky, Alejandro. 2009. *La danza de la realidad.* 2nd ed. Madrid: Ediciones Siruela.

Jodorowsky, Alejandro. 2010. *Psychomagic: The Transformative Power of Shamanistic Psychotherapy.* Rochester: Inner Traditions.

Jodorowsky, Alejandro. 2013. *The Dance of Reality.* Blu-ray. ABKCO Films.

Jodorowsky, Alejandro. 2015. *Where the Bird Sings Best.* Translated by Alfred MacAdam. New York: Restless Books.

Jodorowsky, Alejandro. 2016a. *Poesía sin fin* (Endless Poetry). Sartori Films.

Jodorowsky, Alejandro. 2016b. Twitter June 27. https://twitter.com/alejodorowsky/status/747378734521520128. Accessed January 3, 2022.

Jodorowsky, Alejandro. 2019. *Psychomagic, a Healing Art.* Blu-ray. ABKCO Films.

Jodorowsky, Alejandro. 2021. "The Incal - The Movie." *Humanoids Inc.* November 4. https://www.youtube.com/watch?v=1DkxB75CNvA. Accessed February 13, 2022.

Joyce, Samuel. 2015. "Jodorowsky Crowdfunding to Complete 'Endless Poetry.'" *Screen Daily.* August 11. https://www.screendaily.com/news/jodorowsky-crowdfunding-to-complete-endless-poetry/5091513.article. Accessed January 3, 2022.

Jung, C. G. 1974. *Dreams.* Translated by R. F. C. Hull. Princeton: Princeton University Press.

Kahn, Luis Aránguiz. 2012. "Entre el cuerpo y las místicas: interacción del judeo-cristianismo en dos cuentos de Alejandro Jodorowsky." *Cuadernos Judaicos* 29: 222–39.

Kan, Alianna. 2018. "Buy High, Sell Cheap: An Interview with Alejandro Jodorowsky." *The Paris Review*. March 8. https://www.theparisreview.org/blog/2018/03/08/buy-high-sell-cheap-an-interview-with-alejandro-jodorowsky/.

Kannas, Alexia. 2019. "The Italian Giallo" in Ernest Mathijs and Jamie Sexton, *The Routledge Companion to Cult Cinema*, Oxford and New York: Routledge, 76–84.

Kastrenakes, Jacob. 2015. "Alejandro Jodorowsky Will Give you Fake Money for Backing His New Film on Kickstarter." *The Verge*. February 16. https://www.theverge.com/2015/2/16/8047885/alejandro-jodorowsky-will-give-you-fake-money-for-backing-his-new.

Kelin, T. E. D. 1974. "They Kill Animals and They Call It Art." *The New York Times*. January 13. https://www.nytimes.com/1974/01/13/archives/they-kill-animals-and-they-call-it-art-more-and-more-directors-are.html. Accessed September 29, 2021.

Kenny, Glen. 2020. "'Psychomagic, a Healing Art' Review: Introducing Surrealist Therapy." *New York Times*. August 7. https://www.nytimes.com/2020/08/06/movies/psychomagic-a-healing-art-review.html. Accessed July 18, 2021.

Kerik, Claudia. 2018. "Childhood Chained: Fernando Arrabal and His Theatre of the Absurd." *Signos Literarios* XIV (27): 106–56.

Kermode, Mark. 2021. "Dune Review—Denis Villeneuve's Sci-fi Epic Gets Off to an Electrifying Start." *The Guardian*. October 24. https://www.theguardian.com/film/2021/oct/24/dune-review-denis-villeneuve-timothee-chalamet-zendaya-oscar-isaac. Accessed October 26, 2021.

Kickstarter.com. 2015. "Poetry Without End." https://www.kickstarter.com/projects/276667448/jodorowskys-new-film-endless-poetrypoesia-sin-fin. Accessed December 28, 2021.

Kickstarter.com. 2016. "Jodorowsky's New Film ENDLESS POETRY (Poesia Sin Fin)." https://Kickstarter.com/projects/276667448/jodorowskys-new-film-endless-poetrypoesia-sin-fin?ref=nav_search&result=project&term=%20endless%20poetry. Accessed January 3, 2020.

Kohn, Eric. 2020. "'Psychomagic' Review: Alejandro Jodorowsky Delivers His Solution for All of Humanity's Pain." *Indie Wire*. August 5. https://www.indiewire.com/2020/08/psychomagic-a-healing-art-review-1234578278/. Accessed January 12, 2022.

Kudláč, Martin. 2017. "In *Endless Poetry*, Alejandro Jodorowski Continues to Amaze." *ScreenAnarchy.com*. July 13. http://screenanarchy.com/2017/07/review-in-endless-poetry-alejandro-jodorowsky-continues-to-amaze.html and https://www.academia.edu/35150603/The_Cinematic_Aesthetics_of_Psychomagical_Realism_in_Alejandro_Jodorowsky_s_Endless_Poetry.

Leoni, Roberto. 2019. "When I Wrote *Santa Sangre*." https://www.imdb.com/title/tt11336028/mediaviewer/rm4261514241/?ref_=tt_ov_i and https://www.youtube.com/watch?v=UK3RwKSUcRU

Leonte, Tudor. 2021. "Taika Waititi Will Adapt Ground-Breaking Jodorowsky Comic The Incal." *Superherohype.com*. November 4. https://www.superherohype.com/

movies/507323-taika-waititi-will-adapt-ground-breaking-jodorowsky-comic-the-incal. Accessed February 8, 2022.

Lim, Dennis. 2013. "Cannes 2013: Chile's Onetime Cult Kind Still the Wizard of Weird." *Los Angeles Times*. May 16. https://www.latimes.com/entertainment/movies/moviesnow/la-et-mn-alejandro-jodorowsky-dance-reality-cannes-20130519-story.html. Accessed November 30, 2021.

Lindstrom, Naomi. 2013. "La Expressión Profética y Apocalíptica en la Producción de Alejandro Jodorowsky." *Chasqui: revista de literatura latinoamericana* 42 (2): 125–33. http://www.jstor.org/stable/43589568. Accessed July 31, 2021.

Macnab, Geoffrey. 1999. "Video: Tarot and Toads in Coats: Alejandro Jodorowsky Talks About Making 'The Holy Mountain,' a Film Financed by John Lennon That Saved Him from Therapy." *Sight and Sound* 9 (6): 58–9.

Marques, Tatiana Lee. 2014. "Climbing The Holy Mountain—Alejandro Jodorowsky's Mystical Cinema/Subindo a Montanha Sagrada—O cinema mistico de Alejandro Jodorowsky." *CROMA* 4: 217. https://link.gale.com/apps/doc/A379982355/IFME?u=anon~7230824&sid=googleScholar&xid=9c446711. Accessed July 12, 2021.

Martin, Kenneth. 2009. "The Spiritual Journey of Alejandro Jodorowsky: The Creator of *El Topo* (a review)." *Arizona Journal of Hispanic Cultural Studies* 13: 206–7. https:/doi.org/10.1353/hcs.0.0061.

Martin, Kenneth. 2018. "Mexico City, Koans, and the Zen Buddhist Master: Alejandro Jodorowsky, Ejo Takata and the Fundamental Lesson of the Death of the Intellect." *Transmodernity: Journal of Peripheral Cultural Production of the Luso-Hispanic World.* Fall Special Issue: 114–25. https://doi.org/10.5070/T483041154. Accessed July 29, 2021.

Massmann, Stefanie. 2005. "Arbol genealógico y álbum de familia: dos figuras de la memoria en relatos de immigrantes judíos." *Estudios filolócos* 40: 131–7. http://dx.doi.org/10.4067/S0071-17132005000100009.

Melbye, David. 2010. *Landscape Allegory in Cinema: From Wilderness to Wasteland*. New York: Palgrave Macmillan.

Melia, Matthew. 2019. "Landscape, Imagery and Symbolism in Alejandro Jodorowsky's 'El Topo.'" In Lee Broughton, ed. *Reframing Cult Westerns: From The Magnificent Seven to The Hateful Eight*. London: Bloomsbury Academic. 93–110. https://www.bloomsbury.com/uk/reframing-cult-westerns-9781501343490. Accessed August 2, 2021.

Melnyk, George. 2016. "Surrealism in the Autobiographical Cinema of Alejandro Jodorowsky." *Journal of Surrealism and the Americas* 9 (1): 62–6.

Melnyk, George. 2017. "Octogenarian Carnival: Psychomagic and Phantasmagoria in Alejandro Jodorowsky's Autobiographical Film 'The Dance of Reality.'" *Film International* 15 (3): 56–65.

Melnyk, George. 2018. "The Transcontinental Cinema of Alejandro Jodorowsky: Surrealism, Psycho-Magic, Metagenealogy and the Art of Self-Exile." *Film International* 16 (4): 59–70.

Mouchet, Louis. 1994. *La (The) Constellation Jodorowsky*. Documentary film.
Nadeau, Maurice. 1967. *The History of Surrealism*, Translated from the French by Richard Howard. New York: Collier.
Nardonne, Michael. 2020 "Alejandro Jodorowsky." *Hobomagazine.com*. http://www.hobomagazine.com/interviews/alejandro-jodorowsky-2/. Accessed August 30, 2021.
Neustadt, Robert. 1996. "Las prerrogations de la imaginación: una conversación con Alejandro Jodorowsky." *Confluencia* 11 (2): 203–12.
Neustadt, Robert. 1999. "Alejandro Jodorowsky: Reiterating Chaos, Rattling the Cage of Representation." In Robert Neustadt, ed. *(Con)Fusing Signs and Postmodern Positions: Spanish American Performance, Experimental Writing, and the Critique of Political Confusion*. Milton Park, Abingdon: Francis and Taylor. 81–126.
New York Times. 1970. "'Fando and Lis,' a Film Calculated to Shock." February 3. https://www.nytimes.com/1970/02/03/archives/fando-and-lis-a-film-calculated-to-shock.html#:~:text=%22EVERY%20cinematographic%20trick%20was%20avoided,stripped%20naked%2C%20tortured%20and%20beaten.&text=Repeatedly%20Fando%20is%20misled%20into,to%20serve%20and%20humiliate%20Lis. Accessed February 9, 2022.
Outlaw, Kofi. 2021. "Dune Opening Weekend Box Office Revised Up To $41 Million." October 25. https://comicbook.com/movies//news/dune-opening-weekend-box-office-revised-41-million-domestic-worldwide/. Accessed October 26, 2021.
Pavich, Frank. 2013. *Jodorowsky's Dune*. Blu-ray.
Pecotic, David. 2014. "Mountains Analogous? The Academic Urban Legend of Alejandro Jodorowsky's Cult Film Adaptation of René Daumal's Esoteric Novel." *Journal for the Academic Study of Religion* 27 (3): 367–87.
POV (Point of View). 2004. "A Delirious Surrealist: Alejandro Jodorowsky." June 24. Issue 55. http://povmagazine.com/articles/view/a-delirious-surrealist-alejandro-jodorowsky. Accessed May 16, 2021.
Ramanchandran, Naman. 2020. "Cult Filmmaker Alejandro Jodorowsky Faces Unpaid $200,000 Loan From 2016 Film 'Endless Poetry.'" *Variety*. August 7. https://variety.com/2020/film/global/jodorowsky-unpaid-loan-endless-poetry-1234727763/. Accessed September 9, 2021.
Roberts, James. 2017. "The Sublime Absurdity of *Endless Poetry*." Glidemagazine.com. July 21. https://glidemagazine.com/189116/endless-poetry-review/. Accessed August 22, 2022.
Rose, Steve. 2009. "Lennon, Manson and Me: The Psychedelic Cinema of Alejandro Jodorowsky." *The Guardian*. November 14. https://www.theguardian.com/film/2009/nov/14/alejandro-jodorowosky-el-topo. Accessed June 19, 2021.
Rosmaninho, Joao. 2016. "Citypunk: Transgeographies in Science Fiction Comics." In Erin Vander Wall, ed. *Edgelands: A Collection of Monstrous Geographies*. London: Inter-Disciplinary Press. 107–14. https://core.ac.uk/download/pdf/132798626.pdf.

Rottenberg, Josh. 2021. "'Dune: Part One' Ending Explained: Where Could a Sequel go from Here?" *The Los Angeles Times*. October 22. https://www.latimes.com/entertainment-arts/movies/story/2021-10-22/dune-part-one-ending-explained-sequel-hbo. Accessed October 26, 2021.

Samson, Jacques. 2014. "Modern Strategies for Pictorial Enunciation in Comics." In Ann Miller and Bart Beaty, eds. *The French Comics Theory Reader*. Leuven: Leuven University Press. 147–62.

Santos, Alessandra. 2017. *The Holy Mountain*. New York: Columbia University Press.

Sartori Films. 2016. *Poesía sin fin*. Press Release. https://medias.unifrance.org/medias/210/146/168658/presse/poesia-sin-fin-dossier-de-presse-anglais.pdf. Accessed August 22, 2022.

Schechtman, Marya. 1996. *The Constitution of Selves*. Ithaca: Cornell University Press.

Schjeldahl, Peter. 1971. "Should "El Topo" Be Elevated to The Tops?." *New York Times*. June 6 D11. https://www.nytimes.com/1971/06/06/archives/should-el-topo-be-elevated-to-el-tops.html. Accessed December 2, 2021.

Scott, A. O. 2014 "Family Memoir as Dreamscape." May 22. Print version May 23, 2014, Section C. 1. https:/ 05/23/movies/the-dance-of-reality-jodorowskys-comeback-film.html /www.nytimes.com/2014/. Accessed December 1, 2021.

Scott, A. O. 2017. "Review: *Endless Poetry*, Alejandro Jodorowsky's Surreal Self-Portrait." *New York Times*. July 13. https://www.nytimes.com/2017/07/13/movies/review-endless-poetry-alejandro-jodorowskys-surreal-self-portrait.html. Accessed August 22, 2022.

Seitz, Matt Zoller. 2007. "Modern Life, in All Its Mystery and Madness." *The New York Times*. April 18. https://www.nytimes.com/2007/04/18/movies/18moun.html. Accessed September 30, 2021.

Sharf, Zack. 2020. "Jodorowsky Reviews Villeneuve's 'Dune' Trailer: 'Very Well Done' but 'Everything Is Predictable.'" *Indiewire*. September 15. https://www.indiewire.com/2020/09/jodorowsky-reviews-villeneuve-dune-trailer-predictable-1234586462/. Accessed October 26, 2021.

Sobczynski, Peter. 2014 "The Dance of Reality." May 23. https://www.rogerebert.com/reviews/the-dance-of-reality-2014. Accessed November 30, 2021.

Susik, Abigail. 2021. "The Alchemy of Surrealist Presence in Alejandro Jodorowsky's *The Holy Mountain*." In Kristoffer Noheden and Abigail Susik, eds. *Surrealism and Films after 1945*. Manchester: Manchester University Press. https://www.manchesterhive.com/view/9781526150011/9781526150011.00018.xml. Accessed August 20, 2022.

Treviño, Jesús Salvador. 1979. "The New Mexican Cinema." *Film Quarterly* 32 (3): 26–37. https://www.jstor.org/stable/1212204. Accessed September 28, 2021.

Verrone, William. 2012. *The Avant-Garde Feature Film: A Critical History*, Jefferson: McFarland.

Visser, Margaret. 2002. *Beyond Fate*. Toronto: Anansi.

Weiler, A. H. 1973. "'Niger' Will Flow on Film." *New York Times*. May 27. 103. https://www.nytimes.com/1973/05/27/archives/niger-will-flow-on-film-niger-flows-on-film.html. Accessed October 18, 2021.

Weinstein, Max. 2020. "Is Alejandro Jodorowsky's "Psychomagic" Healing Film or Filmed Healing? Maybe It's Both." *Nofilmschool.com*. August 26. https://nofilmschool.com/alejandro-jodorowsky-psychomagic-interview. Accessed January 24, 2022.

Weiss, Jason. 1999. "An Interview with Alejandro Jodorowsky." *Raintaxi.com*. https://www.raintaxi/an-interview-with-alejandro-jodorowsky. Accessed August 31, 2021.

Weston, Christopher. 2021. "How Much Did it Cost to Make Dune? Budget Explored." October 25. https://www.hitc.com/en-gb/2021/10/25/how-much-did-it-cost-to-make-dune/. Accessed October 30, 2021.

Wilkins, Budd. 2020. "Review: *Psychomagic, a Healing Art* Is a Moving Look at Therapeutic Interventions." *Slantmagazine.com*. August 4. https://www.slantmagazine.com/film/review-psychomagic-a-healing-art-is-a-moving-look-at-therapeutic-interventions/. Accessed January 24, 2022.

Index

Alchemist (The)   69–72, 74–7, 89, 114
alchemy   66–7
Anarchy and Alchemy: The Films of Alejandro Jodorowsky (Cobb)   3, 8
anti-Semitism   7, 14, 61, 125, 126, 131, 134, 154
Antología pánica (Jodorowsky)   67
Argento, Claudio   97–9
Arrabal, Fernando   29
Ascent of Mount Carmel (St. John of the Cross)   63

Benson, Eric   4, 118
Bergman, Ingrid   77
Bischoff, Edgar   26
Bitel, Anton   93
Blade Runner (Villeneuve)   18
Blanc-Hoang, Henri-Simon   154
Bradshaw, Peter   134, 141
Breathless (Godard)   29
Breckenridge, Adam   80, 153
Breton, André   79
Buder, Emily   138, 179
Buñuel, Luis   30, 170, 171

Cabrejo, José Carlos   27, 41, 112, 132, 153–4
Campbell, Joseph   101
Canby, Vincent   44
Catholicism   67, 111, 112
Christianity   56, 58–9
Church, David   8, 41–2, 60, 112
Cobb, Ben   8, 32, 40, 63–4, 66, 83, 90–2, 98, 99, 178
   on *El Topo*   46, 50, 58
   on *Fando y Lis*   33, 38, 42
Cocteau, Jean   28
counterculture   58
crowdfunding   137–8

Daumal, René   63, 64
Decroux, Étienne   14

De Mille, Cecil B.   75
desacralization   80, 148
Divine Comedy (Dante)   32–3
Dominquez, D. Berta   92
Donde mejor canta un pájaro (Jodorowsky)   131
Dossey, Evan   159
Douglas, Alan   46
Dune (Herbert)   17, 82, 89, 91
Dune (Lynch)   18, 85
Dune (Villeneuve)   88–90
Durrell, Lawrence   77

Ebert, Roger   58, 81, 101, 111, 117
Echeverria, Rodolfo   77
El ángel exterminador (*The Exterminating Angel*, Buñuel)   30
El Minotaura (The Minotaur, Jodorowsky)   13
El Topo (The Mole, Jodorowsky)   4, 6, 15–16, 19, 37, 40, 41, 43–62, 78, 113, 127, 130, 133, 171, 174, 182
   audience engagement   46–7
   biblical reference   49–50, 54–5
   controversy   48–51
   critical response   57–61
   cult characteristics   58
   film budget   43
   landscape   60
   people with physical disabilities in   60–1
   psychedelic   46
   psychomagic in   160, 161
   religious aspects of   55, 56, 58, 59, 79
   success of   61–2
   synopsis   51–7
   time span   45
   unknown actors in   67
El Topo: The Book of the Film (Jodorowsky)   45–7, 63
"*El Topo*: Through the Wasteland of the Counterculture" (Hoberman)   58

enlightenment 47, 66
Enneagram 69, 77
esoteric symbolism 134

Fábulas pánicas (*Panic Fables*,
    Jodorowsky) 15
fabulations 169
Fando y Lis (*Fando and Lis*,
    Jodorowsky) 15, 19, 29–32,
    127, 133, 163, 181–2
  critical response 39–42
  cult characteristics 41
  review in *New York Times* 39
  sadomasochistic 42
  synopsis and meaning 32–9
  unknown actors in 67
Fellini, Federico 170, 171
Flores, Pamela 124, 129, 139,
    142, 145
Foss, Christopher 85, 87
400 Blows (Truffaut) 29
Freaks 61
Frye, Northrop 146

Garcia, Luis 79
Giger, H. R. 17, 23, 85, 87
Giraud, Jean "Moebius" 17–19,
    85–8, 93–5
Glidemagazine.com 141
Godard, Jean-Luc 29
Greenfield, Robert 66
The Guardian 81, 134, 141
Guida, Jeremy 80
Gurdjieff, G. I. 63

Herbert, Frank 17, 23, 82, 84, 88, 89
Hernández, Gregorio "Goyo"
    Cárdenas 98
Heston, Charlton 43
Hoberman, James 58
Humanoid Publishing 94

Icahzo, Oscar 65
Indiewire.com 158–9

Jaramillo, Laura 50
Jodorowsky, Adán 1–2, 20, 23, 60, 100,
    126, 133, 139, 144, 158, 172
Jodorowsky, Alejandro

academic analysis of film 7
approach to filmmaking 47, 48, 89,
    161–7, 170, 173
cinematic legacy 177
comic book phase 93–6
composite identity 6
as cult director 4, 171
desacralization 80, 148
enlightenment 47, 66
as fabulist 169
filmmaking period 171
film production 176
graphic comic 18, 19, 21
identity of spiritual master 65–6
Jewish identity 7, 12, 58–9, 123,
    131, 154
Judaism 58, 59, 62, 70, 73, 74
mimes 13–14, 25, 27, 28, 70
modus operandi 66
mysticism 80
nationalities 7, 123, 131, 154, 174
Panic Movement 14, 22, 29,
    172, 175
pictorial enunciation 21
poetic filmmaking 172
Producciones Pánicas 30
psychogenealogy 121
psychomagic 20, 107, 112–13, 118,
    121, 135, 153, 160–8
religio-sacrilegous obsession 80
religious symbolism 7, 58–9, 62, 113,
    130, 171
science-fiction films 15, 17–19
shamanistic practices 17, 31, 43, 55,
    58, 59, 128, 129, 163, 174
significance of color usage 26–7, 53,
    55, 72, 73, 80, 89, 109, 110, 120,
    122, 127, 147, 153, 161–2, 167
spiritual filmmaking 172–3
subconscious filmmaking 173
theatrical filmmaking 172, 174, 175
therapeutic works 175
usage of money 123
as writer of novels, play, and comic
    book 113–14
Zen Buddhism 17, 58–9, 67
Jodorowsky, Brontis 2, 15, 47, 48, 51–3,
    56, 87, 90, 100, 102, 123, 126,
    129, 133, 139, 142, 160, 172

Jodorowsky, Jaime   12, 152
Jodorowsky: El cine como viaje
    (*Jodorowsky: Cinema as Journey*,
    Cabrejo)   41
Jodorowsky's Dune (Pavich)   18, 19, 83,
    85–8, 117, 118, 185
The Jodoverse (Jodorowsky)   94
Jung, Carl   173

Kael, Pauline   58
Kan, Alianna   152, 178, 179
Kickstarter   23, 137–8
Klein, Allen   4, 16, 45–6, 63, 64, 78, 81–3
Kleiner, Burt   66
Kohn, Eric   159
Kudláè, Martin   153

La Constellation Jodorowsky
    (Mouchet)   38, 83, 86, 184
La Cravate (*The Severed Heads*,
    Jodorowsky)   14, 25–9, 181
La danza de la realidad (The Dance of
    Reality, Jodorowsky)   7, 20, 22,
    23, 85, 122, 159, 162, 170, 183
  academic commentary   130–3
  autofictional film as visual
    text   122–30
  journalistic commentary   133–5
  meta-performances   131, 154, 155
  review
    The Guardian   134
    The Los Angeles Times   117
    New York Times   118, 133–4
    Rogerebert.com   134

La Folle du Sacré-Coeur (*The Mad Woman
    of Sacred Heart*, Jodorowsky and
    Giraud)   95
La montaña sagrada (*The Holy Mountain*,
    Jodorowsky)   15–16, 58, 63–82,
    84, 90, 92, 96, 113, 114, 120, 166,
    170, 171, 178, 182
  alchemy   66–7
  chapter by chapter/scene by
    scene   71–7
  critical response   77–81
  DVD   69
  film budget   64–5

  Mexican iconography   67–8
  review
    Ebert, Roger   81
    The Guardian   81
    New York Times   78, 80–1
  storyboards   69
  synopsis   68–71
La vía del tarot (*Way of the Tarot*,
    Jodorowsky)   20

Lennon, John   45
Leoni, Roberto   98–9
Le Sang d'un poète (*The Blood of the Poet*,
    Cocteau)   28
Les Fils d'El Topo (*The Sons of El Topo*,
    Jodorowsky)   62
Les yeux du chat (*The Eyes of the Cat*,
    Jodorowsky)   18, 19
*Le théâtre de la guérison, une thérapie
    panique* (*The Theater of
    Healing: A Panic Therapy*,
    Jodorowsky)   20
Lim, Dennis   117
L'Incal (*The Incal*, Jodorowsky and
    Giraud)   19, 83–6, 93–6
Lindstrom, Naomi   130
Lorenzio, Mara   48
The Los Angeles Times   117
Lynch, David   18, 85, 88

Macnab, Geoffrey   69, 178
Mann, Thomas   25
Manson, Marilyn   170
Marceau, Marcel   28, 29
Martin, Ken   59
The Mask Maker (Marceau)   28
Melbye, David   60
Melnyk, Lubomyr   170
Mélodrame sacramental
    (*Sacramental Melodrama*)
    14–15, 30
Metagenealogía (*Metagenealogy*,
    Jodorowsky)   132
metagenealogy   2, 57, 107, 132, 153
#MeToo movement   49
Mexican Catholicism   111, 112
mimes   13–14, 25, 27, 28, 70
Monroe, Marilyn   71
Mother Courage (Brecht)   33

Mount Analogue: A Novel of Symbolically Authentic Non-Euclidean Adventures in Mountain Climbing (Daumal)   63

Nardonne, Michael   179
Neruda, Pablo   148
Neustadt, Robert   78, 113–14
The New Yorker   45
New York Times   6, 39, 78, 80–1, 101, 111, 118, 133–4, 140–1, 158
Night of the Living Dead (Romero)   41
Nofilmschool.com   159–61
nostalgic emotion   153

O'Bannon, Dan   17, 23, 85
O'Hara, Helen   49

Panic Movement   14, 22, 29, 172, 175
Parra, Nicanor   12–13, 144–5
Pavich, Frank   18, 23, 83, 84, 88, 117
Pecotic, David   64
pictorial enunciation   21
Pink Floyd   18, 85
Poesía sin fin (*Endless Poetry*, Jodorowsky)   1, 7, 13, 23, 30, 60, 126, 142–52, 164, 166, 170, 184
   academic commentary   153–5
   colors usage in   147
   crowdfunding   137–9
   earning   138
   poetic quality of   140–1
   reviews
      of Glidemagazine.com   141
      of *The Guardian*   141
      of the *New York Times*   140–1
      of Slantmagazine.com   141
   surrealism   140–1, 148, 153, 155
Pollack, Sydney   77
Producciones Pánicas   30
psychoanalysis   112, 160–2
psychomagic   20, 107, 112–13, 118, 121, 135, 153, 160–8
Psychomagic, A Healing Art (Jodorowsky)   23, 157, 184
   anti-surrealist claim   162
   assessment   168
   crowdfunding   158
   Jodorowsky's view of the film   159
   reviews
      Indiewire.com   158–9
      RogerEbert.com   158
      Slantmagazine.com   159
   scene-by-scene description and analysis   161–7

The Rainbow Thief (Jodorowsky)   20, 92–3, 113
Roberts, James   141
RogerEbert.com   134, 158
Romero, George   41
Rose, Steve   178
Rosenberg, Moishe   45

Salkind, Alexander   92
Samson, Jacques   21
Santa Sangre (*Holy Blood*, Jodorowsky)   19, 97–9, 113, 114, 120, 182–3
   awards   100
   budget   99
   commentary
      Cabrejo, José Carlos   112
      Church, David   112
   casting of unknowns and street people   100
   critical response   110–13
   ratings   101
   reviews
      Ebert, Roger   101, 111
      New York Times   101, 111, 118
   as a sentimental picture   110
   synopsis of the film   101–10
Sara Felicidad Prullansky Arcavi   12
Satori Films   23, 138, 157, 176
Savage, Carlos   30
Schechtman, Marya   120–1
Schjeldahl, Peter   45
Scott, A. O.   118, 141
Seydoux, Michel   23, 84, 85, 87, 90, 118, 139
Sharf, Zack   90
Slantmagazine.com   141, 159
Spaghetti Nightmares   99

The Spiritual Journey of Alejandro Jodorowsky (Jodorowsky)   17, 22, 44, 57
surrealism   5–6, 140–1, 148, 153, 155

Takata, Ejo   59
Teatro sin fin (*Endless Theater*, Jodorowsky)   30, 31, 181
theosophy   126–7
The Transposed Heads: A Legend of India (Mann)   25
Treviño, Jesús Salvador   77
Truffaut, François   29
Tusk (Jodorowsky)   18, 19, 90–2
2001: A Space Odyssey (Kubrick)   60

Une aventure de John Difool (*The Affair of John Difool*, Giraud)   93

The Village Voice   44–5
Villeneuve, Denis   18, 86, 88–90
The Viper (Parra)   144–5

Viskin, Roberto   45
Visser, Margaret   170

Waititi, Taika   94
Weinstein, Harvey   49
Weinstein, Max   160
Where the Bird Sings Best (Jodorowsky)   11, 21, 152

Yamamoto, Xavier Guerrero   138, 139

Zen Buddhism   17, 56, 58–9, 67

www.ingramcontent.com/pod-product-compliance
Lightning Source LLC
Chambersburg PA
CBHW061829300426
44115CB00013B/2308